# ROARING TWENTIES

## A Portrait of New York City During the 1920's

### By: Noah Moss

© 2016 by Noah J. Moss. All rights reserved to the author.

Feel free to take bits or pieces of this book and replicate them online or in print. But please, always link back to the author and cite appropriately, in good taste and to the best of your ability. If you want to use a few paragraphs, that's great and I encourage you to do so—please contact the author first! I simple head's up in the DM is all you need. But, if you illegally downloaded this book or filched a paperback version, shame on you! The only thing the author asks in that case is that you at least share your lifted copy with a friend or enemy (as the case may be) who might benefit from its words.

ISBN:   978-1533547927
WC: 85,890 (ish)

Typset in Cambria
Written in the U.S.A.
Printed in the U.S.A.

Author Info
Medium:      @nomo
Instagram: @nomolds

*There simply isn't enough space on the page to thank everyone who's supported me and encouraged me to see this through. I'd like to thank my Mom in particular, whose intellect, creativity and love are truly boundless.*

*Last but not least, I want to thank you, dear Reader. I appreciate your patience; it's my first book, after all!*

ROARING TWENTIES

## TABLE OF CONTENTS

| | |
|---|---|
| MANAHATTA, a poem by Walt Whitman | vii |
| INTRO: ORIGINS | ix |
| ROARING TWENTIES | 1 |
|   BOOK ONE: ALL'S FAIR IN LOVE & WAR | 3 |
|     Moving Day | 4 |
|     A Harsh Winter | 13 |
|     A Housing Shortage | 21 |
|     Early Rent Strikes | 24 |
|     Rapacious Rent Hikes | 30 |
|     Stirring The Pot | 38 |
|     A New Kind O'Rent Strike | 45 |
|   BOOK TWO: HANG TOGETHER, OR HANG SEPARATELY | 53 |
|     Moving Day Redux | 54 |
|     All Bark, No Bite? | 59 |
|     Upstate Conservatives (Supposedly) | 66 |
|     What About Public Housing? | 72 |
|     A 'Special' Session | 76 |
|     Turning Tides | 81 |
|     Out With The Reds! | 86 |
|     The Eleventh Hour | 89 |
|     Holding Court | 94 |
|     'Special' Session Redux | 97 |
| INTERLUDE | 103 |
|   BOOK THREE: RISE OF THE TENANT ARMY | 165 |
|     Constructive Eviction | 166 |
|     American Federalism | 168 |
|     Oliver Wendell Holmes & | |
|         The D.C. Rent Commission | 173 |
|     Municipal Judges At The Helm | 177 |
|     Extended Emergency? | 184 |
|     Rise Of The Tenant Army | 187 |
|     Reign Of The Tenant Army | 195 |

MANNAHATTA
By: Walt Whitman

*I was asking for something specific and perfect for my city,*
*Whereupon lo! Upsprang the aboriginal name.*
*Now I see what there is in a name, a word, liquid, sane, unruly, musical, self-sufficient,*
*I see that the word of my city is that word from of old,*
*Because I see that word nested in nests of water-bays, superb,*
*Rich, hemm'd thick all around with sailships and steamships, an island sixteen miles long, solid-founded,*
*Numberless crowded streets, high growths of iron, slender, strong, light, splendidly uprising toward clear skies,*
*Tides swift and ample, well-loved by me, toward sundown,*
*The flowing sea-current, the little islands, larger adjoining islands, the heights, the villas,*
*The countless masts, the white shore-steamers, the lighters, the ferry-boats, the black sea-streamers well-model'd,*
*The downtown streets, the jobbers' houses of business, the houses of business of the ship-merchants and money brokers, the river-streets,*
*Immigrants arriving, fifteen or twenty thousand in a week,*
*The carts hauling goods, the manly race of drivers of horses, the brown-faced sailors,*
*The summer air, the bright sun shining, and the sailing clouds aloft,*
*The winter snows, the sleigh-bells, the broken ice in the river, passing along up or down the flood-tide or ebb-tide,*
*The mechanics of the city, the masters, well-form'd, beautiful-faced, looking you straight in the eyes,*
*Trottoirs throng'd, vehicles, Broadway, the women, the shops and shows,*
*A million people-manners free and superb—open voices—hospitality—the most courageous and*

*friendly young men,*
*City of hurried and sparkling waters! City of spires and masts!*
*City nested in bays! my city!*

# INTRO

## ORIGINS

Do you know Walt Whitman? Of course you do, who'm I kidding? I don't mean to suggest that you know him personally in any way, just that you're likely to have a passing familiarity with his life and work. You might be wondering who I am, but more on that later.

If you remember Walt Whitman at all, you surely know him as a heavily-bearded wordsmith, particularly in old age, who published an impressive number of poems around the turn of the century, in 1900. *MANNAHATTA*, which is a reference to the aboriginal land mass originally occupied by the Lenape tribe and that we know today as Manhattan, is featured prominently among Whitman's, *Leaves of Grass*, a collection widely considered to be a masterpiece of American and global literature. To this day, Whitman is still revered as the "Poet of Democracy" and "America's Shakespeare."

In his time, the sprawling urban landscape of Manhattan was as turbulent and corrupt a'world epicenter as any seen down through American history and where this story really begins. Before we dive headlong into what exactly happened in New York City during the 1920's, we should first find some context for this story, for not a moment in history makes sense without a larger context.

By 1890, population growth in America was off the charts, so to speak. In Walt Whitman's day, New York City's population growth was in no small part the result of a seemingly endless flow of pious immigrants through America's porous borders. 'Where did all those families live?' you might be asking yourself. The luckiest of New York City's newly-minted residents were able to settle in tenement buildings along Manhattan's East Side ethnic neighborhoods, while the less fortunate were relegated to 'rear houses,' which was a proper name for what really were dilapidated old slums haphazardly constructed off the rear of those old tenement buildings pockmarking Manhattan Island. The rear house of any old-law Manhattan tenement building in 1890, having endured nearly 50 years of continuous occupation, was undoubtedly a dark and ramshackle labyrinth of old shanties, run-over by organized crime, alcoholism, tubercular disease, influenza and cholera.

How crowded were these tenement buildings? Consider, for example, that Manhattan averaged in those days roughly 114 residents per acre; whereas a factory district on the lower East Side averaged an astounding 523.6 residents per acre. By 1895, the area below Manhattan's 14th Street—roughly 1.2 percent of New York's total land area—housed some 1.3 million people in an abysmal 40,000 slum tenements! And these cheaply constructed tenement buildings, run-over as they were with poor and working-class immigrants, were often owned by the same, serving as a fast-track to steady income and allowing, for the first time, many poor immigrant families to work their way out of urban squalor into the lower echelons of the city's middle-class.

As author Jared Day points out in his piece, *Urban Castles*, "[d]uring the late eighteenth and early nineteenth centuries, New York experienced an economic expansion that transformed the quality and character of artisanal labor," a transformation that resulted in a diverse labor force that landed New York City as one of the preeminent manufacturing and commercial epicenters in the Union. As America's urban labor force expanded, the price of labor naturally dropped, allowing early American capitalist real estate investors like John Jacob Astor to amass vast real estate fortunes as they harnessed the lucrative potential of cheap labor.

Capitalism, in its purest form, is fundamentally American. I'm sure you know that capitalism, in broad strokes, was founded on the primacy of private ownership and is carried out by individuals or, alternatively, private corporations. Together, private businessmen like Astor, alongside their companies, formed a discrete private sector in early America that operated within a 'free market' economy. Businesses that operated in this private sector of the early American economy actively competed with one another for consumers. The goal of this game was to maximize profit, which was, in those early days, all but entirely uninhibited by law, the only qualification being those unruly economic forces of supply and demand.

Even before 1900, capitalism reigned supreme in America, unhindered for all intents and purposes, and allowing companies from the private sector to employ any number of strategies in a mad scramble to amass as large an individual fortune as possible. Unfettered capitalism has been tempered somewhat since the days of Astor and the Vanderbilt family; for example, the federal government has imposed regulations to prevent private companies from becoming too big or charging prices that are too high. But in 1900, no one would have looked at you sideways if you explained capitalism with stars in your eyes, unfettered as capitalism was in those years. In fact, America's approach came to have symbolic significance and those games players that excelled ascended to incredible wealth and notoriety, in both the U.S. and abroad.

Even today, the few times I've recently come across the names of two of America's most notorious private sector businessmen—names like John Piedmont Morgan or John D. Rockefeller—their names always ring to recognition. Each employed a similar approach to business, particularly with respect to their efforts in the early American railroad industry. Call it what you will, but the gist of their strategy was simple—'Bigger is better. Period.' And why not? No one could stop them (though not for lack of effort).

Massive industrial consolidation by a few wealthy families was the rule of the day in 1900 as J.P. Morgan acquired ever-expanding control over American railroad and banking interests, while John D. Rockefeller likewise wrested control over oil markets and expanded into banking as well. By 1905, both J.P.

Morgan and John D. Rockefeller had consolidated more than a thousand railroad lines into six awe-inspiring companies.

To borrow the words of historians Thomas Cochran and William Miller, "The imperial leader of the new oligarchy was the House of Morgan." J.P. Morgan, alongside John D. Rockefeller and one other contemporary—Director of the First National Bank of New York, George F. Baker—headed a financial empire with holdings that would swell by 1912 to over $22 billion, more than the assessed value for all property west of the Mississippi River in those years.

Ask any politician in 1908, for example, and he or she would tell you candidly about how Rockefeller, Morgan, and a host of contemporary capitalist cohorts, justified their belief in the profitability of stern consolidation by pointing out two overlapping strategies. First, the more of a particular industry a particular company owned, the greater the profits. Second, growth allowed a given company to take advantage of an attribute of American capitalism called "economies of scale," which describes the cost-saving potential gained as a function of growth in output. The result of exploiting these economies of scale? Usually, a trimming of cost per unit of output for a given company; meaning the more a company produced, the greater the potential cost-savings. And so it went.

To say that the House of Morgan thrived due to sheer size alone would be to inexcusably overgeneralize the Morgans' savvy as businessmen in the era of American Taylorism. In addition to sheer size, the House of Morgan valued regularity, stability and predictability. As one Morgan associate described it—

> With a man like Mr. Morgan at the head of a great industry, as against the old plan of many diverse interests in it, production would become more regular, labor would be more steadily employed at better wages, and panics caused by over-production would become a thing of the past.

Despite his best efforts, however, not even J.P. Morgan could exercise complete control over unfettered capitalism. In 1907, the nation experienced a financial panic following a collapse of New York City's third largest trust company, the Knickerbocker Trust Company. The ensuing financial crisis gripped, not only the five boroughs or even the tri-state area, but permeated all forty five states.

With the benefit of hindsight, we now know that one reason for such a wide-spread financial crisis—originating from Manhattan—was that the Union lacked a central national bank in those years and the crisis might have deepened were it not for the intervention of J.P Morgan himself, who personally pledged enormous sums of money to prop up the national banking system. If you're thinking that this is a rare, though telling example of a private sector bailout, you wouldn't be alone in your observation.

Still, the damage had been done. Profits in the wake of the Panic of 1907 were still pouring in but not to the satisfaction of private sector capitalists, a shortage that prompted American companies to begin a ruthless search for further cost-cutting measures. Around the same time, a steel foreman by the name of Fredrick Taylor wrote and published a book on what he coined as 'scientific management,' a term describing an approach to controlling every detail of each factory worker's time and energy while working along the manufacturing assembly line, each detail the subject of close scrutiny and categorization. The goal of American "Taylorism," as it came to be called, was to make every unskilled laborer interchangeable with the next, each of their individual tasks simple and standardized, mindless and requiring minimal skill to boot.

As immigrants gushed through U.S. borders by the millions—stricken by poverty and desperate for work—Taylorism prospered in America, creating an expansive unskilled labor force filling simple, poorly compensated jobs. The result for domestic companies was dramatic. Consider, for example, the nascent auto industry. In 1909 Henry Ford's company sold 10,607 autos; in 1913, 168,000; in 1914, 248,000. When you adopt Taylorism into a capitalist society, ambition shines. Due to Henry Ford's adoption of Taylorism (combined with a singular ambition), Ford Motor Company's production in 1914 accounted for 45 percent of all automobiles produced that year for American consumers.

I may have mentioned this already but as American manufacturing jobs simplified, unskilled laborers were increasingly regarded as interchangeable by their employers who, themselves, were regarded as largely interchangeable by their superiors. And so it went. The bottom rung of the totem pole, however, took the brunt of private sector cost-cutting measures, as working conditions in factories all over the country took a dramatic turn for the worse.

Meanwhile, immigrant families poured into New York City and, given such pervasive poverty, each and every member of the family—children included—was put to work. In garment manufacturing, for example, young children would work as schleppers alongside their grandparents in over-crowded sweatshops, which were usually run out of an equally over-crowded residential tenement building in Manhattan's lower East Side. A contemporary of Walt Whitman, Edwin Markham, wrote—

> Those in the home sweatshop must work cheaper than those in the factory sweatshops. . . . And the children are called in from play to drive and drudge beside their elders . . . All the year in New York and in other cities you may watch children radiating to and from such pitiful homes. Nearly any hour on the East Side of New York City you can see them—pallid boy or spindling girl— their faces dulled, their backs bent under a heavy load of garments piled on

head and shoulders, the muscles of the whole frame in a long strain.... Is it not a cruel civilization that allows little hearts and shoulders to strain under these grown-up responsibilities, while in the same city, a pet cur is jeweled and pampered and aired on a fine lady's velvet lap on the beautiful boulevards?

A cruel civilization, indeed. All told, there were nearly five hundred garment factories in New York City during those years, many of which were densely packed among the city's already over-crowded low-income neighborhoods. A woman later recounted working conditions she had endured as a child—

> [D]angerously broken stairways ... windows few and so dirty ... The wooden floors that were swept once a year.... Hardly any other light but the gas jets burning by day and by night ... the filthy, malodorous lavatory in the dark hall. No fresh drinking water.... mice and roaches.... During the winter months ... how we suffered from the cold. In the summer we suffered from the heat.... In these disease-breeding holes we, the youngsters together with the men and women toiled from seventy and eighty hours a week! Saturdays and Sundays included! ... A sign would go up on Saturday afternoon: 'If you don't come in on Sunday, you need not come in on Monday.' ... Children's dreams of a day off shattered. We wept, for after all, we were only children.

An individual worker, exhausted of these unfathomable working conditions and possessed of an initiative to take action could refuse to work in the hope of coaxing an improvement. But this lone laborer, admirable as his or her efforts and noble as their purpose, would no doubt be disciplined for such antics. In other words, the individual worker was powerless to make any demands on his or her own. 'What if,' it eventually occurred to the individual laborer, 'instead of going it alone, workers banded together? What if we formed a union amongst one another? Isn't there strength in numbers? Wouldn't we have more leverage then?'

As far back as the turn of the century, in 1900, the advantages of banding together as a labor union were well known and had already motivated formation of the American Federation of Labor ('AFL'). Despite its size—a key barometer for a labor union's success—the AFL nevertheless proved problematic in that it was overly exclusive and quite blatant in its racism, barring many immigrant and minority laborers from membership and actively perpetuating a deep-seated xenophobia among its members and organizational leaders. The AFL's meetings were tightly controlled and all but completely impervious to external criticism and internal dissention. The AFL employed, for example, "goon squads," hired thugs directed to intimidate and harass internal dissenters into line. That did not mean, however, that labor unionization fizzled out as entirely futile. Shortly after the turn of the century, the number of union members in the U.S. swelled to over two million. It's true that many of them were AFL members but that wouldn't last long.

Times were tough and the immediate outlook bleak for capitalists and union members alike, but particularly bleak for working-class union members. Factory conditions were terrible and only getting worse. Unskilled laborers wanted radical change, begged for it, even. Many viewed capitalism as the root of all evil, the source of the working class' misery.

Just when it seemed that the AFL had completely squandered any hope of unionization as a possible defense against profit-mongering capitalists, something happened that changed the course of American history. On a summer morning in June 1905, a group of some two hundred—including socialists, anarchists and the more radical sect of union members—gathered in Chicago. All in attendance coalesced during the meeting into a massive labor union whose origins were not capitalist in nature, but rather, socialist.

'What is socialism?' you might be asking yourself. I'm sure you've heard of it, and know it as an ideological opposite of capitalism for all intents and purposes. Here's what I mean. Remember how capitalism is based largely around individual ownership and individual profit? While there are many varieties of socialism, one aspect common to them all is the primacy of social ownership in lieu of private or individual ownership. In practice, as opposed to theory, the differences between capitalism and socialism have proven rather nuanced and for that reason are beyond the scope of this story.

As long as you bear in mind capitalism's emphasis on individual profit and, conversely, socialism's focus on the collective's well-being, you're likely to find interesting the fact that follows—alongside socialism, there was another idea that quickly took hold of Europe at this time, sweeping over Spain, Italy and France. The idea was simple—that workers could take power, not just by unionizing (as the IWW had done) and not by armed rebellion (as the French proletariat had done during their Revolution, beginning in 1789), but by bringing industry to a halt in a general labor strike, then seizing control for the benefit of all. As an idea, the strike was a powerful one that quickly jumped the Atlantic Ocean, landing and taking root on American's eastern seaboard. Take, for example, a group of women laborers who organized a strike at the Triangle Shirtwaist Company in the winter months of 1909. As a participant and witness later recalled—

> Thousands upon thousands left the factories from every side, all of them walking down toward Union Square. It was November, the cold winter was just around the corner, we had no fur coats to keep warm, and yet there was the spirit that led us on until we got to some hall.... I can see the young people, mostly women, walking down and not caring what might happen... the hunger, cold, loneliness.... They just didn't care on that particular day; it was their day.

Union members of the Triangle Shirtwaist Company had hoped three thousand might walk out. Twenty thousand striking workers was the final tally.

Labor strikes were on the rise in America, no two ways about it. In 1904 there were four thousand strikes—general, labor and otherwise. Despite these efforts, the bulk of influence in American politics nonetheless remained disproportionally concentrated in the hands of powerful corporations whose justification for profit drove American policy.

Hopefully it's easy to see why socialism, with its promise that people might together use their collective resources to make life better for everyone, would spread through the hearts and minds of Americans from all walks of life, particularly those housed in densely populated cities housing a poverty-stricken working class. In New York City, socialism expanded its reach beyond small pockets concentrated among city immigrants—Jewish and German migrant workers refusing to communicate in a language other than their respective mother tongues—and became decidedly American.

Socialism soon ascended into the institutions of city, state and national politics. The strongest state organization by all accounts took root in Oklahoma. By 1914, the Socialist party collected dues from over twelve thousand members across the state; voters elected over one hundred Socialist party members to Oklahoma state and local government.

As a necessary aside, you should know that across the U.S., the early 20$^{th}$ century also saw another unprecedented campaign for reform—that of women for full suffrage, including the right to vote and serve in government. In the spring months of 1913, the national press reported from Washington, D.C.—

> In a woman's suffrage demonstration to-day the capital saw the greatest parade of women in its history. . . . In the parade over 5000 women passed down Pennsylvania Avenue. . . . It was an astonishing demonstration. It was estimated. . . . that 500,000 persons watched the women march for their cause.

Despite the best efforts of feminists and labor organizers (who often were one in the same), it was clear that the federal government, with its allegiance and commitment to unfettered capitalism, was ill-prepared, indeed inept, to address the reforms called for all over the country.

Known eventually as the 'Progressive Period,' this time period did not see much in the way of real progress at all, but rather, reluctant and piecemeal reform aimed, at least in part, at quelling popular protest.

True, legal reform from these years did effect some change, bringing enough into the middle class to stem the rising tide of class conflict. But it wasn't enough. For the large swaths of tenant farmers, factory workers and slum dwellers, men and women alike, conditions changed only to the extent that they worsened and at a quickening pace. Perhaps as a result, the challenge of everyday living conditions predisposed those working-class laborers to adopting socialism, lending to the ideology's rapid spread through the lower rungs of New York City's throngs of working class residents and throughout the country during this time. Victor Berger was elected to U.S. Congress in 1910, the first member of the Socialist party to hold a seat in the U.S. federal government. By 1911, seventy-three Socialist mayors had been elected and some twelve hundred lesser officials presided in 340 cities and towns across the country.

It was undeniable—socialism continued to spread like a grease fire after having been dowsed with water, as quick as it was intemperate. The IWW, for its part, continued its agitating efforts, and not long after Democratic candidate Woodrow Wilson took office as America's 28th President in 1913, the state of Colorado saw a bitter conflict between laborers and private sector capitalists, one of the ugliest such affairs in American history.

The episode began when a band of coal miners in the southern mining town of Trinidad, Colorado went on strike against their employer, the Colorado Fuel & Iron Company, a prominent corporation owned almost entirely by John D. Rockefeller. All told, eleven thousand miners walked off the job in September 1913, protesting low pay, dangerous working conditions and complete domination by the mining company, which effectively owned every aspect of the miners' lives in Trinidad and the surrounding towns. For example, the miners lived with their families in veritable shack colonies built and owned by the Colorado Fuel & Iron Company. The shacks were set up by the Rockefellers' coal company and miners were to revere the Colorado Fuel & Iron Company as a landlord. As soon as the miners walked out on strike, they were all immediately evicted from their shacks, families and all.

The United Mine Workers Union (UMWU) stepped in and helped the evicted miners set up a tent colony in the nearby hills of Trinidad from where the miners could carry on their strike and go on picketing in protest. To that end, the UMWU constructed tents on wood platforms and outfitted them with cast iron stoves. The tents sat on land leased by the UMWU in preparation for the strike, strategically chosen near the canyons leading to the coal mines themselves, so that the tents might obstruct any efforts of strikebreakers brought in to keep operations going in the mines. The UMWU's intervention by no means deterred the Colorado Fuel & Iron Company from hiring the Baldwin-Felts Detective Agency to protect all non-striking mine workers—called 'scabs' by union members—and to harass the strikers.

And harassment there was. In one early incident, Baldwin-Felts strikebreakers raided the Trinidad tent colonies with Gatling guns. The miners persisted even though they suffered injuries and even casualties in increasing numbers. In a surreal effort, the striking miners drove back an armored train sent in by Baldwin-Felts in a valiant gun battle. As the miners refused to give in, Colorado's governor—referred to by the Rockefellers as "our little cowboy governor"—called in the National Guard with, as the story goes, the Rockefellers supplying the Guard's wages.

The sight of the National Guard, called in on October 28, 1913, initially calmed the miners who were under the impression that the Guard's sympathies lie with the debilitated union militia. The miners couldn't have been more wrong. Despite the National Guard's best efforts to shuttle in replacement laborers and otherwise break the strike, at times, with no outward remorse for human life, the striking miners persisted in waging on from their tent colonies through the spring of 1914.

On March 10, 1914, the body of a scab worker was discovered on the railroad tracks near Forbes, Colorado—a death publicly attributed by the National Guard to the strikers nearby. In retaliation, Colorado's Governor ordered complete destruction of the strikers' tent colony. The Guard sent strikebreakers in while the miners were attending the funeral of a young child, another casualty of the strikers' resistance. Guardsmen beat the miners, arrested them by the hundreds and chased striking miners through the streets on horseback. The brave and resilient miners fended the strikebreakers and armed Guardsmen off, making it acutely clear that extraordinary measures would be required to break up the strike.

On the morning of April 20, 1914, two squadrons of the National Guard stationed themselves in the hills overlooking the largest of the tent colonies, the tent colony in Ludlow, Colorado, which housed a thousand men, women and children. That morning, the National Guard opened fire in a machine gun attack on the tents and their occupants. The miners fired back and the gun battle that ensued raged on for the entire day. Lou Tikas, leader of a miners' militia in Ludlow, responded to a call for truce by the National Guard. Tikas was lured into the hills and shot dead, in cold blood. Women and children dug pits out from beneath their tents in an effort to find cover from the gunfire.

As the sun set that evening, those companies of the National Guard companies descended from their hilltop perches with torches in hand, callously setting fire to the Ludlow tent colony as they continued their rifle assault from the hills. The incident came to be known as the "Ludlow Massacre" after the location of the tent colony and indiscriminate killing that took place that day. In the aftermath, bodies of miners and National Guardsmen alike lay strewn along the Colorado and Southern Railway tracks for three days in full view of passing trains, left as a gruesome message of deterrence before a railway union finally demanded the bodies be properly buried.

The day after fighting ceased, a telephone linesman sifting through the ruins outside Ludlow found the charred and twisted bodies of four women and eleven children who had taken shelter from the National Guard's gunfire in a pit dug out beneath their tent. Tragically, their safe haven turned to a death trap when their tent was set ablaze.

News of the Ludlow Massacre spread like wildfire across the country and incited an armed response. The UMWU issued a "Call to Arms"—"Gather together for defensive purposes all arms and ammunition legally available." What happened next was not "defensive" by any stretch. In a nearby town, miners attended a funeral service for the twenty-six men, women and children that had died in Ludlow. Following the memorial service, the crowd in attendance marched directly to a makeshift armory housed in a nearby building where they armed themselves with rifles. They set off for the hills where they pillaged and destroyed mines, showing no remorse for the guards on duty. In Colorado Springs, three hundred union members walked off the job and made straight for the Ludlow area, which included the city of Trinidad, with revolvers, rifles and machine guns in tow. The local press reported, "the hills in every direction are suddenly alive with men."

In Denver, soldiers called in to Trinidad as support refused their call to duty in opposition to the strikers. Some five thousand people demonstrated on the front lawn of the state capitol, demanding that the National Guard officers from Ludlow be tried for murder and that the governor, for his part, be tried as an accessory! Other unions stepped in—the United Garment Workers Union in Denver pledged four hundred members as volunteer nurses to help the strikers; the Denver Cigar Makers Union pledged an additional five hundred armed men as reinforcements to Ludlow and Trinidad.

The fervor breached national news. Meetings and demonstrations sprouted up all across the country. Picketers marched outside of the Rockefeller Office at 26 Broadway in New York City. NYPD officers clubbed a New York minister as he protested outside the church where the Rockefellers sat Sunday Mass. The *New York Times* reported, "With the deadliest weapons of civilization in the hands of savage minded men, there can be no telling what lengths the war on Colorado will go unless it is quelled by force."

And President Woodrow Wilson eventually did just that, obliging a request by the Colorado Governor for federal troops. Unsurprisingly, the strike petered out shortly thereafter. Regardless, the message had been sent—at the core of the Ludlow Massacre was ferocious class conflict, no two ways about it. Was it finally past that tipping point which compelled a conversation about fundamental change?

Reflecting on this very question, historian and author Howard Zinn writes—

> The threat of class rebellion was clearly still there in the industrial conditions of the United States, in the undeterred spirit of rebellion among working people—whatever legislation had been passed, whatever liberal reforms were on the books, whatever investigations were undertaken and words of regret and conciliation uttered.

Given the tenuous state of affairs in America, teetering constantly on the razor's edge of all out revolution at home, it may surprise you to know that domestic revolt fell out of the national conversation in the wake of the Ludlow Massacre, along with any chance, for all intents and purposes, of meaningful reform for the time being. Rather, the national media turned America's attention to Vera Cruz, Mexico.

On the morning that the bodies were discovered in a pit at the Ludlow tent colony, American warships bombarded the Mexican coastal city of Vera Cruz, leaving one hundred Mexicans dead and resulting in a seven-month occupation of U.S. troops. Publicly, President Wilson justified the operation on a recent arrest of American sailors by Mexican authorities, coined as the Tampico Affair. Behind the scenes, some speculated that President Wilson had other, more clandestine motives.

Regardless of his intent, the national conversation shifted away from divisive, polarizing domestic dissention (labor struggles, socialism, etc.) to American patriotism, with the goal of galvanizing all against a common, external enemy. Recalling the rising unemployment and hard times gripping the U.S. in 1914, historian Howard Zinn asks, "Could patriotic fervor and the military spirit cover up class struggle?"

The timing is curious, isn't it? That the U.S. attack on Vera Cruz and the true extent of the Ludlow Massacre came to light on the same day?

Believe what you will. I'm convinced the timing is nothing more than coincidence. That, however, by no means detracts from its significance. Indeed, the incident at Vera Cruz was a minor one on the whole, especially when you consider that, in just four short months, Europe would enter World War I.

Not long after, America's foray into the "the war to end all wars," World War I, no doubt changed the conversation at home. There is an old German proverb that goes something like this—*Wenn das Militar sich bewegt, bleit die Wahrheit auf der Strecke.* In English, "When the Military sets itself in motion, the truth is too slow to keep up, so it stays behind." The point is well taken. As war broke out in Europe in 1914, young soldiers perished at an alarming rate, their valiant demonstrations of patriotism in the name of a mere hundred yards of land guarded by a line of trenches. Meanwhile, nationalism bloomed, providing brief reprieve such that it was now possible for European governments to quell class unrest. America was not immune and experienced a similar shift in the national conversation.

A change in topic aside, struggles at home continued to provided a catalyst for the steady spread of socialism in the U.S., which continued to make deep inroads into American politics. Consider New York City's municipal elections in 1917 where Socialist candidate for mayor, Morris Hillquist, garnered an astonishing 22 percent of the popular vote. That year, ten legislators from the Socialist party won elected seats in the New York state legislature. Socialist politicians made remarkable gains in Chicago where the party vote—only 3.6 percent in 1915—jumped to 34.7 percent by 1917. Buffalo saw a similar, though no less jarring jump from 2.6 percent in 1915 to 30.2 percent by 1917.

Socialists, particularly in their outspoken opposition to America's entry into World War I, were formidable and growing into an influential voice in the U.S. Perhaps as a direct result, perhaps not, Congress passed a federal law called the Espionage Act, which took effect in June 1917 and remains in effect to this day. Given its name, you'd be justified in your impression that the statute outlawed spying in every sense of the word. However, the title said nothing of the law's purpose—imprisoning Americans who spoke out or wrote against America's entry into the war.

Here's what I mean. Congress wrote into the statute a clause that supposedly guaranteed, "nothing in this section shall be construed to limit or restrict . . . any discussion, comment, or criticism of the acts or policies of the Government." This language was necessary because, as you know, the *First Amendment of the U.S. Constitution* guarantees to each citizen the freedom of speech. A citizen's freedom of speech is naturally qualified, even today, though in the tradition of *First Amendment* rights, that qualification shouldn't go so far as to prohibit someone in the U.S. from speaking out against the acts or policies of the federal government, which presumably included President Wilson's entry into the war. Now, Congress wrote into the Espionage Act another provision that provided for up to twenty years in prison for "[w]hoever, when the United States is at War, shall willfully cause or attempt to cause, insubordination, disloyalty, mutiny, or refusal of duty in the military or naval forces of the United States, or shall willfully obstruct the recruiting or enlistment service."

Ok, that all sounds fine, right? If the U.S. is at war and imposes a draft, like the federal government did for World War I, it makes sense to outlaw activities that might interfere with the draft. It's in the name of national security after all and mutinies in a time of war are no small matter. So how was it that this statute came to be used for such nefarious ends? Were they nefarious at all?

I'll let you decide. Two months after Congress voted the Espionage Act into law a Socialist named Charles Schenck was arrested in Philadelphia. His supposed crime? Printing and distributing some sixteen thousand leaflets that denounced the draft and America's entry into the war. You see the draft was imposed by another law called the Conscription Act. Schenck's leaflet cited the *Thirteenth Amendment of the U.S. Constitution*, which forever outlawed "involuntary servitude," and argued that the Conscription Act violated the *Thirteenth Amendment* because it sent able-bodied Americans to war in service of the federal government against their will. Conscription, Schenck wrote, was "a monstrous deed against humanity in the interests of financiers of Wall Street." Schenck went further, imploring his fellow citizens, "Do not submit to intimidation," calling for such measures as a petition to repeal the Espionage Act.

Federal prosecutors indicted and tried Schenck, who was ultimately sentenced by a trial judge to six months in jail for violating the Espionage Act. Schenck appealed, arguing that the Act, by prosecuting him for speech and his written leaflet, violated his right of free speech guaranteed under the *First Amendment*. His appeal ascended all the way to our nation's highest, the U.S. Supreme Court, where it danced across the desk of Chief Justice Oliver Wendell Holmes, one of the Supreme Court's most revered legal minds and one of its most famous liberals.

In a unanimous decision penned by Justice Holmes, the Court affirmed Schenck's conviction, finding no doubt as to whether Schenck's leaflets were meant to "obstruct" America's military draft.

Did the *First Amendment* protect Schenck? Justice Holmes didn't buy the argument, writing—

> The most stringent protection of free speech would not protect a man in falsely shouting fire in a theater and causing a panic … The question in every case is whether the words used are used in such circumstances and are of such a nature as to create a clear and present danger that they will bring about the substantive evils that Congress has a right to prevent.

Heavy language, no? Justice Holmes' analogy struck a chord so deep as to resonate to almost universal recognition, surviving through the decades even to this day. Who could argue with him? Few people would think that the *First Amendment* should protect someone falsely yelling "Fire" in a crowded theater, particularly when a panic ensues.

Holmes continued—

> When a nation is at war many things that might be said in time of peace are such a hindrance to its effort that their utterance will not be endured as long as men fight and that no Court could regard them as protected by any constitutional right.

Perhaps Holmes' analogy, though clever, was not as apt as history has made it out to be. Historian Howard Zinn asks, "Was not Schenck's act more like someone shouting, not falsely, but truly, to people about to buy tickets and enter a theater, that there was a fire raging inside?"

Even at the time, Holmes' analogy proved controversial. That did not prevent the U.S. government from prosecuting some two thousand others under the Espionage Act, with roughly nine hundred ending up in prison, sequestering this substantial opposition to American efforts in World War I out of ear shot as the federal government bombarded its citizens with military bands and flag waving. Perhaps subduing opposition was a necessary evil given that the

President and Congress imposed a draft, compelling men of suitable age to mandatory military service. Perhaps not.

If the federal government was actively stamping out opposition through a courtroom campaign of indictments under the Espionage Act, the national media was no less active in perpetuating a national fervor against socialism and radical opposition in the court of public opinion. In the summer of 1917, the *New York Times* quoted former Secretary of War, Elihu Root, as commenting publicly, "There are men walking about the streets of this city tonight who ought to be taken out at sunrise tomorrow and shot for treason."

Efforts to search for and weed out radical opposition became something of a civic duty. The *New York Times* carried an editorial imploring the civilian population—"It is the duty of every good citizen to communicate to proper authorities any evidence of sedition that comes to his notice." In other words, if you see something, say something. By 1918, the U.S. Attorney General soberly declared, "never in its history has this country been so thoroughly policed."

These efforts, for whatever they suggested about the American media, did not prevent militant antiwar protestors in Oklahoma from making plans to destroy a railroad bridge and cut telephone wires with the goal of interfering with military enlistment. Meanwhile, the U.S. Post Office suspended service for magazines and newspapers that had published articles with an antiwar message.

In the City of Angels, Los Angeles, the U.S. Attorney General's office prosecuted a filmmaker under the Espionage Act for making and showing a film entitled, *The Spirit of '76*. Robert Goldstein's film depicted British atrocities committed against American colonist militias during the Revolutionary War over a century before. In a decision ultimately listed as *U.S. v. Spirit of '76*, filmmaker Robert Goldstein was convicted and sentenced to ten years in prison because his film tended "to question the good faith of our ally, Great Britain."

Soon, all left-leaning social agitation was deemed radical and/or socialist. As news spread of the socialist revolution in Russia by 1917, this agitation culminated in the first of America's Red Scares.

The Red Scare at home and World War I abroad gave the federal government the impetus it needed for stamping out the IWW once and for all. The crackdown was nationwide, coordinated by the U.S. Department of Justice (DOJ). Over the course of a single month in September of 1917, the DOJ carried out nearly fifty raids on IWW meeting halls, ultimately arresting some 165 IWW leaders on charges of conspiracy to hinder the U.S. military draft, encouraging desertion and inciting opposition to the war.

At trial, one IWW member took the stand—

> You ask my why the I.W.W. is not patriotic to the United States. If you were a bum without a blanket; if you had left your wife and kids when you went west for a job, and had never located them since; if your job had never kept you long

enough in a place to qualify you for a vote; if you slept in a lousy, sour bunkhouse, and ate food just as rotten as they could give you and get by with it; if deputy sheriffs shot your cooking case full of holes and spilled your grub on the ground; if your wages were lowered on you when the bosses thought they had you down; if there was one law for Ford, Suhr, and Mooney, and another for Harry Thaw; if every person who represented law and order and the nation beat you up, railroaded you to jail, and the good Christian people cheered and told them to go to it, how in hell do you expect a man to be patriotic? This war is a businessman's war and we don't see why we should go out and get shot in order to save the lonely state of affairs that we now enjoy.

Of the hundred and one IWW leaders put on trial in April 1918, the jury found them all guilty—every last one—sentencing all to prison for as many as twenty years. The IWW was shattered by the time World War I ended in November 1918. All told, foray into World War I had cost the nation fifty thousand American soldiers. It didn't take long for an overwhelming disillusionment to sweep much of the country, already weary with bitterness.

Ernest Hemmingway would write his novel, *A Farewell to Arms*, and a Hollywood screenwriter would go on to write a visceral, spine-wrenching novel about a torso and brain, still connected and clinging to life, left for dead on the battlefield of World War I; a work entitled, *Johnny Got His Gun*.

If all the wartime jailings, intimidation and propaganda-driven campaigns for national unity were any indication, many still held a wholesome fear of socialism, fueled on by a deep-seated xenophobia. Even though the IWW leadership lingered in prison, opposition to the IWW was escalating in violence, revealing a troubling dissention boiling under the surface, directed particularly against those IWW members that were still organizing in protest.

In one episode, for example, an anti-IWW protestor named Frank Everett posed as an army officer and emptied a full machine gun clip into a crowd gathered outside the IWW's former headquarters. A chase ensued as Everett fled into the woods, pursued closely by an angry mob. Everett reached a river and was forced to turn back because the current was far too strong to safely cross. As Everett turned back towards the mob, he shot the leading man dead, tossed his handgun into the river, and then engaged the rest of the oncoming mob in hand-to-hand combat. Outnumbered, Everett was captured alive and dragged back to town tied to a car, where he was hung from a telephone pole temporarily before being locked in prison. That night, he was broken out of jail only to be castrated, hanged and riddled with bullets by an anti-IWW firing squad.

And so it went.

Even in the face of such violent opposition, American unions waged on, courageously undeterred. In 1920, some 120,000 New England textile workers walked off their assembly lines in strike. In Boston, the police force even walked off duty in protest—the entire police force! In New York City, cigarmakers, shirtmakers, carpenters, bakers, teamsters, schleppers and barbers walked off the job to join the general strike.

Despite these efforts, it seemed that the crucible of American society, burning with civil unrest, now had a chance to cool. The Socialist party was falling apart and the IWW had all but imploded from a lack of leadership. Strikers were beaten down by force and the nation's economy was hovering just high enough above catastrophe in the wake of World War I to stave off mass rebellion.

So too, did Congress pass legislation directed to putting an end to the veritable flood of immigrants onto American soil, some fourteen million between the years of 1900 and 1920. To that end, Congress imposed immigration quotas for the first time. No African country, nor China, Bulgaria or Palestine for that matter, could send more than one hundred nationals to the U.S. Here are some numbers: 34,007 were permitted from England or Northern Ireland; 3,845 from Italy; 51,227 from German; 124 from Lithuania; 28,567 from the Irish Free State; and, last but not least, 2,248 from Russia. I'm sure you've realized but I'll tell you anyways. The quotas favored Anglo-Saxons, kept out those of African and Chinese descent and severely limited arrivals to America of Jews, Latins and Slavs.

Meanwhile, every year in the early 1920's saw roughly 25,000 laborers lose their lives on the job and another 100,000 permanently disabled from injuries related to appalling factory conditions. Appalling and dangerous working conditions were undeniably pervasive during this time.

Living conditions weren't much better. Nearly two million New York City tenants lived in tenements long condemned by the city as too laden with fire hazards to be fit for human habitation. The ironic thing is that the FDNY stopped responding to reports of fire in those "firetraps," and for good reason. You see, mud and filth had accumulated between the paper-thin walls of Manhattan's lower East Side tenement buildings for years, piling densely from floor to ceiling. Conditions turned so bad that, as I mentioned, firemen were instructed to stop responding to reports of active fire, ablaze in the tenements of the lower East Side. 'Why?!' you may be asking yourself, and rightly so. Well, it turns out that the thick layer of dirt accumulated in the walls deprived any burning fire of fuel. The firefighters knew—along with authorities all over the city—that any fire was likely to be out by the time they arrived, smothered of oxygen by filth. 'How could so many people possibly be breathing the same air and expect to live past thirty years of age?!'

You might also be asking yourself, 'You mean to tell me that the standard of living was that low in these so-called apartment houses (hundred year old dirt in the walls!!), yet filled to the brim, literally spilling into the streets with tenant families?' The answer is, 'Yes. Period.'

Despite such widespread squalor, there was some tempered truth to the portrayal of this decade as the 'Jazz Age' and the 'Roaring Twenties' in the colloquial sense. The times are familiar to us. They include characters we know—Picasso, Hemmingway, F. Scott Fitzgerald. Remember Fitzgerald's, *The Great Gatsby*? Granted, the great Jay Gatsby was a fictional character, but his experience is not entirely unrealistic. Gatsby's was, on the other hand, an isolated experience concentrated among a few wealthy elites. For many, many (and I mean many) others, this decade was another story entirely.

In an article entitled, *Echoes of the Jazz Age*, author F. Scott Fitzgerald lamented that the 1920s were "borrowed time anyway—the whole upper tenth of the nation living with insouciance of a grand duc and the casualness of chorus girls." Fitzgerald foretold ominous omens amid the prosperity—

> A classmate killed his wife and himself on Long Island, another tumbled "accidentally" from a skyscraper in Philadelphia, another purposefully from a skyscraper in New York. One was killed in a speak-easy in Chicago; another was beaten to death in a speak-easy in New York and crawled home to the Princeton Club to die; still another had his skull crushed by a maniac's axe in an insane asylum where he was confined.

For the many authors and well-informed citizens of the time, the pervasive class conflict was undeniable, which is why it's rather surprising to think about how few political figures spoke out for poor, working-class families, many of whom toiled by day in sweatshops, only to go home to dilapidated and condemned tenement buildings by night.

One notable exception was Fiorello H. La Guardia, a Congressman and former President of New York City's Board of Aldermen, hailing from New York City's poverty-stricken neighborhood of East Harlem. For example, poor, working-class tenants in Congressman La Guardia's district came to him with complaints one year about the high price of meat. La Guardia appealed to the Secretary of Agriculture, William Jardine, imploring him to investigate the elevated prices. To La Guardia's dismay, Secretary Jardine replied with a mere pamphlet explaining how to use meat economically.

La Guardia wrote back—

> I asked for your help and you send me a bulletin. The people of New York City cannot feed their children on Department bulletins . . . Your bulletins . . . are of no use to the tenement dwellers of this great city. The housewives of New York have been trained by hard experience on the economical use of meat. What we want is the help of your department on the meat profiteers who are keeping the hard-working people of this city from obtaining proper nourishment.

Though just one example, the 1920's saw tremendous activity from La Guardia. Perhaps it was these efforts that earned him the name-sake of one of New York City's international airports, commemorating his notable role in the annuls of New York City's history.

As late as 1928, La Guardia confessed after touring New York City's poverty-stricken neighborhoods, "I was not prepared for what I actually saw. It seemed almost incredible that such conditions of poverty could really exist."

What Socialist advocates persisted through the 1920's maintained their harsh criticism of capitalism as blind to human needs, its proponents beholden only to the almighty dollar. Down through 1929, on the eve of the Great Depression, critics said of capitalism—despite attempts at refinement and organization—that it was still as centered on exploitation as ever.

Perhaps the critics had a point this time; it was the eve of the Great Depression, after all. But that's a matter for another day. For now, let's again turn back the clock and travel back to New York City as it existed during the incredible rise of the city tenant, a social revolution the likes of which the city had never seen.

# ROARING TWENTIES

## A PORTRAIT OF NEW YORK CITY DURING THE 1920S

# Roaring Twenties

## BOOK ONE

### ALL'S FAIR IN LOVE & WAR

*The law of war is harsh. If there's anything good at all in a war, it's that it brings the best and worst out of people: some people try to use the lawlessness to hurt others, and some try to reduce the suffering to a minimum.*

-Mohamed Ould Slahi

## *MOVING DAY*

I want to tell you the story of a little-known social revolution that began for New York City in the early 1900's, but first things first—we should be on the same page about a few things. For one thing, you should know that I recently moved away from my first Manhattan apartment, which sat on the fourth floor of a five story walk-up building constructed on Manhattan's lower East Side, where Suffolk Street and Stanton Street meet, embrace and then cross. The street address is 157 Suffolk Street if you want to be specific.

When I think about my former apartment building, I don't think so much about our fourth-floor flat, but about the rooftop, sitting two stories or so above the living space. The sights, sounds and smells from this particular rooftop are likely to leave a lasting impression on anyone who's ascended the treacherously crooked staircase to my former oasis, a rooftop perched in such a way as to face downtown, the tower at One World Trade shimmering above the horizon. I remember watching airplanes of all shapes and speeds streak across the horizon past the iconic skyscraper at One World Trade; sounds of children playing shriek over the low hum of building ventilation; the well-timed squawk from a pet parrot down Clinton Street; tracking helicopter traffic; the occasional lightning storm. Home.

Before moving out last week, I lived as a tenant. I didn't own my building or even my apartment, and instead paid a monthly rent to reserve the space. In that way, I shared something in common with some 60 percent of residents living in New York City's five boroughs in 2016, most of whom will likewise pay rent each month to live as tenant-residents of this expansive city. As tenants of New York City, we all pay rent to a landlord, each month and on time (usually). This landlord could be anyone. Maybe the landlord owns the apartment building or a particular unit; maybe the landlord is a commercial lessee, hired by the building owner to manage the property and sublet to individual tenants. Maybe the landlord is from New York, has called the five boroughs home since birth. Maybe the landlord is from overseas or some exotic corner of the world.

Maybe the landlord is opportunistic, raising the rent whenever the chance presents itself. Maybe not. Maybe the landlord makes repairs when needed. Maybe not. Our former landlord (my two roommates' and mine) is likely still a resident of Florida. I can't tell you his name for safety reasons but you should know that he lives in Florida most of the year as a way to try and avoid having to pay state income tax on the rent he collects from his two apartment buildings in Manhattan. Yes, I believe he's Jewish.

Any tenant who's lived in Manhattan's lower East Side neighborhood knows well that there's a harsh reality to living in New York City, particularly in Manhattan. Every year, many tenants across all five boroughs will, without fail, face the prospect of a rent increase at some point during their tenancy, simple as that. This is as true for tenants living on Manhattan's lower East Side as it is for tenants inhabiting the West Village. Upper East, Upper West, Midtown, Financial District, Flatiron, Hell's Kitchen, Kip's Bay, Murray Hill, East Village, Alphabet City, Gramercy, Nolita, TriBeCa, Little Italy, Chinatown. For tenants across all of these neighborhoods and beyond, it's not a question of whether there *will* be a rent increase on an annual or semi-annual basis. The only question will be, 'How much?' Millions of tenants from all corners of New York City come face-to-face with a similar fate every year.

Not to say that this characteristic of New York City is remarkable in any way. Rents in New York City are high, to be sure, but tenants living in many American urban centers—from New York to Chicago, Seattle to San Francisco, and everywhere in between—likewise see their monthly rent go up on a semi-regular basis. Instead, I point this out about New York City by way of contrast to highlight the relative scarcity of a decrease in rent, as opposed to the relative frequency of a rent increase. To be spared the added expense of a raise in rent is widely considered, particularly in Manhattan, to be a minor miracle; while a decrease in rent is almost entirely unheard of. That it does happen occasionally only adds to the lore as tenants, the city over, are imbued with hope that they too, one year, might experience such a fortuitous turn of events.

I don't mean to gloat, but in 2015, we, the fourth-floor tenants at 157 Suffolk Street, were just so struck by luck. In fact, we got lucky in the same way last year, too. You see, after I first moved in during the fall months of 2013, we didn't have to pay a rent increase for our 2014-2015 lease term, nor did we have to agree to a rent increase for our 2015-2016 lease term. Here's what I mean. Living in Apartment 4 would've cost you and two roommates $4,580 per month for the last five months of 2013 and the first seven months of 2014, respectively. Beginning in August 2014, by contrast, renting all rooms together ran precisely $4,300 per month. Before I moved out we had entered into a lease agreement for the same amount, to be paid monthly through the last day of July 2016. As you may have guessed, I have no intention of paying any more in rent to this landlord; but more on that later.

The rarity of a rent decrease in the lower East Side, one of those Manhattan neighborhoods with stock that's always rising, shouldn't go understated. As I may have mentioned, however, a rent decrease is not unheard of and, in point of fact, Manhattan tenants living the city over demanded their rent be lowered on almost a daily basis during the early part of the twentieth century.

Yes, you heard me right. Between the years of 1919 and 1929, New York City's tenants banded together against a fearsome real estate interest that lie deeply entrenched in city and state politics, these tenants overcoming seemingly insurmountable opposition to keep rents modestly stable and, perhaps more importantly, to secure renter's rights that my fellow tenants and I still enjoy today, nearly a century later.

Realizing that you may have caught on to the short window of time between the years of 1919 and 1929, let me assure you that the bevvied onslaught of progress I mentioned was set in motion long before 1919. But in the early days of America's Roaring Twenties, New York City tenants were feverishly, by the tens of thousands, even hundreds of thousands, imploring landlords to hold off raising their rents, even begging for a decrease from the previous year.

Times grew so desperate during the Roaring Twenties, in fact, that tenants turned to increasingly desperate measures. I don't mean to alarm you, but to give you a flavor of the times, consider that there's at least one account of a tenant taking his landlord hostage at gunpoint, demanding a rent decrease of his landlord under threat of imminent murder. Other, more reasonable tenants appealed to politicians and judges for relief, both federal and state Judges, a request that even made its way all the way to our nation's highest, the U.S. Supreme Court.

Such a request for a rent reduction may seem outlandish by today's standards, one that would require an extraordinary amount of leverage to have any chance of being taken seriously. Believe me when I tell you that the same is true today as it was, say, in 1920 or 1921. I mean, honestly, have you ever seriously asked your landlord to lower your monthly rent? I ask you this not to expose you as unreasonable, but to illustrate just how rare a time it was to be a tenant in New York City around the turn of the twentieth century, when this story really begins.

In those days, by 1903 let's say, New York City's tenants began flocking, migrating really, in huge swaths from squalid tenement buildings in Manhattan's overcrowded East Side neighborhoods, so squalid that this corner of the island had been brandished by some as "the City of Living Death." These tenement families migrated out to Brooklyn and, quite literally, greener pastures. When you consider the reality of those old tenement buildings, which were dug into Manahatta's eastern shoreline back in the 1850's, it's not hard to see how "the City of Living Death" got its name.

No two ways about it, by the 1850's, New York City's system of leasing and subleasing resulted in horrific living conditions for working-class families, most of whom were packed endlessly into dense ethnic enclaves, neighborhoods so stricken by poverty and filth that even the grainy photographs that do exist of these areas of early New York City tend to shock the conscience. City tenants were, in effect, at the mercy of property owners, their plight largely lost on lawmakers and tenement building owners. In no small part to address the over-crowding, poverty and disease of New York City's low-income neighborhoods, it was this vile reality that prompted New York's state legislature, sitting upstate in Albany, to pass the Tenement House Act of 1901, a comprehensive overhaul of New York's real estate law designed to regulate future construction with the twin aims of reducing congestion and improving sanitary conditions.

As a result of state legislators' efforts in Albany, New York City saw, beginning around 1903, an unprecedented residential construction boom made possible by plentiful labor, relatively inexpensive building materials and pent-up capital begging for investment into residential construction.

Constructing a residential building on Manahatta required, same as it does today, capital investment whereby a real estate investor takes on financial risk with the expectation of a later occurring generation of revenue. In the context of residential construction during 1903, a real estate investor's financial risk took the form of an obligation, at some future time, to pay off a loan taken on mortgage to finance construction of a residential apartment building, as opposed to paying the full cost of construction in cash up front. Upon completion, a shrewd financier might pay off the mortgage loans for a given building and then, in turn, issue a subsequent loan on mortgage to a committed purchaser of the newly-constructed building.

You should know, however, that these lenders and banks in no way resembled those institutional investors that come to mind today. Rather, real estate investment during the early days of the twentieth century came largely from unchartered "immigrant banks" that were unlicensed and unregulated "phantom institutions" folded into other, equally unregulated business enterprises. And these real estate brokers, immigrant banks and other types of unlicensed amateur lenders bought, sold and financed construction of many early New York City tenement buildings.

Propelled onwards by a strong and, at times, gusting tailwind of capital investment, real estate investors and developers set about a record-breaking stretch of residential construction around the turn of the century, spurred on by the tremendous promise of monetary return on real estate investment and property ownership in New York City's residential real estate market. Builders set upon and completed, often at an astonishing pace, everything from posh high-rise apartment buildings in Manhattan's East and West Side neighborhoods, to more modest five and six-floor walk-up apartment buildings in Brooklyn and the Bronx. So, when thousands of tenant families fled their old-law (pre-Tenement House Act) tenement buildings in Manhattan's lower East Side, migrating across the majestic and recently-completed Williamsburg Bridge, into new-law tenement buildings in Brooklyn and the Bronx, tenant families were greeted by far better apartments with, for the first time, plenty of light and air; even hot water, toilets and bathtubs (oh my!).

Manhattan's tenants in those days had a reputation for moving at the slightest inducement, so consistently and so often as to be known as "the most restless population in the world." As a result, landlords understandably held a wholesome fear of not being able to fill all of their apartments, a vacancy that could mean a hard-felt financial loss for the city's landlords, most of whom operated on a shoestring. And in early 1916, by which time the city-wide construction boom had steadied, New York City's vacancy rate (a measure of available apartments that remain un-rented) settled at 5.6 percent, a figure that Tenement House Commissioner, Frank Mann, publicly announced as nearly twice as high as normal.

A vacancy rate regarded as abnormally high garnered for tenants tremendous leverage to ask for a decrease in rent because landlords, particularly those in Manhattan, were desperate to fill their emptying apartments, going to great lengths to commit restless Manhattan tenants to lease agreements and even more desperate to keep those tenants from succumbing to the omnipresent temptation of flight to greener pastures in Brooklyn and the Bronx. Landlords went to great lengths, not only making repairs at the drop of a hat for requests usually ignored altogether, but also painting and otherwise decorating apartments in order to avoid vacancy. Perhaps most strikingly, landlords were largely willing to grant a "rent concession," which meant that the landlord would simply allow a tenant to live rent-free for a month or two, occasionally longer, without any obligation to repay the rent from those conceded months.

If the idea of a "rent concession" seems strange to you, if it causes you a fit of skepticism—taking root in one or more of your eyebrows and causing it or them, as the case may, to furl with suspicion—you might be on to something. Surely, tenants couldn't hold that much leverage over their landlords, could they? To be able, at a moment's notice, to simply demand that a landlord make repairs on a building that has teetered on the razor's edge of complete disrepair for 50 years or more? To be able, at the drop of a hat, to convince a landlord to simply allow the tenant to live rent-free? 'That would never fly today,' you might be thinking to yourself. And rightfully so. Your inclination that some aspect of the story, some piece of the puzzle is missing, is spot on.

Other than avoiding apartment vacancies, landlords had another incentive to grant rent concessions. Here's what I mean. Most tenement buildings, as many as 90 percent by some estimates, were built in those years, not by prudent, individual investors concerned with how property values might vary over the long term, but rather, by speculative real estate investors and developers who were anxious to sell a building as soon as construction was complete, when the speculator would then pay off the first and perhaps a second or third mortgage, only to turn around and then quickly begin work on another building. Indeed, real estate speculation in this sense became rampant in those early years of the twentieth century, spurred on by loan operators—oftentimes an unlicensed ethnic lender or "immigrant bank"—that lent capital on mortgage to a builder, who then sold to a purchaser immediately once construction was complete, even before. The purchaser would then either rent directly to the public or, alternatively, employ a professional lessee to manage the property and sublet to tenants. Notably, the speculative real estate owner would in no event hold on to the building long enough to be even remotely deterred from granting a rent concession for even a month or two.

A report of New York's "immigrant banks" in 1909 revealed that these unlicensed institutions were entirely unregulated, drawing speculators from all walks of life into banking and real estate investing. Incredibly, this report found that "[i]t is easier to become a banker than to open a saloon or barber shop, or to run a push-cart, or to enter other less responsible occupations which are subject to regulation of some kind." As Jared Day points out in his study, *Urban Castles*—

> While immigrant banks served as critical sources of capital for local real estate investment, they were simply part of a much larger body of ethnic capitalists who operated as unlicensed lenders. Immigrant bankers stood at the center of a broad continuum of unregulated lenders that embraced loansharks and pawnbrokers, on the one hand, and unlicensed bankers whose operations, in all other regards, resembled those of established, chartered banking houses, on the other.

Indeed, some such peddlers—Mayer Lehman, for example, who was one of the founders of Lehman Brothers—went on to amass large fortunes in real estate lending. To be sure, builders and purchasers of these early tenement buildings were unregulated and unprofessional for all intents and purposes.

Another aspect of real estate ownership that favored short-term, speculative real estate investing was the fact that the property value for a given residential building depended, above all else, on the "rent roll," as opposed to simply the rental income for a given year. The rent roll, as it was meant in those years, was a measure of property value accounting for rental income over the entire term of all lease agreements for a given building and assumed, as well, that these lease agreements wouldn't be broken, terminated or held to be otherwise unenforceable by a New York state or municipal Judge. Rent roll calculations also assumed the absolute regularity of rental payments and the integrity of lease agreements, both of which were very often forged or fraudulently accounted for by speculators and landlords alike (believe me when I tell you that this still goes on, even today). For example, by employing rent concessions and fraudulent leases, building owners feigned the illusion of a high rent roll, which dictated whether and for what profit speculative investors could unload their holdings before taking up the next building project. This had the effect of artificially inflating property values the city over, regardless of how generously landlords appeared to be granting rent concessions.

Given the landscape of New York City's residential markets, it's easy to see now, with the benefit of hindsight, that neglect and evasion of the law became less a common practice and more a quintessential strategy for survival as a loan operator, developer or lessee. Even those on this side of the industry readily admitted that the lion's share of buildings in Manhattan were neglected "as a matter of custom and regular business practice."

The higher the rent roll, the higher the property value, simple as that. There was a rule of thumb employed by those in the real estate business that the property value for a given residential apartment building was eight to ten times the rent roll. Still, landlords and speculators alike, try as they might, could not escape the grip of those familiar and often unpredictable market forces—supply and demand. On the supply side, New York City's construction boom saw a dramatic increase in the supply of new living accommodations and, by extension, a rise in the city's vacancy rate. A timeless pillar of economics is that when supply expands, price drops, especially if demand remains constant. Conversely, if demand rises, so too does price, particularly if supply remains constant.

The supply-side of the residential housing market expanded rapidly beginning in 1903. Demand, though steadily on the rise in those early days, did not outpace the rapid expansion of the city's supply of livable apartments. The result, as you might expect, was that landlords and commercial lessees endured years of abnormally low rents leading up to America's entry in 1917 into the fray of a 'war to end all wars,' World War I.

By 1917, when then-President Woodrow Wilson signed the Selective Service Act (also known as the Conscription Act) into law, residential construction in New York City had sputtered and stalled. Even if residential construction had been half as robust as it was only ten years earlier, no amount of construction could keep pace with the massive influx of European immigrants, gushing through America's porous borders into New York City's five boroughs at an alarming rate. As it happened, the influx of immigrants drove a steady and sharp increase in the demand for vacant apartments, the supply of which was shrinking just as sharply by 1917.

The resulting uptick in demand for housing accommodations caught up with a narrowing supply of vacant apartments, this much was inevitable. And by the fall rental season of 1917, looking for an apartment in any one of New York City's five boroughs was akin to looking for an elusive needle in the proverbial haystack. Landlords, brokers, investors, movers, schleppers and others forming the city's deeply-entrenched real estate interest, were euphoric. The fall renting season that year ended with many vacant apartments filled for the first time in a year, some for the first time ever.

Residential construction, on the other hand, continued to stall during the early months of 1917, raising the prospect, for the first time since the city's residential construction boom began, of a potential scarcity of livable apartments. Following the fall rental season in 1917, real estate brokers all over the city advised tenants to remain in their apartments for the year and resist their restless urge to move. A public service announcement published that fall season admonished tenants to meet "slight rent advances" for the coming year before heeding that tenants who refused to pay a slight rent increase might face the imminent prospect of homelessness.

As it turned out, every tenant in every corner of New York City's five boroughs paid a rent after the fall renting season of 1917 that was higher than the previous lease. And for what? Well, as many read in the newspapers, "for [the] privilege of being a New Yorker." That landlords *could* so indiscriminately raise rents was due in part to the relative scarcity of apartments, a supply-side shortage that was worsening by the day. Why, exactly, landlords *did* so indiscriminately raise rents is still the subject of some debate.


Debates often end with the passing of time and the benefit of hindsight, and it's now, with the benefit of nearly a century of hindsight, rather easy to see that these early rent increases were relatively modest. So modest, in fact, that despite a rent increase of say, 40 or 50 percent in monthly rent, even the most conservative and skeptical of minds would readily admit that these years leading up to the winter of 1917 were not a bad time to be a tenant in New York City. Rents were affordable, apartments were abundant and landlords were accommodating. No doubt about it, life was good.

As tenants reaped the benefits, however, landlords brooded, waiting for the opportunity to recoup what they felt was owed to them after several lean years bookending and including World War I. As a result, most landlords grew eager, anxious even, to harvest the tremendous promise of real estate ownership in New York City, a growing rapacity that began to manifest in widespread, albeit relatively modest, rent increases. Even though tenants saw a glimpse of what landlords had in store for them in early 1917, it was, in that day, wholly unclear to the city's tenants just how far landlords would go to squeeze a profit from real estate ownership.

And then the winter of 1917 hit.

## *A HARSH WINTER*

A "hawser," as it was called in the early twentieth century, described a rope or cable, thick in either case, for mooring or towing a ship. Hawsers employed by the U.S. Navy in 1917, for example, were extraordinarily strong, resistant to 50 mile-per-hour winds and sub-zero temperatures. In fact, the right Navy hawser would be strong enough to hold together, intact against the winds and temperature, four large steam-powered tugboats, each weighing some 150 tons; or by a more familiar metric, roughly 300,000 pounds.

And during the winter months of 1917, four tugboat captains did just that, linking together four ice-cutter tugboats by a single hawser with the mission of breaking through a stern sheet of ice, a sheet spanning the entirety of New York Harbor and steadily swallowing up tugboats piloted by other captains who had tried, as single voyagers, to make the ordinarily routine trip across New York Harbor to deliver precious coal to Manhattan's ports from New Jersey. At its longest, the coal's journey from the Jersey tidewater to New York City meant traversing a distance of no more than 30 miles and, along some routes, the last leg was so short as to be within eyeshot of Manhattan's coal yards run by the city's large retail coal dealers. In fact, the final journey through New York Harbor was the coal's easiest leg of an otherwise onerous journey from mine to market.

By December 1917, many a'single tugboat, try as it might, had to be retrieved and towed back to the New Jersey shoreline due to a broken propeller or, far worse, ending up permanently marooned, its icy captor unrelenting.

Remember the four tugboat captains who tied their ice-breaking ships together? The result of those four tugboat captains' courageous efforts, piloting four Navy tugboats knotted together by a single hawser, was a temporary channel through the thickening ice of New York Harbor, which afforded safe and swift passage for tugboats and other coal-shipping vessels from New Jersey's port terminals along the tidewater, to supply all of New York City (and beyond) with precious coal.

New York City during this time was, as it remains today, an untamable beast with an insatiable appetite. The city craved coal back then, which was necessary to power its iconic bright lights during all hours of the day and, more importantly, provide heat to the city's many and growing population of diverse residents. You see, coal was in short supply nationwide that year and by the end of

January 1918, the situation for New York City grew dire. In this way, a temporary channel carved into the ice (four tugboats wide and thirty miles long), stretching from South Amboy, along New Jersey's tidewater to Manhattan, proved, at least temporarily, to be a lifeline for residents living in any one of the city's five boroughs. From a port in South Amboy alone, this temporary channel permitted coal, by the hundreds of thousands of tons, to reach the homes and businesses of New York City. Given such a severe coal dependency, a coal shortage like the one New York City's residents experienced in the midst of 1917 and 1918's winter months would not go unnoticed and, in point of fact, could be catastrophic for the city's quality of life.

If you really want to know about it, this coal shortage was truly a labor shortage, brought on in many ways by an exodus of able-bodied American workers overseas following their enlistment in the U.S. military. Mind you, many in this lot of soldiers didn't enlist by choice, having been drafted by then Commander-in-Chief, Woodrow Wilson, to fight overseas in the name of America's efforts during World War I.

Regardless of your political leanings when it comes to military drafts, you must realize the undeniable impact these soldiers' absence had at home. With labor in such short supply, the country's railroad companies were incredibly short-handed, which wrought havoc with nation-wide commercial transport—shipping in general and coal in particular. As a nationwide labor shortage pinched the collective resources of U.S. railroad shipping companies, the labor shortage begat a transportation shortage, which, in turn, begat a rather public skirmish between those in the railroad industry and those in the coal industry.

New York City's coal interest, through its National Coal Association, did a fair amount of public finger-pointing during December 1917, finger-pointing directed almost exclusively at the railroad shipping companies. For example, the National Coal Association, by public announcement, maintained—

> There need not have been a fuel famine in 1917; there need not have even been a coal shortage. That there was a fuel famine, with its attendant suffering, was due solely to transportation facilities.

The railroad companies and associations (also known as "transportation facilities"), for their part, denied responsibility. Regardless, it is clear today, with the benefit of hindsight, that the tri-state area was ill-prepared for the unprecedented severity of those winter months, lacking the infrastructure and organization required to coordinate a swift solution to the penetrating winds, punishing cold and growing animosity between railroad companies and coal shippers. Fragile, like a dry field of coarse, predatory grass during a drought, New York City's transportation facilities seemed poised to ignite at even the slightest provocation.

What exposed this animosity between the coal shipping industry and railroad companies, lingering just below the surface? The short answer—a harsh winter. For this, America's greatest city, was not immune to a harsh winter. In fact, no New York City winter on record had been harsher than the winter season straddling the years of 1917 and 1918. Temperatures that season, for one thing, were the lowest ever recorded by the Weather Bureau to date, some 46 years since the Bureau started keeping record in 1871.

That winter also brought with it the full force of epic winds, hurling at speeds of 45 to 50 miles per hour, with gusts of 70 to 80 miles per hour one day in mid-December. A series of severe snowstorms, five regional blizzards in total, all but paralyzed the Northeast and Midwest. New York City saw a full foot of snow in December 1917 and another thirteen inches for good measure in January of the following year, 1918.

Precipitation in combination with frigid temperatures is, without fail, a recipe for ice and ice there was—more ice, reported the *New York Times*, than at any time in the past thirty years. Monstrous ice floes clogged New York Harbor, choking off New York City's vital supply of coal; coal burned by millions of residents to keep the city's pulse beating regularly. Indeed, the coal shortage escalated to an acute crisis. For example, residents and business owners in the Bronx required an average of 4,000 tons of coal each day to keep their lights on and heat running. Bronx residents could not stay warm with less, particularly during one of the harshest winters in New York City's recorded history. Yet, during December 1917, Bronx residents had to make due with a mere 1,000 tons of coal per delivery, which came from coal-shippers at intermittent and irregular intervals from New Jersey's tidewater.

Considering the pernicious cold and attendant lack of coal, it was no surprise when New York's Health Commissioner announced that, half-way through December 1917, "deaths from pneumonia were the largest recorded in five years." Almost immediately—within a matter of days—New York's Fuel Administrator, Albert H. Wiggin, declared the necessity of coal conservation, urging businesses to use less electricity for the lighting of signs. If the first to suffer the effects of New York City's coal shortage was residents' health, the first solution was to turn off New York City's lights. Brilliant. What prevented Fuel Administrator Wiggin from talking less and doing more? What did New York City's Mayor, John F. Hylan, have to say? Did he even know? As the winter months wore on it became clear, obvious even, that the city would need far more drastic measures with respect to coal conservation.

I may have mentioned this before, but to say that New York City suffered a "coal shortage" is really a misnomer. You might be surprised to learn, like I was, that there was, in fact, plenty of coal set aside for New York City, piled high by the frozen ton at New Jersey's tidewater where it sat, within sight but tauntingly out of reach for New York City's residents; residents who received intermittent deliveries of some 30,000 tons of coal per day, if they were lucky. By the time Fuel Administrator Wiggin realized that New York City's lack of coal was exposing the city's residents to an acute crisis, the ordinarily benign stretch of New York Harbor separating New Jersey from New York was completely frozen over, a solid sheet of thick ice. At one point, Fuel Administrator Wiggin implored Director General of Railroads, W.G. McAdoo, to lift an ordinance prohibiting the use of Pennsylvania's tunnels—known endearingly as "the tubes"—for freight traffic so that coal might be delivered into New York City by freight train. Director General McAdoo more or less fell in line behind this proposal.

Fuel Administrator Wiggin's efforts, however well-intentioned, proved, in the end, to be in vain. In outward opposition to any and all requests, railway shipping companies were unrelenting in their refusal to ship coal any further than New Jersey's tidewater, arguing adamantly that they did not have enough able-bodied employees to carry coal shipments all the way into the yards of New York City's large retail coal dealers. Coal dealers, on the other hand, persisted otherwise.

The two groups, coal and railway, and their respective employee unions all stood at a stubborn and unrelenting standstill in December 1917 during this, a formally-declared city-wide crisis that was now threatening to deprive all of New England of coal. To that end, Fuel Administrator Wiggin requested a few government tugboats to loosen the logjam of coal accumulating along New Jersey's tidewater, a request outspokenly supported by New York City's Mayor, John F. Hylan. Indeed, New York City's competing coal and railroad interests feuded with such bullheadedness that federal officials of the U.S. Government saw no choice but to intervene, and ultimately assumed complete, albeit temporary, authority over coal-shipping, an aspect of American infrastructure typically reserved to the private sector.

And four of those very tugboats, held together by a single hawser, were used to carve a channel through the ice floes from South Amboy, through New York Harbor, to Manhattan and beyond, providing temporary, but nonetheless critical, reprieve.

As the winter months of 1917 and 1918 pressed on, the weather did not improve. Unprecedented cold continued to pinch the city's supply of coal and, at the same time, caused demand for coal to soar. Recall those timeless pillars of economics, supply and demand? Do you remember how, as supply expands (and demand stays constant), price generally decreases? Well, supply and demand can work the other way too. For example, as supply narrows, price tends to increase, particularly when demand remains constant. Conversely, if demand grows, price also tends to increase, particularly when supply remains constant. If supply narrows as demand grows, there is a compounding effect on price, which has the potential to skyrocket.

That is exactly what happened to the price of coal during the winter months of 1917 and 1918. The skyrocketing price of coal meant higher expenses for landlords and residential building owners alike. In those days, landlords and building owners had two options when faced with an added expense; a long-term option and a short-term option. Over the long-term, a landlord could absorb the added expense as a cost of doing business and hope to recoup any loss over a given period of time, usually measured in terms of years or even decades. In the short-term, by contrast, a landlord could minimize the impact by passing the added expense immediately on to tenants in the form of a rent increase, for example. Naturally, landlords and building owners often chose the latter and that winter was no different. Landlords in unison answered the bell rung by the added expense of coal by raising tenants' rents during those punishing winter months, no two ways about it.

At this point you should be asking yourself an obvious question. 'How is it possible that landlords could raise the rent that quickly? Hadn't the tenants signed a lease that effectively locked in their monthly rent for a full year? Landlords surely didn't have the power to raise rents whenever the pleased to whatever they wanted, did they?' As you may have guessed, the answer is an unequivocal and resounding, 'Duh!' particularly when you consider that rent control, as we know it today, did not exist yet in New York City as of 1917 and 1918.

In order to understand how landlords could wield such unchecked power to raise the rent, you must absolutely understand something fundamental about tenants' lease agreements in New York City in those years. Even among the well-off, long-term written leases of a year or longer were the exception to the rule, not the norm, for all but the city's wealthiest tenants. In high-class buildings like the Tomahawk gracing the upper West Side's Riverside Drive, for example, any written leases were to run only from October 1, say of 1919, to September 30, one year later. By contrast, written leases of any duration were unheard of for nearly every other tenant throughout the city's five boroughs who relied, instead, on oral lease agreements on a monthly basis, an informal, oral agreement that did fix the rent, but only for a month or so at a time. Consequently, landlords in those days could, at least in theory, raise the rent every month, indefinitely and without restraint, then shrug their shoulders at one another and confess, "Hey, that's just capitalism for ya's."

In 1917, you won't be surprised to learn that every tenant in each corner of New York City's five boroughs paid a higher rent than the year before, a harbinger of things to come. For some, the rent increase was within their family's means. For others, the increase in rent squeezed the family's finances to such an extent as to be cause for serious concern. For example, there was a police officer that lived near Southern Boulevard in the Bronx, a working-class, predominantly Italian neighborhood. With the officer's yearly take, he and his family couldn't afford to pay more than $17.50 towards monthly rent. This police officer lived with his family in a four-room apartment that the landlord, notably, neglected to regularly heat. The officer and his family first faced the prospect of a rent increase in 1916, when the landlord raised the monthly rent from $28, an exorbitant amount to the officer as it was, to $32 in 1917 and, eventually, to $40 in 1918. This was an increase of over 40 percent! This police officer was not alone in his plight as some claimed that rents had nearly doubled in working-class neighborhoods over the course of a mere two or three years' time.

Recall that real estate brokers cautioned, by public announcement, of "slight" rent increases for that year's rental season? Does anything about a 40 percent increase in rent seem slight to you? Before you answer, consider that many of the city's tenants had, for generations, allocated their finances so as not to spend more than a week's pay for a month's rent. Following a third round of rent increases, that police officer living in the Bronx was committing nearly 60 percent of his yearly income to paying rent.

With the supply of apartments dwindling, that landlords used a city-wide coal shortage to again raise rents only added insult to injury, further deepening a firmly entrenched resentment landlords had for tenants (and vice versa), an animosity that took root during those lean years endured by landlords before World War I. It went on like this, landlords passing the increased price of scarce coal on to tenants by raising rents and, at the same time, not only neglecting, but flat out refusing to provide heat, leaving many frigid tenant families to fend for themselves.

'Did tenants just take the rent increases lying down?' you might be asking. 'Did they take any action?'

Most tenants had no choice but to pay the rent increase due, in no small part, to landlords' threats of eviction by summary proceeding. The threat of eviction by summary proceeding was no empty threat when you consider how these lopsided legal proceedings were stacked so undeniably against tenants and in favor of landlords. Consider that a landlord could seek to evict a tenant by simply accusing a tenant in open court of being an "undesirable," a term formally referring to a tenant whose presence in an apartment was so destructive or whose disposition so recalcitrant that the landlord was left no choice but to have the tenant forcibly removed from the building. By law, the landlord need not offer any proof of a recalcitrant tenant's undesirability, but need only to make the claim and a municipal Judge presiding over the summary proceeding had no choice but to rule in favor of the landlord, regardless of fact or circumstance.

Tenants' only recourse seemed to be to hone in on an aspect of their apartment that had gone into disrepair—a lack of heat, for example—and partially withhold the month's rent commensurate with the degree of disrepair. With respect to a landlord's failure to regularly provide heat—by far, the most common complaint during the winter months of 1917 and 1918—tenants would intentionally pay less than the full amount of rent if the landlord failed to provide heat, withholding the unpaid rent as collateral in a desperate attempt to goad the landlord into more regularly providing heat. In practice, a tenant's tactic of withholding rent often proved fruitless because landlords would simply seek to evict such a tenant for being an "undesirable," rather than for non-payment of rent, and if charging that the tenant is undesirable, be all but guaranteed a victory in municipal court. As one tenant organizer put it, "When it comes to a squabble between [the tenants] and the landlord [the tenants] haven't got as much a chance as a wax candle on a stove."

For those tenants who did suffer eviction, and there were many, some had places to go but others were far less fortunate. It was common practice for tenant families to be forcibly removed, their furniture shoved to the sidewalk without reproach or fear of reprisal.

As the winter months of 1917 and 1918 eased and temperatures rose, coal again flowed normally into New York City, easing the shortage that had gripped city residents during those frigid winter months. To ensure that New York City would not run short of coal again, public officials urged New Yorkers to stock up on coal during the summer months, to overhaul their furnaces and clean their flues. And, if necessary, wash dishes and take baths in cold water.

As for coal dealers, public officials urged dealers to find a place to store spare coal as a precaution against the prospect of another harsh winter. All involved strongly considered, at one time, storing coal in Central Park.

More disheartening than the thought of storing sooty coal among the sprawling green space of Central Park, the coal shortage that year exposed a growing rapacity of landlords, callously going to great lengths to squeeze every last dollar from their often poor and working-class tenant families, a greed that fueled a growing fire between landlord and tenant that had been again sparked while the U.S. was spread desperately thin as a result of a military foray into World War I. And the tension would only grow worse.

## *A HOUSING SHORTAGE*

If there was finger-pointing and confusion to be had over what, exactly, caused the coal shortage New York City experienced in 1917 and 1918, there was very little dispute over what caused a housing shortage that was beginning to take hold of the five boroughs around the same time, a shortage that was worsening by the day. For as booming as residential construction was in the frothy wake of the Tenement House Act of 1901, residential construction had largely come to a grinding halt by 1918, a year in which tens of thousands of immigrant families continued to pour into New York City from Ireland and Italy, Germany, Russia and Poland, to name a few.

It was simply a matter of numbers. By 1918, demand for apartments was skyrocketing. Meanwhile, only a dozen more apartment buildings were built in 1918 than were demolished. That's right, twelve new buildings for all of New York City! Why so little residential construction? Well, for one thing, even before the U.S. entered World War I in April 1917, the price of building materials was on the rise, nearly doubling in cost between the years of 1914 and 1918. Compounding the issue was a persistent labor shortage that lasted well after America's withdrawal from World War I.

Many argued that the severity of the labor shortage was attributable to an expansive military campaign that eroded America's work force by drafting so many able-bodied American workers to the armed forces, shipping them overseas, or else driving laborers to other jobs in war-related industries. Regardless, given such a pervasive labor shortage, it wouldn't be long until the cost of construction rose again by nearly 50 percent in 1918.

By early 1919, New York City's housing shortage was so severe that, of the city's nearly one million apartments, fewer than 22,000 were vacant; down from more than 53,000 in 1916 and a hearty 67,000 vacant apartments in 1909. Of the 22,000 vacant apartments in 1919, a great many of them were confined to old-law tenement ghettos carved into Manhattan's lower East Side prior to the Tenement House Act of 1901. In the words of Tenement House Commissioner, Frank Mann, these tenement buildings were "habitable 'legally,' but not humanly fit places to live." Even among new-law tenements, the vacancy rate was a jaw-dropping 1.0 percent in Manhattan, 0.5 percent in Brooklyn, less than 0.2 percent in the Bronx and, incredibly, less than 0.1 percent in Queens. Even by 1918, it was obvious that there was not a single decent apartment available for rent in all five boroughs.

True, that building materials were no longer in short supply by 1919. With the end of the American war effort overseas came the end of munitions and military manufacturing, at least for the time being. Nonetheless, building materials continued to be very much in high demand and, rather surprisingly, went to almost every other purpose except construction of residential housing accommodations for the city's working-class residents.

Bricks needed for constructing apartment buildings were instead being used to build theaters; glass needed for apartment windows was being installed as car windshields. Despite some rosy predictions, prices that had been prohibitively expensive during the war years remained high and didn't fall, save for structural steel. But an apartment building frame made of steel, as strong as it can be, would be of little use without bricks or glass or wood to fill out the living space. It would be akin to constructing a human being of skeleton bone alone, strong and miraculous in its own right, but entirely devoid of life absent the musculature, organ, cardiovascular and nervous systems required to constitute a fully alive human being.

Perhaps more important to the sudden cessation of residential construction than the shortage of materials and laborers was a debilitating lack of capital available for backing the mortgage loans required to finance residential construction. Institutional investors—unlicensed immigrant banks and other, larger institutional investors alike—began in 1919 moving capital assets away from real estate and into stocks and bonds, which were more attractive given that they paid a higher percent yield than residential mortgages. First-in-time mortgages took an especially hard hit, even though considered during New York City's construction boom to be highly lucrative investments.

The city's housing shortage, it should come as no surprise, had absolutely no deterrent effect on New York City's population growth, which was rapid as a rabbit patch, if you catch my drift. By 1919, the population of New Yorkers grew by some 115,000, roughly a full 2 percent increase in the city's population, these new residents having poured in from all corners of the globe. By year's end, New York City was widely believed to be 80,000 to 100,000 apartments short, leaving roughly 400,000 to half a'million people without a place to live.

A widely-employed barometer for the severity of New York City's housing shortage in those years was the city's overall vacancy rate. An acute housing shortage might, for example, drive the vacancy rate down to uncharted territory, leaving a significant portion of city tenants without housing accommodations. By April 1920, the city's vacancy rate had plunged from a hearty 5 percent to just above 2 percent. In terms of actual vacancies, this meant that an abysmal 3,500 of the city's more than one million apartments stood vacant. And this estimate itself can be misleading because five of every six vacant apartments were housed in old-law tenement buildings, more than three-quarters of which were almost entirely uninhabitable and largely concentrated in Manhattan's lower East Side.

If the coal shortage of 1917-1918 was an opportunity to raise tenants' rents, then the acute housing shortage that followed was a veritable gold rush for landlords who, it should come as no surprise, took full advantage of the acute supply-side apartment shortage to hike rents, and hike them by leaps and bounds.

Eventually it became clear to everyone who investigated the housing shortage in New York City that the only recourse for such a severe and penetrating housing crisis was to build more apartments, thereby restoring the vacancy rate to acceptable levels. Even during the coal shortage that gripped New York City during the winter months of 1917 and 1918, most recognized that there would be no reprieve until the price of building materials declined and America's labor force returned *en masse* from the battlegrounds of the Great War, allowing for some restoration of balance to the city's housing market. Until lenders began lending for residential construction again, suffice to say, there was no end in sight.

## *EARLY RENT STRIKES*

Given the sordid tendency New York City's landlords shared for raising rents at even the slightest opportunity, relations among the city's tenants and landlords were tenuous at best, and constantly teetering on the razor's edge of confrontation. You should know also that landlords and tenants the city over had a history of skirmishing over rent increases, among other attendant disputes such as landlords' neglect of residential buildings to the point, in some instances, of complete and utter disrepair.

Faced with early rent increases, New York City's tenants fell into one of several camps. Some bit the bullet and paid a rent increase for fear of being dragged by their landlord through the muck of a summary proceeding, which involved navigating the thorny labyrinth of legal proceedings conducted in a language—English—that many of New York City's immigrant tenants had taken up only upon their recent arrival in the U.S. Other, more provocative tenants took a different tact, choosing instead to join together in protest. Recall that common practice among them was to withhold rent, at least in part, thereby hoping to exercise some leverage as a group over their landlords.

The most militant of tenants, however, not only withheld rent, but banded together and engaged in a rent strike in a collective attempt to strong-arm their landlord or building owner into rescinding the rent increase. Collective action such as a rent strike was, at the time, widely associated with socialism as it manifested in European cities such as Paris, and which held a legitimate hold on New York City politics by this time. An isolated series of past rent strikes, unheard of in the U.S. before the Civil War, along with various documented riots in the early 1900's, provide, to this day, a ready glimpse into the practice of organized protest as it reared its head in New York City.

As an example, consider the eighty or so families living in one Manhattan apartment building who, during the spring rental season of 1904, saw their rent increase to "what they declare to be an unjustifiable and unreasonable advance in their rents immediately after sale of the building to a new owner." The new owner promptly raised the rent for each flat (four rooms each), which formerly cost $8 or $9 a room in monthly rent, to $12, $13 and even $15 per month—a raise of 50 percent or more for some tenants.

The tenants of this building, for their part, initially appealed directly to their landlord to rescind the rent increase and allow the tenants to remain in their homes at the former rent. What followed when the landlords refused was that hundreds of tenants went on strike, a strike that endured for nearly a full month. The tension escalated to the point where NYPD officers were called in to preserve order.

This militant camp of city tenants who organized in strike against these early rent increases was led, by and large, by local women, housewives of the day, who had already led a successful boycott in 1902, only two years earlier, against kosher butchers of the lower East Side and other neighborhoods in Manhattan, Brooklyn and the Bronx. Outraged by the rising cost of kosher meat in 1902, up to $0.18 from $0.12, these pugnacious women stopped buying kosher meat altogether and encouraged others to follow suit. I use the word "encourage" in a facetious way given that these furious female organizers denounced women who rebuked the boycott as "scabs," often breaking into their homes, looting all the meat inside and tossing it by the pound into the street.

The boycott organizers went further in their demonstrations, dragging huge slabs of meat from hooks hanging in vendors' storefronts and, without even a hint of compunction, making a scene of trampling the slabs in the streets. They impaled meat on painted sticks and marched around in public, a delectable symbol of boycott.

By 1904, the city's women were at it again. Tenant protesters, spurred on by the city's housewives, organized again in 1904, ultimately forming the New York Tenant Cooperative Association, which offered legal counsel to tenants summoned to appear in court and provided financial support to those tenant families who had suffered eviction. Many predicted that the 1904 rent strikes would prove futile, but these predictions underestimated those marching in protest. Their persistence and, at times, violence, but their cohesion most of all, was unrivaled to that time in New York City. As a result, many landlords responded to these quarrels the only way they could, by rescinding rent hikes and tempering their tendency to bring summary proceedings.

A relatively larger rent strike, involving some five hundred tenants, took hold of Williamsburg a few months later, in 1904. Recall that Williamsburg had recently received a large migration of tenants formerly of Manhattan's lower East Side and also from other of the city's many over-crowded, working-class neighborhoods. This prewar rent strike sparked after a synchronized ring of Manhattan real estate investors purchased several Williamsburg apartment buildings and coordinated a rent increase from $1 to $3, a tripling of the monthly rent! Tenants living in these buildings publicly charged that these real estate investors were increasing rent for the sole end of artificially boosting property value and quickly reselling at an inflated profit. These particular tenants not only withheld rent, they threatened their landlords, called mass meetings, built up a fund to pay for legal fees and intimidated prospective tenants with signs reading, for example, "This House Is On Strike," or "Don't Try To Rent Rooms Here If You Know What's Good For You!" Many striking tenants were so aggressive that city marshals and movers tasked with carrying out evictions often called in police reinforcements.

Adding insult to injury, a nationwide depression in 1907 (dubbed the "Panic of 1907") left Manhattan's lower East Side residents unemployed by the tens of thousands, even reaching 100,000 jobless by some estimates. The Panic of 1907 and attendant unemployment drove city tenants to beseech their landlords to rescind the recent round of rent hikes and even to reduce the rent. "When you are hungry and out of work," explained one east side tenant to the national press, a "$2 [rent reduction] is something big. And in twelve months the saving will more than pay a whole month's rent." Indeed, a $2 decrease in monthly rent, though modest by today's standards, would've certainly gone a long way to feeding a given tenant family in those years.

When landlords refused, as they almost always did, city tenants again went on strike, led by militant housewives to be sure, but also under guidance this time from dedicated community activists and even members of the Socialist party. Operating out of party headquarters on Grand Street, advocates from the Socialist party intervened and advised tenants about how to approach landlords and, if that failed, how to organize a strike.

By December 1907, tenants were far more organized, displaying an unprecedented militancy as they came together in droves for the largest of the prewar rent strikes. This round sparked on Manhattan's lower East Side but soon spread, and spread rapidly to Brownsville and Harlem, ultimately reaching as far as New York City's Italian neighborhoods and even spilled over across state lines, to Hoboken, Newark and Jersey City.

In Manhattan's lower East Side, a young woman emerged as a prominent leader of the tenant resistance. Pauline Neuman—whose experience organizing rent strikes would soon translate into organized protest against low wages and poor working conditions—worked by day at the Triangle Shirtwaist factory on Grand Street and, by night, diligently visited tenant families, arousing their interest in pledging support to efforts directed at lowering rents. As the national press reported, "[Neuman] has organized a band of 400 women, all of whom earn their own living, whose duty it is to promulgate the doctrine of lower rents."

Tenant organizers in 1907 would point out that evicting tenant families was a futile exercise for landlords in any event, ultimately costing the landlord $8 when tenants are only requesting a rent reduction of $1 or $2 in monthly rent. As one Socialist party organizer put it, "houses are easier to get in Harlem and Brownsville," and "once an east side family gets to those places they never go back into the stifled atmosphere of the east side," which left landlords in those neighborhoods particularly vulnerable to a costly vacancy. One East Side organization adopted a foreboding slogan, "We will all be dispossessed, if necessary, but we must have a reduction of $1 to $2."

Though isolated, these early efforts at agitation galvanized some support, perhaps providing a glimpse of things to come. For one thing, representatives of 125 labor and other organizations committed their efforts to cooperate as much as possible with the rent-reduction movement. For another, organizers succeeded in gathering tenants to hear rousing speeches by, most often, Socialist leaders, targeted at rousing support for a collective movement to lower rents. Consider Benjamin Rosenfelt who, at one meeting, argued—

> This is the richest and best developed country in the world. Who made it so? The rich? No. The Police Commissioner? No. The poor made it so. The only cure for this rent evil and all these evils is Socialism. We must work together, one for all, all for one. Down with the rents!

Despite the oration and commitment of tenant organizers, most landlords facing such organized resistance fought back, if not against the tenants themselves, than out of principle against the Socialist party. To be sure, few landlords acknowledged the legitimacy of tenants' complaints, let alone the need for a rent reduction. Landlords and building owners took solace in the fact that summoning these tenants to court through a summary proceeding usually meant a legal victory, the law being on their side and municipal Judges, for their part, deeply troubled by the Socialist party's role in inciting these early rent strikes. Katz & Co., one of the East Side's largest building owners by 1907, threatened publicly to close down each one of its more than 100 tenement buildings rather than yield to demands for a rent reduction.

With respect to quelling tenant unrest, New York City's landlords could also count on the city's police force who, by and large, suffered from a scathing xenophobia and anti-Semitism. Not surprisingly, most of the city's police force viewed these early rent strikes as a direct offshoot of the Socialist party movement. Perhaps they had a point given the provocative nature of the Socialist party's creed, which sounded in revolution—

> There is a deeper cause for this misery than high rents alone, and that is the present capitalist system of private ownership of the means of life, and we therefore demand the entire abolition of the present system, and declare that the land, dwelling places, and means of production of wealth should be the common property of the whole people . . . We demand that the working class receive the full product of its labor . . .

Such sentiments drove the New York Police Department's inclination to deny tenants demonstration permits and forcibly break up organized protest, often invoking use of a billy club. In the words of the Police Commissioner, "If you don't like your rents get out. If you are not satisfied with our system of rents go back where you came from. No, I won't give you any permit."

Faced with such opposition, most tenants naturally paid the rent increase, moved or otherwise succumbed to eviction. Though more widespread, these early rent strikes had no deterrent effect on landlord's practice of freely raising the rent.

Even more widespread were the food riots of 1917, which revealed a more rambunctious side of New York City housewives who, by this point, were openly predisposed to organized protest. In 1917, many of the city's housewives again coalesced around a cause, this time in an attempt to drive down the soaring price of bread, milk, vegetables, meat and eggs.

For example, when the price of eggs climbed to $0.80 a dozen, up from $0.32 only a year earlier, bands of cantankerous women threatened shopkeepers, attacked peddlers and vendors alike, overturned their pushcarts and scattered produce in the streets. Many lashed out at police officers as well, who had been called in by the dozen to try their heavy hand at restoring order. In contrast to early protest against high rents, early protest against the cost of food proved far more effective. Maybe there was a lesson to be learned?

Though perhaps a presage of things to come, the reality was that the prewar rent strikes had very little impact on rents, particularly when compared to the success of strikers against the rising cost of food. The prewar rent strikes were too sporadic, too isolated and largely confined to Manhattan's lower East Side neighborhood, along with other predominantly Jewish neighborhoods like Brownsville and Harlem. The success of these isolated efforts depended largely on harassing a landlord or building owner to such an extent as to leave no choice but to accept an agreement to rescind a rent hike and, in more extreme cases, secure a commitment not to raise the rent for another 12 months. While some landlords did succumb to such agreements, they did so out of convenience rather than fear. To be sure, most viewed the agitation as isolated and, in turn, lacking the ethos of a legitimate threat (though there was certainly no shortage of pathos). Wrote one historian, "From the beginning, this was a Jewish strike; the organizers were Jewish, the tenants were Jewish, and, for the most part, the landlords were Jewish."

Lacking the poignancy hoped for by many, the prewar rent strikes were not devoid of valuable lessons for New York City tenants. To have an impact, tenant organizers now understood that they would have to strike, not by the hundreds or even thousands, but by the tens or hundreds of thousands and they must corral dozens of neighborhoods. A rent strike, to have any real impact, would have to transcend social class and ethnicity. Only by organizing on this grand and unprecedented a'scale would tenants stand a chance of making a difference in a legal and political system stacked firmly in favor of landlords, this much was for sure.

## *RAPACIOUS RENT HIKES*

Not to belittle the atrocity of human life that was World War I, we must jump ahead again from 1917 to New York City's housing shortage, which was, to that point in 1919, a famine unparalleled in New York City's history. Demand for apartments was never higher and continued to accelerate at a surreal pace. For example, consider that an apartment, vacated on Moving Day of 1919, would be easily rented to a new tenant family within hours of being vacated, and would never remain vacant for less than a single day. Meanwhile, a worsening supply-side shortage of livable apartments gave landlords tremendous leverage to set the rent at essentially any rate they saw fit and, likewise, to callously brush aside tenant requests for repairs and basic necessities.

Notoriously, brazen landlords would ask each other often and aloud, "Why should we ask'a $500 raise when we can get $1,500? Why indeed?!" These were rare times for landlords, who didn't want to miss out on what they perceived as a clear opportunity to recoup losses sustained prior to and during World War I; losses stemming from the coal, labor, equipment, building material, construction and housing shortages that simultaneously gripped New York City (and the rest of the country) during those lean years. Less tangibly, but no less critical, these lean years left both landlords and tenants resentful and confrontational towards one another, sowing the seeds of a deep-seated animosity. This animosity only deepened as landlords again capitalized on a supply-side shortage of apartments to raise rents the city over during the renting season of 1919.

Why did landlords persist in raising the rent any chance they got, even in the face of such harassment and protest? Recall that property value at the time was tied directly to the rent roll for a particular building. Rental income aside, landlords continuously hiked residential rents with the aim of inflating a building's rent roll, thereby increasing the property value.

Take the case of a typical five-story walk-up with four apartments per floor. Assume that each room rented for $25 to $30 per month. Even a rent hike of $5 for the month would translate to a $1,200 increase in property value for the year and a whopping $12,000 total evaluation—or one-third the total cost of constructing such a building! Rising rent rolls, by virtue of their being tied to property value over a longer period of time, allowed private-sector speculators to invest, owning just long enough to be able to quickly raise the rent, thereby raising the rent roll, before reselling just as quickly at a higher property value. This practice left tenants vulnerable and largely without recourse against landlords' rapacity.

Also leaving tenants vulnerable was a common aspect of most tenants' lease agreements, something almost unheard of today. Recall that written lease agreements were extremely rare among even the city's well-to-do tenants and, by the same token, virtually non-existent for working-class and poor tenants. In this way, almost all tenants of New York City took possession of their rented apartment units under an oral lease agreement with their landlord.

Notably, there were two types of oral lease agreements whose origins can be traced back to early England. The "monthly tenancy" was said to be a hiring of definite duration, automatically expiring at the end of each month. A tenant could, however, renew a monthly tenancy rather easily, at least in theory, by simply continuing to reside in a given apartment—called "holding over"—which in turn created by default an oral monthly tenancy on the same terms as the month before. The "month-to-month tenancy," by contrast, was said to be of potentially indefinite duration, carrying no expiration date, only a requirement that the tenant pay rent, *in full*, each month. In neither case could an oral lease agreement extend longer than a single year and all leases that did not specify a duration were deemed, by statute at the time, to expire on May 1st, a day endearingly referred to as "Moving Day." In this way, all lease agreements ended on either May 1st or October 1st, earning each day the nickname, "Moving Day," one for the spring rental season and one for the fall rental season respectively.

If the distinction between a "monthly tenancy" and a "month-to-month tenancy" seems esoteric to you, you're in good company. As you might imagine, differentiating among the two, like differentiating among identical twins that have adopted the same style of dress and physical manicuring, proved difficult, giving even trained and experienced Judges fits. The elusiveness of a common-sense distinction between the two types of oral lease agreements perpetuated a tremendous uncertainty as to the scope and nature of a landlord's relationship with his or her tenants.

Given this pervasive uncertainty, a strong lobby on behalf of landlords, building owners and real estate investors (referred to collectively for convenience as the "real estate interest") lobbied New York's state legislature, sitting upstate in Albany, to address the issue in 1918. Significantly, New York's state legislature was renowned as opaque at best and largely beholden to a powerful, wealthy real estate interest or, at the very least, fearful of falling out of favor with real estate investors, many of whom were also campaign contributors. The result of these efforts upstate was the Ottinger Law, a new statute named after its sponsoring lawmaker, which Senator Albert E. Ottinger designed to relieve New York's municipal Judges of the onerous ask of discerning among different types of oral lease agreements, their differences largely existing only in the abstract as opposed to practice.

However well-intentioned (or not), the Ottinger Law might have been, it had the effect of essentially nullifying all prior oral lease agreements between landlord and tenant. All of them, every last one. As you might imagine, this only exasperated the plight of New York City tenants who were already extremely vulnerable due to the unprecedented supply-side shortage of apartments undeniably taking hold of the five boroughs. Imagine bringing a knife to a gun fight and being told by state politicians that you had to enter the ring of physical confrontation with nothing but your bare fists, stripped by law of your only weapon and also any chance of success save for some minor, though not insignificant twist of fate.

In the wake of this ill-timed legislative folly, landlords again had an opportunity to raise rents—à la the recent coal shortage—now unencumbered by supposed oral promises to refrain from imposing a rent increase. Remember, too, that landlords facing a recalcitrant tenant could evict a tenant by way of a judicial card game where the deck was always stacked against tenants—the summary proceeding, also known as the summary dispossess proceeding.

I'd be remiss if I didn't tell you that not all landlords took the bait. One celebrated landlord, Max Dick, never gouged tenants during the city's housing shortage. Max was an orthodox Jew who owned a large tenement building near the corner of Rivington Street and First Avenue in Manhattan's lower East Side neighborhood. Aside from keeping the rent unfathomably stable—Max never raised it, not once, while he owned the building—Max and his family adored his Jewish tenants' many children. He gave parents in the building a gift every time they birthed a child—prizes for "a pair of deuces" (twins) and for every ninth child, if born a boy (the Jews of this day were know for the prolificacy). He was beloved, so much so that one day, an over-excited tenant took to painting a tribute verse on Max's door! It read—"He is the greatest landlord in New York town, we saw / Because he doesn't raise the rents from day to day."

The rest of the city's landlords, by contrast, were nothing like beloved Max. No, no. In the wake of the Ottinger Law, a great many landlords answered the bell by again hiking rents early and often, usually by a lot as well.

Rent increases became systemic, even hegemonic, settling into a vicious cycle. It went something like this. Many building owners would raise the rent repeatedly until either age or conscience took over, at which time the owner would transfer ownership of the property to a near relative—mother-in-law, sister-in-law, brother-in-law—who would then impose another round of rent hikes early and often, often relentlessly. On and on, residential apartment buildings were passed around like the city's many working girls, who used to congregate over on Vandam Street to recruit an evening's clientele. This cycle turned so sour that one prominent New York City citizen, Judge Jacob Strahl, jested that it was a "case of in-laws becoming outlaws," before stating the obvious—that this extortionary practice had become rampant "at the expense of the community."

If the city's landlords differed in their practice of raising rents at all, it was only a matter of degree. The more extreme rent hikes, one hundred percent or more in some cases (!), were indefensible but that didn't stop landlords and real estate investors alike from crying out in pallid justification that a raise in rent was necessary to cover the increasing cost of construction, maintenance and upkeep. There was some merit to this when you consider that, between December 1914 and June 1920, the cost of housing rose 32 percent, the cost of food doubled plus an additional 5 percent, the cost of furniture and furnishings rose a whopping 205 percent and the cost of clothing? An unfathomable 240 percent.

These figures, it should be noted, can be misleading in the sense that, while invoking a certain reverence due to the sheer scale of the percent increase in cost, the increase pales in comparison to the exponential rise in monthly rents for New York tenants following the state legislature's enactment of the Ottinger Law. True, rents in New York City rose at a rather slow pace before and during World War I, undoubtedly slower than the cost of living. Shortly after the war ended, by contrast, rents rose much faster than the cost of living, roughly fifteen times as fast as the cost of food, four times the cost of clothing and six times as fast as the cost of furniture and furnishings.

The reality was that, sure, some landlords may have been raising rents exclusively to cover the soaring costs of labor and building materials and not, as charged many tenants, to profiteer or gouge tenants. As one real estate investor told the national press in 1919—

Tenants have had their own way so long that perhaps they are a trifle spoiled. They have almost always dictated to the owner in the past, and now that the owner, for the first time, is able to dictate to them, they show a different spirit than the owner did when the situation was reversed. It must be remembered that pea coal, which is largely used in the heating of these buildings, has increased in price from $3.25 per ton to over $7; that the wages of elevator men, hallmen, firemen, [etc.] have been doubled. Repairs of all kinds, including redecoration of apartments have doubled in cost. The tax rate, which a short time ago was $1.80 per $100, has now become $2.36. Labor, besides being higher priced, is less efficient.

However, it shouldn't go unnoticed that many, and I mean many, landlords were determined to raise rents to the point where they could recoup their losses from the lean prewar years, and do so in as little as a year or two! Much like the housing shortage, this round of rent hikes was a city-wide affliction, affecting all five boroughs, all ethnic and racial groups and, in a rather surprising way, all social classes.

Bearing in mind the ubiquity of rent increases, it's easy to imagine how nerve-racking rent day could be in those years, the day when a landlord or agent came to collect and oftentimes raise the rent. Indeed, Mary Ganz, whose experience was the result of being a Jewish immigrant raised in the bustling and squalid tenements of Manhattan's lower East Side neighborhood, wrote about how a knock at the door announcing arrival of the landlord or the landlord's agent meant not only that the rent was due, but also that the rent was going to be raised. Though Marie Ganz would go on to become a well-known anarchist, renowned for once threatening to shoot John D. Rockefeller, Jr. "down like a dog," her description of how a knock at the door came to be a dreaded moment for tenants associated with a rent increase, and the enormous sacrifice to follow, was both apt and deeply unnerving. Marie Ganz, for her part, was not alone in her observation. Others morbidly described this exchange occurring within the first few days of every month to be "absolutely as unpopular as the unbidden presence of the 'Grim Reaper' at the wedding feast, and just as appropriate."

I may have mentioned this, but New York City residents had a rule of thumb in those days—spend no more than one week's pay for one month's rent. In view of the rampant rent hikes, however, many tenants were already committing far more than a quarter of their income to rent, sometimes more. Especially for those tenants who had trouble finding steady work, and only earned a meager wage when they did, it was no stretch of the truth to say that a hike of as little as $1 or $2 in monthly rent for a working-class tenant made it exceedingly difficult to feed their families. In fact, one Brooklyn tenant, speaking on behalf of a group of knitters, waiters, drivers and vegetable dealers whose rent had been raised from $15 to $16, and then again to $18 per month, recounted how she pleaded with her landlord, "We can't pay for it." The landlord then callously suggested the tenant feed her children less milk and fewer eggs, to which the tenant lamented helplessly, "Why should we be asked to take bread out of our children's mouths so that we can give more money to the landlord?"

Hopefully it's easy to see how landlords' incessant rent hikes left tenants in a no-win situation, between a veritable rock and a hard place. Recall that this was a time when the cost of just about everything was rising sharply, leaving tenants a difficult choice. Tenants could either 'stint' on necessities—buying cheap cuts of meat or going altogether without meat for a few days, putting off new coats and dresses, stretching clothing further, doing without newspapers and going to the movies once a month instead of once a week—or, alternatively, tenants could move to a different, hopefully cheaper, apartment.

Prior to World War I, you should know that those among New York City's tenantry who refused to move from their neighborhoods did so mostly out of principle, particularly when it came to tenants living in the city's working-class neighborhoods where they had settled as distinct ethnic groups. Many tenants preferred to stay in the slums even when their factories moved to New Jersey in the early 1900's where, for the same or less, tenant families could have rented more spacious living accommodations with functioning sanitary facilities to boot. Faced with the choice, however, many tenant families resisted, preferring instead to remain among residents of the same descent and culture, with a shared language, shared religion, even a shared diaspora. Whether from Ireland, Italy, Germany, Russia or Poland, most tenants felt at home in the ghettos and moving to any other neighborhood made little sense if it meant severing the ties that bound them together, giving meaning to their lives as they acclimated to a foreign country thousands of miles from where they were born.

The alternative, of course, was to move to a cheaper apartment. "Voting with their feet," as it was known, was probably the most widespread tactic employed to avoid rent hikes before World War I. In many ways, it was easier to move than to pay a higher rent. With only a few notable exceptions, recall that New York City tenants had, by this time, earned a reputation as "the most restless population in the world," and rightfully so.

However, by 1918 and 1919, as the city's housing supply dwindled, tenants across the five boroughs were far less inclined to give up their apartments, even in light of landlords' incessant rent hikes. Even a tenant who was lucky enough to find a new apartment at a reasonable rent knew his family's troubles were far from over. By 1919, many tenants who did decide to move found that the apartments they'd reserved and hoped to occupy had not been vacated as yet by the prior tenants, who were similarly resistant to moving, leaving many tenant families with otherwise legitimate lease arrangements all packed up with nowhere to go.

As you can imagine, tenant families were hard-pressed to find space for their belongings and everywhere from empty storerooms, barns and other spaces were commandeered to accommodate the overflow of furniture and household belongings. Household belongings aside, there was the pressing question of where to house these tenant families who were physically prevented from moving into their new apartments by holdover tenants stubbornly remaining past the expiration of their lease agreements. Hotels booked up weeks in advance, whether high or low-end, and were relentlessly filled to the brim. Instead, many tenants were forced to move back in with their parents or double up with friends or neighbors. In the lower income sections of the city, current and former tenants doubled up, forced to live on top of one another under one crowded and dilapidated old roof.

Apartments in Manhattan's lower East Side were so overcrowded that some lodgers and boarders had to sleep on a mattress placed on the floor or, incredibly, on a board balanced between two kitchen chairs. Renting such a makeshift bed, if it can even be called that, was known endearingly as "renting a sheet." Times were so desperate that working-class families would send small children out to forage and scavenge for small, loose and discarded pieces of wood or coal to be burned for heat.

It was undeniable by this time that rampant postwar rent hikes were here to stay, a long-term and chronic practice rather than a short-term nuisance for the city's many tenant families, particularly those working-class families living in poverty. With residential construction sputtering and stalling, many among the city's residents were at a loss.

Some took to desperate measures, selling off most or all of their earthly possessions—family heirlooms in some instances—to meet the rising cost of rent. A good many tenants, however, contemplated a far more dramatic measure, one few landlords expected despite some precedent sprinkled throughout the early twentieth century—tenants began to consider as a legitimate solution, ignoring landlords' ultimatums to pay a higher rent or move and, instead, pondered joining forces with other tenants in a collective protest.

As one tenant organizer of the day put it—

> We know that the statute book law is on the side of the landlords ... Where we have succeeded in organizing only one house in a hard block we advise that not much energy be lost on it. We are bending efforts to organize whole blocks of houses. Where we have such a block we tell the tenants simply to refuse to pay unless the reductions are granted. We know that they can't dispossess that many families; it is a physical impossibility.

In other words, the tenants considered rent strikes on a scale never before seen by New York City.

## *STIRRING THE POT*

By 1918, a good many New Yorkers were understandably irate as a result of landlords' ruthless rent hikes and, adding insult to injury, many tenants were notified by their landlords of another imminent rent increase set to kick in as of Moving Day in the coming year, 1919. *En masse*, three thousand New York City tenants attended a meeting of the Brooklyn Tenants League, one of many such organizations that had coalesced throughout the city with the aim of advocating on behalf of the city tenants' cause. In attendance at this particular meeting was a Socialist Assemblyman who had been elected to New York's state legislature and who solemnly declared at one point, "If everything else fails, why there is nothing left for us to do but strike."

Of course, if tenants withheld rent and went on strike, the city's cadre of landlords wouldn't take it lying down. At stake at this point for landlords was more than money. Said one landlord seeking to evict a recalcitrant tenant, "It was not the 50 cents I wanted, it was the principle of the thing." Landlords taking tenants to task, and *vice versa*, out of principle was a symptom, no doubt, of the lingering but so far latent animosity among tenants and landlords, lurking just below the surface but bubbling rapidly.

You should know that, at least initially, many city tenants were hesitant to organize in protest. A wholesome fear of eviction ordinarily deterred even the most indefatigable of tenants from going on strike and for good reason. Recall that once a landlord initiated a summary proceeding in pursuit of an eviction warrant from one of the city's municipal Judges, a tenant became immediately and irreversibly embroiled in the arcane world of legal notices, precepts, orders and warrants, a world likely to be incomprehensible to almost anyone but a trained attorney or an experienced municipal Judge. What many first and second-generation immigrants, for whom English was a second or third language, made of these documents is hard to imagine.

The sum of all fears was a warrant of eviction, issued by a municipal Judge against a tenant and carried out by a city marshal vested with the authority to forcibly remove a tenant, his family and belongings, usually to the street, then turning over possession of the vacant apartment to the landlord.

When a tenant was unable to find other accommodations before a municipal Judge issued an eviction warrant, what happened next in the city's streets was even more horrifying than what went on the courtroom. With tenants and neighbors looking on, a city marshal, undoubtedly accompanied by a team of schleppers, would descend on a tenant's home, breaking down the door if he had trouble gaining entry. This often meant that marshals would break the locks, batter down the doors and even climb up the fire escape, forcibly gaining entry through the apartment windows. Schleppers would unapologetically carry out tables, chairs, household appliances, children's toys and even tenants' beds, piling all possessions on the sidewalk, often with so little care that what once adorned the abode of a tenant family lay simply in a smashed and broken pile on the street for all to see.

At least as heartbreaking, and in cold weather even more so, was the sight of evicted tenants and their families huddled on the sidewalk alongside their furniture and household belongings. Tenant activist Marie Ganz recalled the heart-rending sight of a poor woman, having been recently evicted, standing beside "the wreck of her home. Clinging to her dress were three frightened little children, the largest of which was surely not more than six years old."

Sadly, it was unusual in those days to pass a street without furniture riddled out front of a tenement house, spread desperately askew across the sidewalk and spilling over into the streets. Evicted tenants and their families were forced to take shelter in churches, temples and other quasi-public spaces like army barracks.

With so many tenants also working from their homes, particularly on Manhattan's lower East Side, eviction also meant unemployment. One time muckraker and New York City's first photojournalist, Jacob Riis, recounted how, in his *How The Other Half Lives*–

> You were made fully aware of [the fact that peoples' homes doubled as daily workshops] before you traveled the length of a single block in any of the East Side streets, by the whir of a thousand sewing-machines, worked at high presser from the earliest dawn till mind and muscle give out together. Every family, from the youngest to the oldest bears a hand.

Tenants regularly rolled cigars and made artificial flowers, as well as washed laundry from their apartments. So long as these city tenants had a home to work from, running a tenement building as a workshop by day and living quarters by night enabled immigrant women, especially Jewish and Italian women, to supplement the household's irregular income without leaving the home. It goes without saying that these make-shift businesses were impossible to run from the sidewalk.

Given the tumultuous and visibly destructive nature of evictions, most East Side New Yorkers felt that unsympathetic city marshals charged with carrying out eviction warrants were running amuck, leaving the marshals as adversaries of tenants all over the city. Importantly, city marshals were not public employees, but rather, independent contractors who were authorized to collect a fee for carrying out an eviction warrant, a fee set by New York City's administrative authorities. Set up to be paid by litigating landlords and tenants themselves, the fees for such tasks ran fairly low on an individual basis; though you should know that when landlords brought summary proceedings by the tens of thousands, city marshals made out quite well in the execution of eviction warrants. And they carried out eviction warrants in droves. On most days, city marshals had to remove dozens of families at once, families who, quite literally, had nowhere else to go and no place to store their belongings, save for the sidewalk.

Naturally, city marshals faced resistance. For one thing, they were often outnumbered by angry tenant mobs, leaving city marshals no choice but to call in the support of the city's heavy-handed police force. If New York City's tenants had any hope that police officers would be sympathetic towards them, this hope was dashed by how the city's police force had engaged tenants during a rash of minor strikes and skirmishes that boiled up prior to World War I. Both before and after the war, city police officers were especially heavy-handed when dealing with tenants and protesters these NYPD officers perceived to be socialists.

With respect to socialism, police officers and citizens alike shared, during this time, a visceral fear of socialism and other radical ideologies. If asked in earnest, most would eagerly point out that the ongoing rent strikes represented more than just a dispute by and between landlords and tenants, but indeed served as a proxy conflict waged by capitalists intent on suppressing radicals who actively revolted, and did so with the worst intentions. This conflict surfaced in the late-nineteenth century, intensified around the time of World War I, and ultimately culminated in the first of America's "Red Scares" in 1919 and 1920.

This was no doubt a time of widespread hysteria in the U.S. and New York City was not immune. Undoubtedly caught up in the Red

Scare, police officers openly refused to grant city tenants demonstration permits, openly badgered tenants in the streets and even enforced a police department directive (later held unconstitutional) that banned anyone from speaking at a public gathering in any language other than English.

You may be as puzzled as I was to learn that, like city tenants, most city police officers were also first and second-generation immigrants, nearly all of them falling into the working-class as well. What was their problem then? Why so unreasonable? Why so heavy-handed? Was it really just the Red Scare? Could that really be it? Perhaps if we look back a little further in time, there might be something there, right?

Sure enough, there is. There always is. As it turns out there was a deep schism amongst first and second-generation immigrants living in New York City during this time—two sides of the line, so to speak. You see, many striking tenants, including many of the most militant among them, were Jewish Americans who had recently emigrated from Russia, Poland and elsewhere in Eastern Europe where they fled open persecution.

On the other hand, most NYPD officers hailed from Ireland, ancestors of those who fled to the U.S. after the now infamous potato famine of 1845. Like most Americans, these city police officers were not only open racists, but also suffered from a scathing xenophobia and anti-Semitism. Notoriously, police-driven anti-Semitism was on full display during the Hoe Riot in Manhattan's lower East Side neighborhood, which erupted in July 1902 after city police officers, by the tens and twenties, lashed out at thousands of Jews who were mostly formed into a large funeral procession and who were already under attack by a group of furious factory workers wielding fists and even billy clubs.


Given their greed-ridden landlords, calloused city marshals and heavy-handed police force, city tenants were bitter, feeling oppressed on multiple fronts with no end in sight. If you were around then, you would be sure to feel helpless and frustrated as these fronts closed in, painting you in a corner while at the same time caging and mocking you so.

Adding salt to an already gaping wound was the fact that, despite higher rents, landlords neglected even the most obvious of repairs needed to keep the city's residential tenement buildings—tenants' homes—from falling into complete disrepair. Paint blistered, wall paper peeled off the walls in endless layers, looking from afar like oversized pencil shavings as the flakes accumulated in building common areas. Calk hardened and fell from the windows to such an extent as to easily allow rain to pour in by the bucket during a storm and to likewise allow pernicious cold to seep in during the city's frigid winter months. Stairwells and hallways filled with garbage, the floors threatened to collapse under residents' feet, cellars overflowed with needless junk and dumbwaiters refused to run. Fire escapes rusted and then rotted, flaking onto the street. There was even one account of an East Side apartment where mushrooms thrived by feeding off the rancid water filling the basin of an unworkable toilet!

Obviously, most tenants charged that there was no limit to the lengths landlords would go to capitalize on the housing shortage gripping New York City following World War I. Tenants saw their landlords as rapacious, greedy and merciless. Perception was that landlords indiscriminately jacked up every tenant's rent for no other reason than to live in posh apartments on Riverside Drive, adorn their neckties with diamonds and their wives with decedent fur coats. The old, the young, the sick, women who had just given birth—no one was immune from the over-grasping landlord. If these city tenants could not pay the rent demanded of them, landlords would seek to evict them regardless of their obvious vulnerabilities.

If relations between tenants and landlords were bad in the prewar years, they had taken a sharp and irreversible turn for the worse shortly after. Landlords' open greed and relentless rapacity sowed the seeds of a deep animosity which swelled and swelled, boiled and boiled, built and built; gathering so swiftly at times as to even outpace the well-entrenched tension between wage-earners, unions and capitalists. One stray spark and the city might explode!

Regardless of the undeniable turmoil, whether to go on strike over a rent increase was still a decision that was not to be taken lightly. It was deliberate and well thought out, mulled over from every angle, talked-over and weighed. And it was a decision that largely fell to the veritable and literal head of the tenant family household.

In those days, the housewife ran the household as a matriarch and was responsible for balancing her family's modest and often irregular sources of income between food, clothing, housing and other necessities. When a landlord raised the rent, it often fell to the woman of the house to figure out whether the family could afford to pay the increase and, if not, whether the family should move, cut back on expenditures or withhold rent entirely and go on strike.

These women were clearly well organized and displayed a growing militancy to boot. As you might remember, this willingness to resort to collective action drew inspiration from the trade union movement and the Socialist party, both of which had made deep inroads into the lower East Side and other poverty-stricken ethnic neighborhoods around the city by this time.

By the end of World War I, many New York City housewives—working-class, middle-class and upper-class alike—were ready to join forces to stop, or at least slow down, over-grasping landlords whose pernicious rent increases wrought havoc with tenant families and quite literally took food out of children's mouths. Recall that women had already, several decades earlier, mobilized successfully to bring down the price of food. Was it not, then and there, a natural progression to mobilize to hold down the price of housing?

The answer? A resounding 'YES!' Hence, for droves of tenant families—fed up with frequent rent increases, outraged by merciless and greedy landlords, confident in the potential of collective action and, perhaps most importantly, feeling that the fate of their families hung in the balance—no longer hesitated to go on strike.

In this light, it should be easy to see now that a rent strike was viewed, not so much as a struggle between landlords and tenants, but instead a grander, more ideological struggle between profiteers and patriots. It was a struggle of epic proportions, even biblical, among those who were taking advantage of a housing shortage to enrich themselves and, in opposition, those who were doing their part to drive down the cost of living and uphold the American standard of life. This sentiment was no more on display than at a gathering of perturbed tenants where a veteran soldier spoke, "We went to war to protect our homes, and now that we have returned we find them wrested from us by an enemy more insidious, more villainous than even the Hun... the war profiteer."

And profiteering landlords, right then, became Public Enemy No. 1. The concern over skyrocketing rents had become widespread, sure, but it was especially concentrated in New York City, the most densely populated of America's many urban epicenters. New York City's Mayor, John F. Hylan, went so far as to publicly brand rent profiteers as "a public menace."

Then it happened, the match had been struck and tenants went on strike the city over, banding together by the tens and hundreds of thousands. Beginning around 1919, tenant activists covered many more buildings than during the comparatively modest prewar rent strikes, covering some hundreds and maybe thousands of apartment buildings, even corralling the exclusive, posh and well-to-do circles of Riverside Drive. Unlike the 1904-1905 rent strikes, which were taken over by the New York Rent Protective Association, an offshoot of the Jewish labor movement, and the 1907-1908 rent strikes, which were driven by the lower East Side branch of the Socialist party, the postwar rent strikes were driven by a host of organized and militant tenant leagues. Counterpart organizations formed on behalf of landlords, lessees, real estate investors and the rest of a well-entrenched real estate interest, all of which collectively opposed these tenant leagues.

With that, the stage was set—bear witness to New York City's Great Rent Strikes.

## *A NEW KIND 'O RENT STRIKE*

If New York City's Great Rent Strikes revealed anything in those early days, it was that the city, for all of its staying power, was at the time one of America's most fragile urban ecosystems. Like the influenza epidemic that swept through New York City in 1917 and 1918, the rent strikes that swept and subsequently engulfed New York City's five boroughs were no picnics—they were serious matters fraught with incredible risk. And the stakes couldn't've been higher. Tenant activists might lose their homes, for one thing. For another, tenant families might end up on the street. They might be attacked while on strike, beaten up by thugs or arrested by the police. Their children might fall ill, which happened with striking frequency, especially for those rent strikes conducted during New York City's frigid winter months. Tenants risked losing or damaging their household and other family possessions.

The postwar rent strikes saw more passionate resistance than ever before because many tenants perceived their efforts quite literally as a fight to protect something sacred, something more important to them than any collective social cause—their individual families. With that in mind it should come as no surprise that the rent strikes beginning in 1919 were fierce, often violent struggles that had profound repercussions for tenants and their families.

Despite the obvious motivations of individual tenant families, I'd be remiss if I didn't mention that, to many in New York City and beyond, the postwar rent strikes represented a larger struggle, one carrying consequences for city, state and country. Particularly for leaders of the Socialist party, the rent strikes served as a brand of proxy struggle against the perceived evils of capitalism, part of an ongoing campaign to transform American society. Rent increases, believed nearly all members of New York City's Socialist party, were less a symptom of rising prices, or even profiteering landlords, but rather a result of capitalism and its foundational notions of private property and boundless individual profit.

These larger concerns did not resonate with most tenants, however. To them, a rent strike was initially nothing more and nothing less than a necessarily desperate measure to force landlords to rescind or reduce the recent rent hikes. Period. End of story. Landlords, many tenants conceded, were entitled to a fair and equitable profit and, at a time of rising prices, even a modest rent increase. But for the recent round of rent hikes, which ran as high as 100 percent or more, there was no excuse.

For as high as landlords hiked rents in those years, surely it seemed as though they had all of the leverage, leaving tenants entirely helpless to their plight, right? I mean, did landlords even bat an eye at the rent strikes?

Yes, they did as it turns out and here's why—even though tenants faced an uphill, seemingly insurmountable climb at the courthouse and calloused city marshals ready to unapologetically carry out eviction warrants at a moment's notice, landlords were, in fact, vulnerable to long-term rent strikes. For one thing, most landlords relied heavily on rental income, not only to support their families, but also to maintain their properties. Landlords paid taxes out of rental income; paid down first, second and sometimes third or fourth mortgages out of rental income; and paid coal dealers, utility companies and employees out of rental income. In this way, rental income was the financial lifeline that kept most landlords afloat. While some landlords could put off paying certain bills (or stint on heat, hot water, routine maintenance or non-emergency repairs), at some point suppliers and utility companies would suspend service or, in particularly egregious cases, cut off service altogether. And worse still, neither the city nor lenders showed any hesitation when it came to foreclosing on landlords' or building owners' mortgages if payments remained delinquent.

Faced with the loss of even one or two months' rent, not to mention the expense of ousting so many striking tenants through summary proceedings, it was clear that landlords all over the city were vulnerable to a well-organized strike. And tenants knew it. Tenants knew that if they could corral every family in a particular building, for example, and drag a coordinated rent strike on for weeks or perhaps months, that this battle of attrition would expose landlords' vulnerabilities.

Despite a growing fervor, you should know that not all tenants fell in line right away and there were certainly a number of dissenters and holdout tenants among the neighbors. Though that did not, by any means, deter appeals to the more trepid tenants. If holdout tenants ignored initial appeals by their striking counterparts to join in protest, tenant strike organizers would often resort to vicious ostracism, intimidation and even violence. For example, trepid tenants were deemed "scabs," and many striking tenants were so hostile toward scabs that, where a landlord caved to a rent strike and was willing to reduce or rescind a rent increase, striking tenants would nevertheless refuse to break up the strike until the landlord provided assurance that the scab tenant would be evicted.

Consider, as another example, a rent strike that took hold of Lexington Avenue in the Bronx where an elderly tenant named Esther Domowitz broke ranks with striking tenants and paid a $5 rent increase to her landlord. Word spread like brush fire and Esther was, in response, accosted in the street outside her home one day by a neighbor angered at Esther's crossing the line, so to speak. Ultimately, the feuding women had to be separated by bystanders and Esther returned home, understandably shaken. When her son, Solomon, found his mother hysterical that day, and discovered what had happened, he retaliated against the neighbor who had accosted his mother. The altercation landed the neighbor in Harlem Hospital. Rumors spread that Solomon had, in fact, killed the neighbor during the altercation, prompting a large, frenzied crowd to descend on Solomon's home, billy clubs in tow. Fortunately, police officers took Solomon into custody before further escalation, the episode a symbolic reminder of how tenants turned even on one another.

For landlords, it was bad enough when striking tenants stayed in their apartments while withholding rent. That did not deter landlords, however, from seeking to replace striking tenants with new, less confrontational tenants willing to pay a higher rent—a practice that prompted striking tenants to go further in their efforts to deter prospective tenants from renting the would-be vacant apartments.

Tenants' efforts to that end saw virtually no boundaries. To be sure, striking tenants would amass picket lines in front of their apartment buildings. Some striking tenants would confront and verbally warn prospective tenants that if they moved into the apartments of evicted tenants, they would be beaten and forcibly removed, head-first, out a window, which often sat several stories above the street level.

As if the threat of being thrown out a window head first (!) wasn't enough, some striking tenants went further. Here's what I mean. Some resorted to urging the city's craftsman unions, whose members were responsible for decorating vacant apartments before they turned over, to refuse to do any work on any apartment from which a tenant had been evicted. Striking tenants also called on the Moving Van Workers Union, which represented many of the schleppers charged with removing furniture and household belongings, to refrain from moving a new tenant into an apartment whose prior tenant had been evicted for withholding rent. A group of tenant activists in Brownsville and East New York went even further, snooping into whether a prospective tenant had any labor union affiliations. The striking tenants would then report a prospective tenant to his union organization and demand that he be expelled, making it difficult or impossible for the prospective tenant to find gainful employment.

Besides withholding rent, or collecting and withholding rent, as the case may be, and deterring prospective tenants from moving in, striking tenants also employed several tactics to foil attempts at eviction. Some of these efforts were geared towards making eviction, which required a landlord to hire an attorney and bring a summary proceeding in municipal court, as expensive and as burdensome as possible. For example, tenants in a summary proceeding could demand a jury trial, a right guaranteed by the *Seventh Amendment of the U.S. Constitution*, a demand that served to drag out the proceedings, costing impatient landlords precious time and money. Other tenants, against whom a municipal Judge had issued an order of eviction, sought to interfere with the efforts of schleppers and city marshals charged with carrying out an eviction warrant.

I'm sure you recall that city marshals and schleppers were, by and large, uncompassionate to tenants, rousing some tenants to the point of taking rather drastic measures. Consider a group of Bronx tenants who piled pianos, stoves and other heavy household items in front of their apartment door, barricading themselves inside and forcibly preventing a team of schleppers and marshals from gaining entry. At this particular building, the tenants' efforts proved successful. Faced with the prospect of removing the stacked pianos and stoves from in front of the door and schlepping the load down five or six flights of stairs, city marshals on site that day convinced the landlord to reduce a recent rent hike by more than 50 percent and sign an agreement for good measure that he would not raise the rent for another twelve months! Other tenants resorted to attacks on city marshals, deputies and schleppers with bricks and stones and, in one particular show of frustration, charged a team of schleppers as an indefatigable band armed with furniture and bedding polls as weapons. These tenants, not surprisingly, were successful in driving marshals and schleppers from their building that day.

Aside from the widely held belief that their family's livelihood hung in the balance, a legitimate cause for optimism drove much of the tenants' avidity. For one thing, tenants could reliably count on tenant leagues and social organizations as a safety net to provide attorneys to represent them in summary proceedings. Striking tenants also had cause for hope that their case might be heard by one of several well-known municipal Judges who were openly antagonistic to rent profiteers. Tenants who ultimately did face eviction, could count on neighbors, churches, synagogues and armories to take them in and provide shelter, albeit temporarily. Given this moral and logistical support, striking tenants were confident they could force landlords to abandon efforts to raise rents if only they stuck together long enough.

Between May 1918 and April 1920, there were thousands of rent strikes in New York City, covering virtually all socioeconomic classes and ethnic groups. The strikes spread and raged like a grease fire after having been doused with cold water, engulfing every corner of the five boroughs. *Crackle—POP! ROOOSSHHHH*, the flames of civil unrest raged on.

Meanwhile, landlords stubbornly persisted in their belief that the quickest and surest way to break up a rent strike was to initiate a summary proceeding in municipal court against each individual tenant. Landlords flocked to the courts in droves, swelling the city's caseload and turning courthouses into public spectacles. Indeed, the crowd in front of Judge Harry Robitzek's courthouse in the Bronx was consistently so large that police reserves were often called in to help organize tenants into lines stretching from the courthouse stairs, down to the sidewalk and out onto the street. The tenant mobs were so vast that they brought pedestrian traffic to a complete halt. Remember, too, that housewives and community women spearheaded many rent strikes? Well, this was on full display as police reserves set aside an open space opposite the courthouse for parking baby carriages.

New York City's municipal courtrooms themselves were so jammed up that many litigants were unable to navigate through the densely packed courtroom audience to the witness stand when their case was eventually called, forced instead to give testimony from their seats in the rear of the courtroom. For those witnesses fortunate enough to make it to the witness stand, their only exit after completing their testimony, often arduous in and of itself, was to climb through the courthouse window and down a rickety and rusty old fire escape.

Overwhelmed by so many thousands of summary proceedings, it seemed that New York City's municipal court system was on the verge of complete collapse. True or not, one thing was clear—tenants were losing confidence in the court system for protection against exorbitant rent hikes and the profiteering landlord.

Desperately taking matters into their own hands, some tenants blatantly threatened to destroy property if landlords didn't reduce their rents. Other tenants threatened landlords' life and limb. Tenants made good on these threats as well, beating and mugging their landlords as reprisal for the raise in rent. Some doused their landlords with boiling water.

In one particularly desperate episode, a tenant lured his landlord into his apartment under the auspices of a peaceful negotiation only to take the landlord hostage at gunpoint, threatening cold-blooded murder unless the landlord rescinded a recent series of rent hikes.

The threat of physical confrontation was as acute as the housing shortage for some landlords who couldn't safely pass through certain parts of the city without being verbally and physically accosted by rambunctious, desperate and militant tenant activists. Take, for example, Herman Kaufmann, a Bronx landlord who had a reputation for being a rent profiteer of the worst sort. Whenever Kaufmann passed within as few as five blocks of his buildings, he was greeted by several recently-evicted families who launched rocks at him, the barrage forcing him into retreat. For his part, Kaufmann was so leery of physical confrontation that he carried a police whistle with him at all times.

There's no doubt that this brand of confrontation between landlords and tenants, in and of itself, was a threat to public order. The threat escalated far more seriously when city marshals, schleppers and police got involved. The presence of police officers and city marshals achieved very little except for further provoking already furious tenants.

As the city's unrest spread, it transcended the obvious rancor and suspicion among New York City's landlords and tenants, even pitting landlord against landlord and, as we've see already, tenant against tenant. Perhaps more significantly, the gripping housing shortage and attendant rent increases only aggravated xenophobic tension, which had already torn along ethnic and religious fault lines. Indeed, many New Yorkers blamed soaring rents indiscriminately on foreigners, observing, "It is a curious state of affairs when a foreigner can come to America and by thieving tactics throw an American onto the street." Closely related was a pervasive anti-Semitism, leading New Yorkers to blame rent profiteering on "dirty Russian Jews."

The postwar housing crisis, as it was clearly by then, deeply divided the city along ideological lines as well, in addition to the ethnic and religious rifts. Exacerbated by news of Bolshevik revolution in Russia, Americans feared that anarchism, radical socialism and Bolshevism were taking root in American society at an alarming rate and with revolutionary ends. Along with many other Americans, New Yorkers were caught up in the Red Scare that swept the nation after World War I.

The city had self-immolated, set ablaze by a housing shortage, merciless rent increases and proliferating rent strikes that seemed to be eroding the city's social fabric from the inside out. A heavy burden fell to the city's municipal Judges to be sure, whose courtrooms remained packed to the brim from open to close; morning, noon and night. As the crisis waged, it became clear to everyone that municipal Judges alone were ill-equipped by themselves to handle the burgeoning civil unrest.

Naturally, some New Yorkers believed that the U.S Government should step in and impose a nationalized system of rent control that would prohibit rent increases in excess of, say 25 percent, for example. Received by national consternation, Congress voted definitively against a nationalized system of rent control, further exasperating New Yorkers. By 1919, Congress was not in a position to follow the lead of many European countries that had adopted a nationalized system of rent control. As a result, pressure mounted on state and local officials all over the country to take action to curb rent profiteering.

And nowhere was this pressure more intense than the smoldering crucible of New York City.

## BOOK TWO

### HANG TOGETHER, OR HANG SEPARATELY

*New York City sighed and pulsed as though Manhattan itself were an unharmonious wire plucked by the hand of some brazen and busy demon.*

-Jack Kerouac

## *MOVING DAY REDUX*

Have you ever lived in an apartment with so little insulation or heat that, when the air temperature dropped below a certain threshold, you could visibly see the moisture on your breath condense the moment it left your lips?

I have, and let's be straight about something—when the year's first cold snap set in during 2013, only a few months after I moved into my first Manhattan apartment, I realized that the apartment was exposed to all the elements and my bed might as well have been on the roof. Why it took me till the year's first cold snap to realize this about my apartment could've been for any number of reasons, but that's not important. What matters is that reality did eventually sink in, especially when our excessive use of multiple space heaters of all sizes and varieties ran us an apocalyptic total for electricity, something like $600 for the month of January that year and, for good measure, we received a bill of over $900 for the month of February!

Maybe it took longer than it should've, but it finally occurred to me, 'We shouldn't be paying this much for heat.' Without paying such an exorbitant amount for electricity—and still suffering, mind you—it would've been like our apartment had no heat at all. The first time this thought crossed my mind, of course, I immediately wanted to see our residential lease and what it said, if anything, about the landlord's obligation to provide basic heat, or lack thereof! What I found was worse than I could've ever anticipated. There it was, plain as day. The words "and heat"—boilerplate language indicating a landlord's obligation to provide heat, language that cannot be amended by agreement in New York—had been *CROSSED OUT BY SHARPIE MARKER!!* It suddenly made perfect sense that our landlord, after being all but unreachable for weeks on end, had showed up abruptly at 6 o'clock in the morning one day around when we were to sign a new lease, adamant that we had to urgently sign the lease agreement at that early hour, before our eyes had acclimated to daylight let alone the fine print of a residential lease agreement.

Ask any lawyer or Judge about residential leases and they're liable to delve into the archaic realms of topics like the right to "quiet possession" or the "implied warranty of habitability," to give two examples. What these well-intentioned jurists mean to say is that, no matter the fact or circumstance, a landlord may be charged as criminally liable for failing to provide heat, regardless of how a written lease reads or even if a tenant agrees to waive this right. The criminal penalties are harsher for a landlord who intentionally alters a lease, such as by sharpie marker, as a pretext for committing fraud or forgery.

Our landlord, you won't be surprised to know, also forged our signatures on our lease, fraudulently altering our agreement without our consent in order to raise the rent. In a curious turn of events, our bathroom ceiling then collapsed due to a water leak, which released into our shower an avalanche of gravel and rock that hadn't seen the light of day since our building was first constructed around the time of World War II. Between the lack of heat, the windows, the loose tiles, the loose floorboards, the unstable ceiling, the treacherous staircase, the fraudulent lease agreement, the fact that you couldn't run the microwave and space heaters at the same time without blowing every circuit breaker in the place, I'd finally had enough! *Get me out of here! I can't live like this!!* would usually be my first thoughts each morning.

I don't mean to be provocative and I share this with you because what happened next is as much a story about the tenants of yesteryear as it is about the present day. To be sure, for the way I was able to take matters into my own hands, the essential rights on which I relied and the basis for the remedy I sought, I owe a debt of gratitude to New York City's tenant activists, who reached the peak of their influence during the Roaring Twenties. What did I do? I evicted myself; more on this later.

As for New York City's tenantry in 1920, what the tenants of that bygone era were able to achieve, stacked against seemingly insurmountable odds, is nothing short of remarkable. Tenant activists from all five boroughs banded together and gave a timeless demonstration of the everlasting vitality of strength as it exists in numbers. Tenants challenged—by sweat, blood and tears—a pervasive and deeply-entrenched legal and political bias in favor of landlords and building owners by virtually any means necessary. And, I'll be damned, they won!

Here's what I mean. Because New York City's tenantry banded together by the legion during a concentrated period of time between 1918 and 1921, tenants living in New York today, almost a century later, still enjoy certain absolute rights, rights that cannot be ignored or neglected by a landlord, even where a tenant has no written lease. Take, for example, one of the most sacred of our rights as tenants in New York City—heat. Recall that frosty morning I mentioned when I could see my breath in my bedroom as I tried to shake off the morning cobwebs? The conversation I had with my landlord over the phone that day is likely similar in context to that between a landlord and tenant in 1921—namely, that a landlord might be subject to a criminal penalty for failure to provide basic necessities like heat and that, if not, the apartment was decidedly unlivable.

Today, this basic right to essential services such as heat is provided, not by contract as between a tenant and landlord, but by law written upstate in Albany or ordinances enacted by a municipal government. It wasn't always this way but believe me when I tell you that the foundation for those modern aspects of the landlord-tenant relationship, whereby a landlord *must* provide basic necessities, was forged by the collective action of New York's tenantry during the early years of the Roaring Twenties.

Given that, by 1919, five out of every six New Yorkers lived as tenant-residents of the five boroughs, as opposed to owning their residence, you might be surprised to learn that elected city officials largely ignored the housing shortage that gripped New York City following World War I and the attendant plight of working-class tenant families. Mayor John F. Hylan, elected in 1917 on behalf of New York City's Democratic party, resisted what little pressure there was to take any action. True, that the city's housing shortage was unprecedented, catching city politicians off guard and leaving many admittedly befuddled, if not dumbfounded as to the best way to go about addressing the issue. And yet, there were those prominent citizens of New York City who fully realized that conditions might only get worse—

> The result of the cessation of building during the war is becoming apparent in the raising rents throughout the city . . . The average growth of population in New York City from 1913 to 1916 was 107,000 annually. The population has grown probably even more rapidly than this in the last few years in spite of the lack of immigration, on account of the centering of so much war work in New York and the surrounding region. As yet, no really constructive program has been offered to relieve the housing situation.

For all of Mayor Hylan's and fellow Democrats' public rhetoric about standing up to "the moneyed interests," *e.g.*, the city's wealthy real estate interest, the reality was that most of New York City's elected officials were deeply conservative and reluctant to tamper with the city's free market economy in general and the real estate market in particular; reserved unabashedly to the notion that New York City's housing market was and should remain a product strictly of the "natural laws" of supply and demand.

So too, were businessman largely opposed to the idea that public officials carried the power to jump in and actively compete as a market participant in an otherwise private sector, *i.e.*, to provide public housing. You should know that, in those years, political opposition to housing reform came less from individual landlords—a group sharply divided along socioeconomic and ethnic lines, who relied more on corruption than organized advocacy—and more often from trade organizations in the building trades, for example, that exerted tremendous influence over both city and state housing policy. Indeed, through an affiliated group of builder associations, it was New York's construction industry that proved most influential in both Albany and across the five boroughs in shaping New York policy to favor real estate owners, investors and landlords. Down through the early part of the twentieth century, this opposition usually proved decisive and served as a seemingly insurmountable barrier to housing reform.

It shouldn't surprise you that this faction of the city's citizens—also deeply conservative—were vigorously outspoken against any resolution targeted at legislatively bringing down or otherwise regulating rents. In this way, New York City's housing shortage and attendant problems of rent profiteering were less a new challenge facing city politicians than perhaps a continuation of more chronic issues plaguing the city, and only now, in 1919, emerging at a severity that city organizers and politicians could no longer ignore.

By 1919, dissatisfaction was widespread among tenants, so much so that many continued to turn to the Socialist party for reprieve as a last resort, a drastic measure for drastic times. Upon learning of only the latest in a series of rent hikes, one Manhattan tenant declared, "I thought of murder, suicide and court proceedings. But upon contemplation I discovered they did not offer any relief. I resolved to be a Bolshevist [radical socialist]."

Tenants across all five boroughs likewise faced an uphill battle to secure livable rents, to be sure. However, they seemed up to the task, bringing an admirable energy to their efforts. As an organized measure to address citywide rent hikes, tenant leagues proliferated throughout Manhattan, Brooklyn and the Bronx. As concern over soaring rents became more widespread, these tenant organizations began to consolidate their efforts, resulting in an organized and coherent leadership structure. The result of such consolidation, the Greater New York Tenant's Association, for example, emerged as one of the most prominent such groups of the day.

With the immanency of Moving Day 1919, Mayor Hylan's administration came under mounting pressure to take action, pressure that came not only from tenant leagues, many of which were funded by Socialist party members, but also labor unions, settlement houses, civic groups, newspapers and clergymen. Heightening the tension, rumors spread that some 200,000 tenants would go on strike in Brownsville alone if rents didn't stabilize soon. Charles Solomon, a Socialist party member elected to the New York State Assembly, predicted that, if rents did not stabilize, if profiteering landlords remained unchecked, tenants all over the city would have no choice but to organize on an unprecedented scale, coming together for "the greatest rent strike New York has ever seen."

The Hylan administration, for its part, might have withstood pressure to take action had it not been for the rousing and persistent efforts of Socialist party members, citizens and politicians alike. Socialism and its many representatives had made deep inroads in Manhattan's lower East Side and throughout the city by this time, their ideas coating the city in flammable grease, leaving all five boroughs susceptible to widespread revolt given only the slightest spark.

As long as rents continued to soar, Mayor Hylan and other politicians soon realized that Democrats and Republicans together faced socialism as a common enemy in the fight for votes, as well as the loyalty of New York City's many and diverse tenants. As a result, city politicians were left no choice but to face the city's growing housing shortage head on, if not for the sake of maintaining a quality of life for city tenants than to garner votes to maintain political office.

## *ALL BARK, NO BITE?*

Given the tension over rising rents and deteriorating living conditions, New York City's tenants and landlords alike bombarded the Mayor's Office with complaints of all kinds, related to both the housing shortage and the rising cost of living. According to Nathan Hirsch, former tax commissioner for New York City and key leader in the Mayor's efforts to curb rent profiteering, "People have no idea of the number of complaints we are receiving, or of what a mean, rotten deal many people are receiving." Of all the remonstrations, what stood out from the herd were the inordinate number of complaints related to rent profiteering, a "condition," in the words of Mayor Hylan, "which is most despicable in the eyes of all our citizens." Or so he said.

According to the Hylan administration, the *profiteer* is one who, for the benefit only of himself, seeks to make an excessive or unfair profit, which often comes only at the expense of one in a less favorable position. The *rent profiteer* is a landlord or building owner who seeks to exact an excessive rent from a tenant, often a working-class tenant living in poverty. As the city's unrest seemed to reach a crescendo, pressure mounted on Mayor Hylan's administration to take action to curb accusations that rent profiteers were proliferating to every corner of the city's five boroughs, their efforts bleeding city tenants dry and taking food from their families' mouths.

To that end, Mayor Hylan finally bowed to mounting pressure during the spring renting season of 1919 by forming the Mayor's Committee on Rent Profiteering mere weeks before Moving Day. Mayor Hylan's efforts came around the same time as New York's state Senators unanimously passed a bill appropriating state funds so that the state's municipalities might be able to better appoint a rent investigating commission.

Initial impressions were optimistic, particularly after Mayor Hylan tapped New York City's tax commissioner, Nathan Hirsch, to head the Mayor's Committee. Following his appointment, Chairman Hirsch confidently announced that, by focusing on Manhattan's lower East Side neighborhood, the Mayor's Committee could eradicate rent profiteering from New York City in six short months.

Was Chairman Hirsch's bark worse than his bite? Was Mayor Hylan all bark and no bite? How did they intend to take on the city's rent profiteers? Not by any traditional route to be sure.

For one thing, Chairman Hirsch was himself a wealthy property owner and a well-regarded real estate man, earning him the trust of landlords and wealthy real estate owners during his tenure as New York City's tax commissioner. Chairman Hirsch's credentials curried very little favor among the city's tenants and Hirsch's appointment appeared, by some accounts, to be only the latest grandstanding in a long line of fruitless efforts by Mayor Hylan to appease the city's poor, working-class residents without falling out of favor with wealthier, campaign contributing factions of New York City's citizenry.

For another, the Mayor's Committee had virtually no meaningful authority or subpoena power to be effective against the city's rent-gouging landlords. The Mayor's Committee could hold public hearings, sure, but had no legal authority to compel a landlord's attendance or testimony. In effect, this meant that Chairman Hirsch could ask a landlord why he raised the rent but, importantly, had to accept whatever answer the landlord gave without any ability to question, cross-examine or pressure-test the answer. Of course, a landlord could also simply refuse to answer or even acknowledge Chairman Hirsch. Likewise, the Mayor's Committee had no authority to compel landlords to submit financial records or otherwise give testimony in defense of one rent increase or another.

Soon, even Chairman Hirsch readily acknowledged the Committee's glaring lack of authority. By Chairman Hirsch's own admission only months into his new appointment, "When a profiteering landlord is recalcitrant, we have no legal means of bringing him to terms." If a landlord was determined to capitalize on the city's housing shortage by exploiting vulnerable tenant families, Chairman Hirsch was not shy in recounting how the Mayor's Committee was "powerless to prevent him from doing so."

To be sure, the Mayor's Committee did galvanize some public confidence by taking what measures it could despite a glaring lack of subpoena power, or any legal authority, for that matter. The Mayor's Committee instead focused its efforts on easing the plight of city tenants and their families by, for example, making arrangements to house homeless tenants in churches, synagogues and armories. To that end, the Mayor's Committee lobbied to ease restrictions on evicted tenants as well. In one instance, Chairman Hirsch lobbied the Bureau of Encumbrances to disregard a city ordinance requiring tenants to remove their belongings from the sidewalk within forty-eight hours of eviction, an impossible task if you have nowhere else to store your household adornments. The Mayor's Committee also held mediation and arbitration proceedings in an attempt to resolve disputes among tenants and landlords expeditiously, without having to resort to the city's inundated municipal courts.

It may come as a surprise, given the Committee's lack of subpoena power, that some of these efforts did prove fruitful. For example, in May 1919, the national press announced that the Mayor's Committee had entered into an agreement with a landlord association in Brownsville providing that all landlord-tenant disputes would, from now on, be referred to the Mayor's Committee for arbitration, successfully diverting these disputes away from the over-crowded municipal courts. In an encouraging turn, this particular association of landlords pledged to help in any way it could to alleviate the situation in the Bronx's Brownsville District including, for example, endeavoring to make repairs, granting some rent reductions and even giving tenants a year-long lease whereby the rent was fixed for twelve months.

What drove some landlords to settle with tenants? For some, it was the fear of public hearings and especially the threat of being subjected to scrutiny by the city's Department of Taxes and other municipal agencies, most of which, in contrast to the Mayor's Committee, had a robust subpoena power. This threat was especially frightening for the small ethnic landlord, hailing from abroad and predisposed to a wholesome fear of government in general. For others, it was the ordeal of a public hearing at which landlords were notoriously heckled and insulted to be sure, and even faced the legitimate prospect of physical confrontation.

Despite some marginal success, however, the lion's share of landlords simply neglected to comply with and even openly flouted the Mayor's Committee. No sooner did landlords elucidate the Committee's strategy—which usually involved urging tenants and landlords to split the difference between any rent increase proposed by a landlord and the lower rent demanded by a tenant—did landlords take to exploiting the Committee's efforts for their own benefit. Due to the busy efforts of city landlords, the Committee's strategy for bringing down rents through compromise had been turned on its head, having the opposite effect—instead of demanding a small increase of $1 or $2 per month, landlords demanded exorbitant increases in monthly rent, ensuring that when they appeared before the Mayor's Committee, they would have plenty of room to compromise, resulting more often than not in a higher rent than tenants were willing or able to pay.

Those landlords that refused to settle with their tenants—and there were many—insisted that no public authority had the right to impose rent control or otherwise interfere with what landlords and real estate owners perceived as private-sector business governed exclusively by principles of free-market supply and demand. Those adhering to this school of thought maintained that landlords were setting rents according to established notions of supply and demand, attempting only to get the fair market value for their property and, as some boldly maintained, nothing more.

On the one hand, that the grease fire of civil unrest did not overtake the entirety of New York City during Hirsch's tenure as Chairman of the Mayor's Committee was lost on most critics. Indeed, as one municipal Judge put it in 1920, "I really believe that if it were not for the Mayor's Committee . . . we would have had bloodshed in the Bronx." Still other critics overlooked the fact that, without the continued effort and support of the Mayor's Committee, landlords all over the city might've faced the prospect of strict legislation and, more ominous, the threat of total anarchy. "There are probably over 200,000 potential anarchists in the city, only [a]waiting a favorable opportunity to raise the flag of soviet government, and their leaders utilizing the rent and housing situation to accentuate the discontent that exists" already, wrote President of the United States Real Estate Owners Association, Stewart Browne, while imploring landlords "to 'go easy' on rent increases during the Winter" of 1919.

On the other hand, New York City was a'buzz with gadflies that openly criticized the Mayor's Committee as being completely ineffective and called for its immediate dissolution. For example, Socialist advocates brazenly declared that the Mayor's Committee "had done nothing except to legalize rent profiteering." It shouldn't be lost on you at this point that tenants in Brownsville, for example, had protested less against the landlord as an individual and more "against the system of increasing rentals every few months because of the frequent changing of landlords." To be sure, this sentiment was widespread and was less an indictment of particular landlords but, instead, a more pointed criticism of the real estate system in general, which allowed for such frequent, unrestrained and undocumented transfer of real estate ownership as to render the identity of a building owner at any given time impossible to nail down in some cases. Still others dubbed the Mayor's Committee hearings an "inquisition" for tenants, permitting public badgering of landlords in the hope that these public exhortations would deter future rent increases.

Even more unnerving, many critics held a documented concern that the Mayor's Committee investigation into rent profiteering and rent strikes covered as a pretext for exposing "certain east side organizations which have been operating on Bolshevik and Soviet lines in an effort not only to prevent landlords from legitimately raising rents, but from maintaining the schedule of rents which has been in force the last year." In response to this allegation, Mayor Hylan urged Chairman Hirsch to lobby Manhattan District Attorney, Edward A. Swann, and his counterparts in the outer boroughs to bring "John Doe proceedings" against leaders of the East Side and other socialist tenant leagues in which prosecutors were not required to identify defendants by name. And Swann did just that, empaneling a grand jury in one case that, for more than a month, heard testimony from a host of policemen, judges and tenants about how the East Side and other tenant leagues were puppets of the Socialist party whose only goal was to incite strikes and agitate rebellion.

These allegations aside, critics and pundits were adamant that the Mayor's Committee had succumb to the Red Scare, convening grand juries in a seeming witch hunt to weed out socialism and other disruptive ideologies the Committee members alone deemed as radical. Outwardly, as the argument went, it seemed that political leaders—New York City Democrats, Republicans and Socialists alike—were exploiting tenants for political purposes. Considering the length of some grand jury proceedings, many surmised, and not unreasonably, that the Hylan administration and New York City's landlords had aligned in their efforts against the Socialist party, using the city's tenants as pawns to carry out their own agenda.

Whatever their intentions, these hearings petered out and resulted in no indictments, but revealed more about the duplicity of the Socialist party and tenants leagues, who Chairman Hirsch himself had alleged were swindling working-class tenants out of association fees, than about the greed of over-grasping landlord profiteers. Chairman Hirsch explained publicly—

> Those engineering these [tenant] associations collected money from tenants ostensibly for legal services, fomented strikes against landlords, and brought about dissention. As a result thousands of tenants have not only paid for legal services never performed, but have lost their homes and been actually thrown

upon the streets . . . Evidence collected by the committee shows that some of these promoters were Bolsheviki.

There's an irony to all of this that shouldn't be lost on you at this point—despite accusations of carrying great importance and responsibility, the Mayor's Committee on Rent Profiteering was undeniably limited in its authority from the very beginning, preventing its members from achieving anything of significance, severely handicapping the Committee's efforts and allowing rent profiteering to continue its advance across the five boroughs.

In this way, it would be fair to say that the Committee's shortcomings were less for lack of effort and more due to the permanence of an ill-prepared legal machine, utterly incapable, in the end, of doling out justice with any efficacy, efficiency or balance. As Socialist candidate for the New York State Assembly, Gertrude Weil Klein, described it, the Mayor's Committee simply and unequivocally made a grandstand play of curbing the city's supposed profiteers without stepping on the toes of New York City's real estate interest. In light of a glaring lack of progress, perhaps Assemblywoman Weil Klein had a point.

For all of the criticism, one thing was certain—the Mayor's Committee on Rent Profiteering did not hold down rents, head off strikes, relieve the swelling dockets of municipal courts or address the pressing concerns of tenant leagues that continued to refine their tactics and sharpen their message. Down through the latter months of 1919 and into early 1920, tenant leagues were stronger than ever, in some ways due to their close association with the Socialist party, which looked more appealing by the day as a source of relief for the plight endured by city tenants.

As if the Mayor's Committee had not come under enough scrutiny, its chairman, Nathan Hirsch (who, if you recall, had predicted total eradication of rent profiteering in six short months) resigned abruptly on January 2, 1920. Naturally, his sudden resignation fueled the debate over the Committee's effectiveness, a debate that started well before Chairman Hirsch stepped down and would continue long after.

As 1919 gave way to 1920, it became increasingly clear that the Mayor's Committee was incapable of resolving New York City's housing shortage on its own, a reality obvious to most even before Chairman Hirsch's resignation. Nor was Mayor Hylan's administration up to the task, which had neither the authority nor the gumption to take on what was becoming less an acute housing shortage and more a problem of far more permanence. Some called for New York City's Board of Aldermen to take action to amend the city's municipal code so as to spur on residential construction, stabilize rents, or both. With city officials floundering, it became clear that if there was any chance of easing the city's housing shortage, it couldn't be solved by city officials, but required state-level intervention; not from New York City, but from upstate, in Albany.

## *UPSTATE CONSERVATIVES (SUPPOSEDLY)*

Upstate in Albany, most state lawmakers—Senators and Assemblymen, Democrats and Republicans alike—dismissed rent profiteering in New York City and across the state in one of two ways. First, some believed that rent profiteering was an isolated issue, confined to New York City itself, as opposed to an issue demanding statewide attention. As the argument went, while rents were on the rise throughout New York, rents were not rising at an altogether alarming rate. By 1919, however, most recognized that the drought in residential construction seen in New York City was actually a statewide issue. As John A. Hamilton (no, not the founding father), a state Senator from Buffalo, maintained—

> Overcrowding in all the towns [of New York] is becoming a menace. In the smaller places there are few tenements and the congestion is apparent chiefly in the fact that families everywhere are taking in boarders to such an extent that the practice is becoming dangerous to health and morals.

Hamilton's contemporaries in the state legislature, for their part, continued to dismiss high rents as an issue isolated to New York City's five boroughs.

Second, by contrast, were those few state lawmakers that did regard rising rents as a serious problem. This camp of politicians, however, held firm to the belief that it was not incumbent on them to address the problem, being Senators and Assemblymen for but one state of the Union. In other words, even those state lawmakers that recognized the gravity of rent profiteering nevertheless persisted in apathy. Like most Americans, New York's state lawmakers were fully aware that rising rents were a national, even international, phenomenon. Other European countries, for example, had already imposed nationalized systems of rent control in response to the exorbitant cost of housing, and many believed that it was incumbent on the federal government of the United States, instead of the New York State Legislature, to resolve the issue of nationwide rent profiteering through federal legislation.

State acedia aside, U.S. Congress, for its part, came close to reigning in New York's landlords in late August 1919 when the House of Representatives voted by a narrow margin to expand the scope of a certain federal statute to cover the nation's landlords. Enacted in 1917, Congress originally passed the Lever Act to curb rampant profiteering among over-grasping capitalists in other industries—coal dealers, retail grocers and retail clothiers, to name a few—with the intent of providing a measure of consumer protection against exorbitant price increases. However, the bill that would have brought landlords and real estate under the Lever Act was shelved in the U.S. Senate, largely due to the efforts of conservative-leaning Republicans.

One New York state politician stood out from the rest, however, finally catapulting New York City's pervasive housing shortage to the forefront of state politics. Only after Alfred E. Smith, Democrat and acting President of New York City's Board of Aldermen, was elected to the New York State Governor's Office did the city's housing shortage truly emerge as a statewide political action item.

In the months after Governor Smith took office, a host of committees, both public and private, began looking more intently at New York City's housing shortage, which had escalated by this time to a citywide crisis. Chief among the public committees, and by far the most visible, was the Joint Legislative Committee on Housing, formed by New York's state legislature at the behest of Governor Smith and colloquially referred to as the "Lockwood Committee" after its chairman, Senator Charles C. Lockwood of Brooklyn.

After initial assessments, the Lockwood Committee came to the same conclusion as most everyone else who had seriously set about investigating emergence of the rent profiteer in New York. The problem, found the Lockwood Committee, was a housing shortage perpetuated by a severe and unrelenting drought of residential construction. In this way, rent profiteering was really a symptom of a more systemic problem. Governor Smith agreed and insisted, "[t]he crying need is for more housing," and "nothing short of an active resumption of building on a large scale will bring adequate relief." Lawson Purdy, a prominent city organizer by 1919, was unequivocal—

> The popular talk of the evil of increased rents is nonsense. The problem is far more deeply rooted, and unless capital can be attracted to building investments and builders encouraged to erect new houses instead of renovating old and dangerous ones, the housing problem will become an even more menacing one. The public should be brought to realize this situation.

An editorial published by the *New York Times* in 1919 began, "Unemployment and unprecedented demand for housing accommodations have focused the public attention upon the building industry. When the need is so great, why are not houses being built?"

Many agreed on the problem, but few saw a clear solution, though not for lack of a thorough search. Some pointed to a glaring "[l]ack of confidence in the continuance of present high prices." To be sure—

> The builder is afraid of being the lender on bond and mortgage, is afraid to lend on the present cost of production, and the outside investor, though beginning to be tempted by the attractive returns offered by some buildings, does not dare put his money into new construction. The general opinion seems to be that, in a period of five years the cost of building will decline to some level not as low as in pre-war times, but lower than at present.

As another real estate developer explained—

> The paralyzing factor that, in my opinion, is interfering to the greatest degree with the construction of low-priced apartment houses is the fact that all self-respecting builders are fearful of an effective and humiliating interference with the natural operation of the law of supply and demand, in which event New York is destined to go through the worst congestion in its history.

There were, in fact, many overlapping problems facing state lawmakers related to New York City's housing crisis; some minor and some major, but all of which had a splintering effect on state lawmakers' efforts. For example, given that thousands of apartments, particularly on Manhattan's lower East Side, were so dilapidated as to be unfit for human habitation, it was difficult to take a proper census, let alone calculate precisely how many livable apartment units actually existed in Manhattan. Without being able to come to a reliable figure in this regard, it was nearly impossible to reach a consensus among politicians about how many units needed to be built to minimize the opportunity for rent profiteering.

There were other, perhaps more practical roadblocks to be sure, particularly with respect to exactly where and how new residential apartment buildings would be built. You shouldn't take for granted, as many tenant activists seemed to in 1919, that residential construction was a job for private enterprise. What did this mean? It meant that real and sustained growth of residential construction required a sufficient incentive for speculative builders to jump in, as they had in the past (recall the construction boom that followed the Tenement House Act of 1901).

But in 1919, there was simply no incentive for any builders, speculative or otherwise, to invest, nor for lenders to lend. Driven by the soaring price of labor and materials, the cost of construction had gone up some 80 percent by some estimates, relegating private sector construction as too expensive and onerous a task for even the most speculative of private developers.

It was during this time that many started to publicly recognize that the persistent drought in residential construction continued largely at the behest of banks and other institutional lenders, who continued to hold off lending on mortgage to fund much needed residential construction. Was there not anything that could be done? Was there not some middle ground or compromise measure that would spur on residential construction? Some went so far as to propose Richmond County, on Staten Island, as a ready area of the city that could be developed in a cost-effective way for residential purposes. As the President of the Staten Island Civic League wrote to the Mayor's Committee in May 1919, Staten Island itself constituted a full 18 percent of the city's geographic territory, an area equivalent to Manhattan and the Bronx combined, and yet, Richmond County housed at that time a mere 1 percent of the city's population. The reality was that Staten Island remained an impractical solution given the difficulties of getting to and from Manhattan's business districts on a reliable basis. The suggestion, instead of being taken as a serious proposal, should, instead, serve to show just how dire conditions were becoming for New York City.

Those looking to Staten Island seemed to be grasping at straws, forced into proposing far-fetched measures at a time when the city's apartment supply was narrowing by the day and evictions were on the rise. In 1919, the national press reported—

> With evictions increasing in number, hardship frequent, and discomfort and increased expense in general, is new building to remain dormant until all the doubts of all the doubters as to the permanence of prices are dispelled? Cannot reserves be set up from rents to protect new buildings against possible future losses in capital value? Is there no economic, no business solution? Is loss inevitable? Must we wait until rents reach such levels that the present hardships are doubled before capital can be tempted into building?

In fact, conditions in New York City were such that private sector real estate developers were not only refusing to look for new building projects, but were actively pulling out of existing commitments. At least as far as 1919 went, most readily conceded that, "it is too late even now to correct the conditions making for higher rents this Autumn." Adding insult to injury were the "growing evils" of commercial leasing companies, which, by nearly all accounts, were—

> [C]orporations organized and existing only for the purpose of paying as low a rental as possible to the [building] owner, and of charging as high a rental as may be obtainable from the tenant. They have absolutely no responsibility to any one, except to their stockholders.

At one point during 1919, the Mayor's Committee, Governor Smith's administration and the Lockwood Commission were all simultaneously investigating New York City's housing shortage. Though some optimism percolated from major news outlets, the incredible reality was that New York City saw no reprieve during this time from a suffocating drought in residential construction, which persisted in choking the city's tenants, droves of whom, as a measure of last resort, banded together in protest against excessive rent increases.

In terms of organized protest, New York was not alone among the world's cities. Many countries also saw mass throngs of wage earners gathering to protest in the name of such causes as labor rights and minimum wage, likewise speaking out against perceived social evils such as profiteering, unhindered private sector corporations, unhinged socialism and other radical ideals battling behind the scenes for worldwide adoption.

For example, Mexico, while undergoing a nationwide revolution led in part by the now infamous Emiliano Zapata, also saw many strikes and protests—though some notably broke down into ineffective fiascos. Canadians, for their part, were, broadly speaking, well organized. Some would say they bordered on militant given the right motivation. The same, of course, was true of Europeans in general and Parisians in particular.

Meanwhile, America was proving on a daily basis why, as organized protesting went, she deserved to be near the top of the heap. Though whether this designation was a good thing is still a matter of some debate. Consider an incident in Texas, for example, where a group of war rioters protesting World War I took to a county politician they believed to have abused the Red Cross and, by extension, American soldiers. The demonstrators showed their consternation by dousing the city official in tar, coating him in feathers, draping him in a banner inscribed, "Traitor; Others Take Warning," and marching him through the streets, ultimately running him out of the county for good.

While tarring and feathering can be good fodder for newspaper headlines, it would prove useless on the battlefield of New York City in 1919. During those delicate times, protestors that proved tactless were condemned as radicals, anarchists and, the worst by far, Bolshevists. No, no. There was no American city in that day that saw more organized or effective peaceful protest than New York City. And the city's tenantry continued to refine their tactics with every passing day.

## *WHAT ABOUT PUBLIC HOUSING?*

Easing New York City's housing shortage required more apartment houses and residential buildings to be built; this much was obvious to everyone by 1919, politicians and citizens alike. On the eve of Moving Day 1919, a special committee of New York's state legislature published a report evincing no sense of equivocation—"The removal of wartime restraint has caused no large-scale resumption of building operations."

As I may have mentioned, however, New York City's tenant activists largely took for granted that residential construction, though subject to government oversight, was really reserved to private enterprise. The private sector, for its part, operated on the promise of American capitalism. As an idea, American capitalism became synonymous with the "American Dream," providing the lure of unrestrained profits and boundless growth. Spurred on by that promise, a contagion of speculative real estate investment proliferated, taking New York City by storm leading up to World War I and continuing to spread well after. Evil or not, speculative builders were necessary if the housing shortage was going to see any relief from private sector real estate developers. Most accepted that, incentivizing private sector real estate developers to jump in required freely available capital to back investment in residential construction.

To that end, many New Yorkers urged federal and state officials to act on a proposal, or perhaps even more than one, to attract capital investment back into the state and spur on residential construction. One widely supported proposal involved exempting payment towards the interest carried on a mortgage loan from federal and state income taxes, a measure that may have made real estate mortgages competitive with other investments again and, perhaps as a result, would provide the impetus needed to attract investors back into real estate development. Both Governor Smith and the Lockwood Committee fell in line behind this proposal.

To the dismay of many, however, this proposal never saw the light of day, providing a stark example of how most proposals of any gravity were diluted down by political jogging to the point, even if passing a vote by some miraculous alignment of untamable political forces, of having no practical effect.

Short of building anew, some proposed converting single-family homes into three and four-family tenement houses. Strictly speaking, such conversion would have added, by some estimates, thousands of apartments to New York City's housing stock. Many New Yorkers on both sides of the line supported such a measure. As one prominent real estate attorney explained—

> For instance, on the lower and upper East Side, there are vacant rooms which will accommodate 100,000 people. If these rooms were made available for proper living accommodations it would go a great way toward solving housing facilities in this city. In most cases all that would be necessary would be for the Government to make appropriation for each building sufficient to install hot water, steam heat, bathtubs, and proper plumbing in each house. These improvements, together with the proper painting of each house, would transform these houses into most desirable living quarters.

Residential conversion, as opposed to building anew, would have the twin benefits of, at the same time, providing much needed housing for the city's tenants while turning these otherwise vacant buildings into valuable real estate investments. Significantly, however, the Tenement Housing Act of 1901 expressly prevented this type of conversion, leading many to call for the state legislature to amend New York's real estate law in targeted ways that would facilitate conversion of single-family homes to multi-family tenement houses.

Though several bills actually made it through a vote in the state legislature, all geared towards providing an investment incentive for residential conversion, as opposed to residential construction, few building owners took advantage, relegating conversion as another non-starter to address the city's housing shortage.

With so much skepticism of private enterprise swirling about, and the housing shortage worsening by the day (by the hour, even), socialist ideas gained more attention, spreading among the ranks of tenant activists and bubbling more often to the surface of public debate. To the Socialist party, the solution to New York City's housing shortage was natural. If private builders were unable to supply housing, it was incumbent on the public sector—state or city government—to step in, building public housing and renting directly to tenants.

Recall how even the loosest association with socialism incited fierce and principled opposition from all ranks of society? If so, you don't need me to tell you just how adamant an opposition there was to public housing.

Consider, for example, the united front presented by private sector real estate advocates and some tenant activists, two groups ordinarily sitting in stubborn opposition to one another and actively engaged in a feud for the hearts and minds of city residents. Public housing, opponents charged, was decidedly un-American and a form of radical socialism that had no place in a country founded on the primacy of private enterprise. As the argument went, if the state provided housing, why not food, clothing, cars, and even theater tickets?

But desperate times called for desperate measures and, aside from the Socialist party, public housing did garner some support, though it was largely unenthusiastic and ultimately gained no traction as a legitimate solution. One notable supporter of public housing, Fiorello H. La Guardia, then-President of New York City's Board of Aldermen, declared the necessity of public housing by pointing out that "[p]eople are robbing themselves of food in order to pay the landlord who robs them with excessive rent, and families already indecently crowded are taking lodgers." Underlying Alderman La Guardia's comments, of course, was the widely held belief that private sector builders were wholly incapable of stepping in under current market conditions.

Aside from ideological opposition, public housing faced tremendous practical opposition as well. Landlord advocates charged that it was not possible for New York's state and city governments to put up housing any cheaper or quicker than builders from the private sector. These advocates argued it was likewise impossible for New York's many city governments to economically rent to the state's underserved tenants at a rent that was any more affordable than what tenants were already paying. As the Advisory Council of Real Estate Interests maintained, "No one can now contend with any show of reason that an activity conducted by public officials can compete on the same basis of costs with private endeavors." Many critics went further, arguing that public housing would exacerbate rather than alleviate the city's housing shortage by actively deterring private sector builders from further investment. Put bluntly, a builder "will not take the risk of so building if the city stands over him with power, whenever it pleases to go into the business of producing space for less than it is worth and destroying the value of his property."

As if this weren't enough, there was also a documented concern that public housing was unconstitutional, violating both the U.S. and New York State constitutions. Relying on an opinion submitted by

New York's Corporation Counsel, William P. Burr, to Mayor Hylan in 1919, opponents of public housing argued that New York City was barred by the New York State Constitution from spending public funds for anything other than a "public purpose." As Burr testified to the Lockwood Committee, to erect buildings and rent apartments directly to tenants was a "private purpose," plain and simple, black and white. Even for some incidental public benefits, undeniable in their own right, Corporation Counsel Burr argued that public housing, funded and constructed by the city's municipal government, should not be regarded in the same way as city water and sewer systems, nor electric and gas plants for that matter.

To proponents of public housing, it was preposterous to charge that public housing was a form of radical socialism given that rent profiteering itself was to blame for the spread of radical ideas. Hence, it made little sense that rent profiteering itself and, in the same breath, a solution meant to curb rent profiteering should be attacked on the same grounds. Supporters further pointed out that public housing was a precedented solution because, while not yet adopted in the U.S., it had already been implemented as a measure with some success in many European cities, including Paris.

With respect to public housing, the opposition largely won out during these years, as you've probably guessed. Any chance public housing had was soon eclipsed by the widespread belief that authorities could do more to ease the housing crisis by subsidizing residential construction—lending money or extending credit to private builders—rather than itself building homes for underserved tenants.

Hopefully by now, you can see that residential construction, though undeniably the ultimate solution to New York City's housing shortage, faced, for all intents and purposes, insurmountable opposition. By early 1919, even those New Yorkers who eagerly advocated in favor of those measures geared towards spurring on residential construction had come to believe that neither private enterprise nor public authority could do much of anything to alleviate the housing shortage in time to head off further calamity.

## A 'SPECIAL' SESSION

Given the abject shortcomings of the Mayor's Committee on Rent Profiteering and a pervasive ideological opposition to public housing, it was no stretch, then, when many concluded that New York's state lawmakers had to take action to curb the city's profiteering landlords, and do so quickly.

By 1919, it was widely regarded that relief must come in one of two ways. First, the state legislature could impose rent control on residential property, preventing landlords from raising the rent above a certain amount for a given tenant. Despite the charge that this was too heavy-handed, there was precedent for rent control both abroad and at home, having been already implemented in some form or another in many European cities abroad and Washington, D.C., the nation's capital. New York City's Real Estate Board, a formidable lobbying group that kept a close eye on what went on upstate in Albany, vigorously opposed rent control for New York, contending, for example, that proposals to regulate rents or revise landlord-tenant law were unfair, if not unconstitutional. Unfair, as the argument went, because most landlords were not greed-ridden profiteers, but simply free-market capitalists who, operating exclusively in the private sector, raised rents to cover skyrocketing expenses and to offset heavy losses suffered during the lean years leading up to World War I. Nor was it fair, as the argument continued, for politicians to single out landlords when the price of food, clothing and other items was rising at a quicker pace than the cost of housing.

New York's Real Estate Board also charged that regulating rents was impractical and that rent control would stand no chance of easing the plight of city tenants. Rents, they argued, should remain a product exclusively of free market forces—namely, the "natural laws" of supply and demand. Rents would accordingly drop only when the cost of labor and materials fell to a level where it was again profitable for private sector developers to build residential apartment buildings, and not before. Any legislative meddling would only exacerbate the problem, they maintained. Many, including some prominent municipal Judges, had doubts about the constitutionality of rent control as well.

A second option would be for the state legislature to revise New York's landlord-tenant laws to make it more difficult and expensive for landlords to bring summary proceedings to evict tenants. The added time and expense of evicting tenants would, as the argument went, have a deterrent effect on further rent increases and level the playing field when it came to evictions. To that end, one proposal drew particular attention—that of giving New York City's core of elected municipal Judges broader discretion to craft a remedy given the particular circumstances of a landlord-tenant dispute instead, as was the *status quo*, of being compelled in case after case to *carte blanche* grant landlords' requests for eviction warrants without the benefit of even a modicum of discretion. Unsurprisingly, there were critics who spoke out that broader judicial discretion would leave landlords and tenants alike "dependent upon the whim of the men on the bench, who may be sober or drunk or half-drunk or straight, or half-straight," ready to do almost anything to stay in the good graces of voters.

In the end, most of the bills proposed that year during the state legislature's regular session never saw a vote. Even those that did never stood a chance. State lawmakers, to the consternation of many, adjourned in mid-June 1919, having shelved, voted against or outright neglected each housing bill that came to a vote.

Fortunately, however, the legislature's adjournment was short-lived. Soon, a campaign gathered steam to persuade Governor Smith to call state lawmakers to a special session, intended as a targeted gathering with the singular goal of addressing New York's lingering housing shortage and rising rents. Governor Smith was initially resistant to calling a special session despite a new round of rent strikes—which occurred by the tens of thousands—and municipal courts being continually inundated with summary proceedings brought by landlords to evict tenants who refused to pay a rent increase. Tension mounted and many municipal Judges, including the prominent Judge Robitzek, joined the fray and insisted on legislative action.

Meanwhile, New York City's sidewalks remained clogged with furniture and household belongings, a visceral image of the city's plight.

At the same time, Congress made a momentous, though merely incidental, decision that brought the matter of a special legislative session to a head in Albany. That year, the U.S. Senate voted in favor of an amendment to the *U.S. Constitution* that gave women, for the first time, full suffrage, including the right to vote.

Governor Smith, for his part, wanted New York to be one of the first states to ratify the *Nineteenth Amendment*, which necessitated, at least at this time of year with the legislature adjourned, a special legislative session. After some squabbling among city and state officials, New York's housing shortage was added to the agenda, ultimately setting the stage for much needed reform. Would it be enough?

State legislators made headway during the special session, you might say, passing two resolutions and, perhaps more importantly, four new laws directed to New York City's housing shortage, which had escalated by 1919 to a citywide crisis.

A resolution of the state legislature is tantamount to a non-binding act by lawmakers (as opposed to the binding nature of a statute) and those resolutions adopted by New York's state lawmakers in 1919 were no different. Both resolutions implored the federal government to enact legislation that would attract essential capital investment back into New York in general and into the real estate market in particular. The first resolution urged Congress to create a federal building loan bank that would serve to provide reliable capital investment to builders, in effect subsidizing residential construction, as opposed to building directly. A second resolution urged Congress to exempt those bonds issued by the New York State Land Bank from federal income taxes. In broad strokes, both resolutions were directed at making residential construction less costly in the hope of coaxing private sector developers to again begin investing in residential construction for both the city and state of New York.

It shouldn't surprise you at this point to learn that, despite their best efforts, New York's state legislators were unable to convince Congress to do much of anything, let alone create a new federal loan bank that would subsidize residential construction in New York.

Fortunately, for New York City's working-class tenants continued to suffer relentless rent increases at the hands of over-grasping landlords, New York's state legislators passed four new state laws in an attempt to ease the plight of city tenants. These special session housing laws essentially came in two flavors—the first two amended the landlord-tenant laws, while the second two were targeted amendments designed to increase the state's housing supply.

To that end, the first required that landlords looking to terminate a lease agreement give a tenant more notice so that the tenant might be able to find other accommodations should a rent increase put the cost of living beyond the family's means, requiring a full 20 days' notice prior to termination of the lease agreement as compared to the prior requirement of five days' notice. To be sure, this amendment was also an attempt to curb the number of tenant families forced to live (if even temporarily) on the sidewalk alongside a pile of their household adornments and belongings.

In the same vein, the second new statute amended the state landlord-tenant laws in order to empower a municipal Judge, when granting a landlord's request to evict a given tenant for failure to pay rent, to prevent (by granting a "judicial stay") a landlord from evicting that tenant for up to 20 days provided, however, that the tenant deposit with the court an amount equivalent to the prior rent, reduced *pro rata* for the length of the tenant's holdover.

Remember the Tenement House Act of 1901? Remember how it prevented the conversion of single-family homes into three and four-family tenement buildings? Well, the New York state legislature's third new statute tweaked the Tenement House Act of 1901 to better allow for residential conversion while still ensuring that these new tenement buildings retained adequate ventilation, insulated stairways and stable fire escapes.

Finally, the fourth new statute passed during that special session amended New York's Banking Law with the aim of attracting more capital investment back into residential construction. You should know that, prior to this amendment, savings banks in New York were prohibited from providing a loan on mortgage to residential builders in an amount exceeding 40 percent of the property value for a given project. Under the new law, savings banks would be permitted to lend on mortgage up to 60 percent of the property value for a given building project. The thought behind this last measure was that, with more capital available for lending on a given project, then more private sector real estate developers (who, whether speculators or otherwise, do not fund construction out of their own pockets) would jump in and start building.

Faced for the first time with laws passed to address the housing shortage, reception of the new special session housing laws split along familiar lines. Some were elated, including the outspoken Judge Robitzek and Governor Alfred Smith himself. Those aligning with the real estate interest, for their part, were up in arms, arguing that the new laws went too far and gave tenants an unprecedented amount of leverage as against their landlords. Tenants likewise spoke out against the new legislation, urging, unsurprisingly, that the new laws did not go far enough to have any real impact. No one seemed satisfied.

For all the controversy, however, these special session housing laws were as notable for failing to impose any measure of rent control as they were for the schismatic effect they had on an already deeply-fractured New York City. The Greater New York Tenants League outspokenly pointed to the lack of rent control as a glaring omission in the special session housing laws, arguing that the city desperately needed rent control as a targeted measure to prevent landlords from raising the rent more than once in a given year, especially where a building changed hands multiple times in the interim. Recall that, in the past, rent had been set by private agreement between tenant and landlord, which could only be enforced as between the parties as a private contract. Rent control, on the other hand, would effectively impose, by law, a rent-related covenant to run with the property, a fundamental transformation of the tenant-landlord relationship. Regardless, nearly all concerned maintained that the special session housing laws were deficient in one way or another, leaving much to be desired by all accounts.

However, one notable aspect of the special session rent laws should not go understated—for the first time, the state legislature, for as conservative as it leaned, had actually risen to the occasion by enacting legislation to curb rent profiteering. It had actually come to a consensus and acted, something that could not be said for the Mayor's Committee on Rent Profiteering, Mayor Hylan's administration or any other municipal agency. For the first time since the city-wide housing crisis set in, state legislators gave the city's hard-pressed tenants reason to believe that if rents continued to soar in the months or years ahead, lawmakers might even be willing to take more drastic measures.

## *TURNING TIDES*

It goes without saying (though I will anyways) that the drought in residential construction exasperated New York City's chronic housing shortage. Following a long, hot summer in 1919, there was no denying that the special session housing laws only obscured New York's otherwise gaping and more chronic injury—a nagging lack of residential construction. By, for instance, merely requiring landlords to give 20 days' notice to tenants prior to eviction, some charged that legislators "simply put[] off for a short time the evil that's sure to come."

For all the talk of rent control, municipal Judges' discretion, summary proceedings and public housing, that the simple and unequivocal lack of livable apartments garnered so little attention as a political action item was enough to make your head spin. Many agreed that unless the cost of labor and building materials fell, builders could not afford to build and lenders would remain unwilling to lend. And yet, it was a well-known fact that, despite those resolutions passed by the state legislature, the special session housing laws passed in early 1919 were failing to have any stimulating effect on residential construction.

It was simply a matter of numbers. Consider that only ninety-five multi-family buildings went up in 1919—just six in Queens and only three in Manhattan. According to New York's Tenement House Department, fewer apartments went up in New York City during 1919 than in any year since the Tenement House Act went into effect in 1901. The city's vacancy rate, which had risen as high as 5.6 percent in March 1916, plummeted to 2.18 percent three years later and then again, down to an unprecedented 0.36 percent by April 1920. Of the nearly one million apartments in New York City, only 3,500 stood vacant, most of them "cold-water flats" in the city's slums, devoid of any hot water and barely livable, *e.g.*, air was barely breathable or the apartment building entirely run over by rats, roaches, tuberculosis, influenza virus or cholera.

New York City's Tenement House Department, meanwhile, was forced to ignore the flagrancy of these violations for fear of, in the event of shutting a building down, being vilified publicly as an active contributor to the city's housing shortage. According to the Lockwood Committee, "[i]t has become necessary to practically suspend operation of our sanitary and building laws so as to preserve any sort of roof over the heads of the poorer population."

The outlook was bleak and all New Yorkers were fearful. City tenants feared that it was going to be nearly impossible to find vacant apartments by Moving Day 1920. For real estate investors, the fear was that if landlords did not ease up on tenants, there would be hell to pay from lawmakers and "potential anarchists" alike, the latter of which stood two hundred thousand strong and teetering on the razor's edge of revolution.

As feared, landlords the city over refused to relent in 1919, unapologetically raising rents anywhere from 10-50 percent, if not more. By the end of the year, "there were very few neighborhoods in which 'the increase has not been at least 25 percent.'"

According to the U.S. Bureau of Labor Statistics, rents in New York City really took off in 1919, rising as rapidly in the second half of the year after the special session housing laws took effect, as in the first half. Especially hard hit were New York City's working-class wage earners, whose rents skyrocketed some 51 percent on average between July 1914 and July 1919, according to the National Industrial Conference Board. Down through 1920, rent continued to outpace the cost of food, clothing and other necessities. In point of fact, rents in New York City were increasing faster than most other of the nation's major cities, adding salt to an already gaping wound.

A good barometer for the extent of unrest gripping New York City might be the bevy of additional housing bills that built up across the desks of state lawmakers in Albany during those days. Most of these proposals fell into one of two broad categories. The first category was directed at curbing the practice of rent profiteering by, for example, prohibiting real estate speculators from arbitrarily raising rent for the purpose of quickly reselling the very same property at an inflated profit. To that end, as well, were several bills designed to curb rent profiteering by authorizing New York City, for example, to establish an independent rent commission to closely monitor and administer rent control, similar in kind to the D.C. Rent Commission convened to resolve rent control in the nation's capital. In contrast to the Mayor's Committee on Rent Profiteering, such a rent commission would be cloaked with the legal authority of an official administrative agency, empowered to hold hearings, issue subpoenas, determine a reasonable rent and issue binding decisions.

A second category of bills introduced that year were targeted at protecting vulnerable tenants, particularly against profiteering landlords hell-bent on obtaining eviction warrants. Before

December 1919, a landlord could terminate a residential lease by simply alleging before a municipal Judge that a particular tenant was "undesirable," a charge for which a landlord, incredibly, need not provide any proof to support before a municipal Judge was compelled by law to rule in the landlord's favor. As the Lockwood Committee found, this aspect of landlord-tenant law (stemming from a ruling of New York's appellate court in *Waitt Construction Company v. Lorraine*) left tenants at the complete and utter mercy of their ill-intentioned landlords, many of whom claimed that even the most peaceful of tenants were "undesirable" as an obvious pretext for evicting tenants unwilling or unable to pay a rent increase. As a measure of protection, the Lockwood Committee introduced a bill under which a landlord bringing a summary proceeding to evict an "undesirable" tenant must, for the first time, prove to the satisfaction of a municipal Judge that a tenant is, in fact, so recalcitrant as to warrant eviction.

The Lockwood Committee also found that some landlords—most of whom were "professional lessees"—attempted to drive out tenants by threatening to rescind or, worse, intentionally depriving tenants of essential services such as light, water, heat, telephone or elevator service. Indeed, some landlords would cut off heat until the tenant made a complaint to the city housing department, only to have the heat suddenly return without explanation but just in time to be functioning when city personnel came to investigate. To protect such defenseless tenants, the Lockwood Committee proposed an unprecedented amendment to the state's criminal code making it, for the first time, a criminal misdemeanor for a landlord or commercial lessee to willfully fail to furnish any essential service.

Most of the remaining bills were designed to stimulate residential construction, though, as before, these bills garnered very little support as the drought in residential development, so pervasive and obvious, continued at the behest of high costs and a labor shortage.

It won't surprise you to learn that these housing bills met virulent opposition, much of it stirred up by the New York City Real Estate Board and their persistent upstate lobbying efforts. Though I'd be remiss if I didn't mention that, despite the outcry, many a'landlord advocacy group relied on their own agendas reflecting their own interests, splintering their efforts and undermining their efficacy. They persisted no less.

As I may have mentioned, drawing particular opposition was a bill that would make it a criminal misdemeanor for a landlord to withhold heat and other essential services to which tenants were entitled as a matter of law. What made the bill so pernicious to critics was not only that the law would swell the ever-increasing tide of litigation among landlords and tenants clogging municipal court dockets as it was, but also, that it would make an alleged breach of a contract made exclusively between tenant and landlord, a crime, punishable as an offense against the public at large. Those that aligned with the real estate interest were vehement in their objection, vocal in particular about the prospect of imposing a criminal penalty for failure to provide heat and other essential services—an allegation that had previously been confined to civil court as a breach of contract concerning private property.

The New York Real Estate Board was not alone as others objected on several by-then familiar grounds. Most familiar were those who maintained that the extent of these proposed bills was simply unjustified, tantamount to killing a mouse with a hand grenade. As the argument went, the average landlord was not an over-grasping profiteer but a capitalist businessman who needed to raise rents just enough to cover the rising cost of operations and maintenance, costs that had more than doubled since World War I. To be sure, most acknowledged that the housing shortage was still waging in New York City. But that was no reason, even in those trying times, to deprive landlords of nearly every element of real estate ownership.

There was public and private outcry as well over punishing the great majority of landlords for the undeniable greed of a small minority, most of whom were commercial lessees and speculators, responsible for inflation of property values and Russian Jews to boot. Some reasoned, "No one expects the shoemaker to sell $15 shoes for $7, much less to sign an agreement with his customers to sell the shoes at that price for an entire year." You wouldn't be mistaken as unreasonable if you inferred at this point that xenophobia still drove much of the opposition to further housing reform.


Something curious happened in that year, though. By this time, after years of stalled progress and relentless rent increases, the mendacity of landlords' claims to the legitimacy of recent increases in rent was never more apparent than in 1920, a year when the tide turned for a great many tenants of New York City. In that year, it was undeniable that rent profiteering had spread rapidly among landlords, like rabies among a disaffected and irreverent pack of afflicted wolves.

Were you to downplay this rampant profiteering, dismissing it as the unavoidable outcome of those free market forces of supply and demand, there would be cause for serious concern among those closest to you and might even provoke anyone overhearing you converse openly about it to question your lucidity.

The Lockwood Committee, convened by state legislators in Albany, took exhaustive hearings, reports and studies over the course of considering a round of proposed legislation related to New York's housing shortage. The Committee's Report was unimpeachable and state legislators had, at that point, more than enough information to reach a reasoned conclusion on the necessity of rent control, or so most thought. To deny the existence of the rent profiteer in 1920 would have required you to be inexcusably oblivious to the Lockwood Committee's publicized hearings at which scores of witnesses—experts and layman alike—testified about the severity of New York's housing shortage, the greed of the state's landlords and the distress of many distressed tenant families.

Nor could state legislators continue to object to further housing measures based on a lack of severity. By Moving Day 1920, most feared that landlords would attempt a "wholesale ousting of tenants," bringing summary proceedings in record numbers, as many as 30,000 alone that year by one estimate. Adding insult to injury, virtually no livable apartments stood vacant and movers were overbooked months in advance. Despite the best efforts of tenants and municipal Judges to head off those landlords hell-bent on carrying out evictions, many tenant families were forced into homelessness and vagabondery that renting season.

Judge Robitzek warned that New York City was "on the verge of a revolution." Loring Black, a Democratic Senator from Brooklyn, likewise warned that New York City faced "a social eruption" if, as predicted, there were "wholesale evictions" on Moving Day 1920.

## *OUT WITH THE REDS!*

Surely, with so many tenants living on the streets from Buffalo to Rochester to New York City, you'd think that addressing the plight of New Yorkers across the state would be a priority of the highest order for state lawmakers, right? To be sure, New York City itself had self-immolated, set ablaze by the continual and unrelenting friction sparked between tenants, landlords, Democrats, Republicans, Socialists and socialists alike. Legislators—both Senators and Assemblyman—must've had little else on their minds during the regular legislative session in 1920, right? I mean, a significant percentage of the state's residents were homeless for goodness sake! Might there be another round of legislation passed to address the obvious shortcomings of the special session housing laws? Wasn't housing reform at the top of everyone's list?

The short answer? No, and as you might imagine, landlords still managed to put their tenants out on the street on a rather unnerving scale.

In truth, there was something else brewing that year in Albany, something else entirely that would not only prevent state lawmakers from addressing the plight of New Yorkers across the state, but would land the entirety of the State Assembly under allegations of treason!

Let me set the stage. First, the characters. In 1920, New York's Republican party controlled a majority of the State Assembly, with Speaker Thaddeus C. Sweet at the helm. In his sights? Five fellow Assemblymen, all of whom were members of the Socialist party *elected* to one of the highest political offices in New York. If you want to be specific, the five assemblymen were Samuel Orr and Samuel A. DeWitt of the Bronx; August Claessens and Louis Waldman of Manhattan; and Charles Solomon of Brooklyn.

Next, the charges. And this is where things get interesting. Led by Assembly Speaker Thaddeus C. Sweet, state lawmakers charged these five Socialists with disloyalty to their country and state, ultimately seeking to expel all five from their elected seats for no other reason than their membership in the Socialist party, which, according to the Assembly's Judiciary Committee, was a "disloyal organization composed exclusively of perpetual traitors" intent on a *coup d'état* by force and violence.

Hardly two hours into the regular legislative session that year, Thaddeus Sweet called the five Socialist members of the Assembly to the front of the house, charging openly that the Socialist party was a criminal conspiracy and calling for an investigation into whether these elected officials should be allowed the privilege of retaining their seats.

After a debate that lasted nearly the entire legislative session, including a full twenty-four hour debate on the eve of the session's scheduled end, the New York Assembly voted on April 1, 1920 to oust all five Socialist Assemblymen from their elected seats, and did so by an overwhelming vote. For example, state Senator Charles Solomon was expelled by a vote of 116 to 28! Given the time of year, you wouldn't be unreasonable if you concluded that the vote was some sort of elaborate (though ill-humored) April Fool's Day joke. Incredible as it seems, you'd be mistaken, for the Judiciary Committee itself had expressly found that "the right of the Assembly to exclude members is fundamental, inherent, and exclusive." This meant that these five Socialist politicians were ousted from their elected seats for no other reason than their political affiliations, the same affiliations that garnered them the votes to win election in the first place!

As the national press reported, Thaddeus Sweet had spearheaded a historic vote—

> By its action, the Assembly established a precedent altogether unique in legislative history in the United States, as never before has an entire party delegation been ejected from any legislative body.

Even the outspoken Assemblyman, Charles Solomon, was nearly rendered speechless by the vote as he, almost too overcome to speak, told an audience at Library Hall in Yonkers the night he lost his seat—

> I was born an American, educated an American, taught to love this country of freedom, typified by the Statue of Liberty at its entrance. We believed that this was a country in which it would never become necessary to have [to] resort to violence. This act tonight is only the beginning. Fellow Americans, the action of the Assembly tonight signalizes a spirit that we believed had been buried long ago.

Prominent labor lawyer and outspoken Socialist party member, Louis Waldman, was equally appalled and openly accused the New York State Assembly itself of treason. "The Constitution has been lynched, and the perpetrators of this outrage must be brought to justice... The right of the ballot is an American right, and those who deny it are traitors."

Why do I make a point of this unholy mess? Well, it's easy to imagine how, with such rancor and suspicion among state lawmakers over whether radical socialists had infiltrated their ranks that the statewide housing crisis almost completely slipped through the cracks during the regular legislative session in 1920. Not that legislators had the proper wherewithal to debate the housing crisis in any event, for, despite alcohol having been recently prohibited by Congress, "[a] great deal of liquor was on hand and was used for the purpose of getting votes over on the other side the night [state legislators threw] the Socialists out." As one Senator recalled, "[s]ome even got so drunk that they had to be *carried* out of the Assembly chamber."

This episode, for whatever it revealed about the Red Scare that swept across the U.S., had the certain effect of undermining lawmakers' efforts to deliberately consider legislation meant to address rent profiteering or New York City's oppressive housing shortage. For what it's worth, expulsion of the five elected Socialists from New York's state legislature seemed to discredit the Red Scare, further bolstering socialism's ethos as a legitimate solution for New Yorkers seeking reprieve from greed-stricken landlords.

What would it take to make meaningful progress? As the regular legislative session of the Assembly neared an end in 1920, any hope of assuaging tenants' plight seemed to be fading quickly, deliverance tauntingly out of reach.

## *THE ELEVENTH HOUR*

Forgive my digression but there's something that bares repeating and we might as well not belabor the point—the timing might seem funny to you, but bare with me while I jump back from April 1, 1920, when five Socialist Assemblymen were summarily ousted from their elected seats in Albany, to March 23, 1920 when state legislators held an all day hearing to decide the fate of all nine housing measures proposed during that regular legislative session. Just before dawn on that morning, there was already underway a veritable migration by public transit bound for the state capital. Many more than those boarding the Empire State Express—packed to the brim with only those who could afford to bare witness to the public debates to take place throughout the course of the day— should have been in attendance were it not prohibitively expensive to travel by train and the roads, not fit for travel by foot.

Still, over a thousand of the city's tenants nonetheless managed to be in attendance, led by Fiorello H. La Guardia, Arthur J.W. Hilly, David Hirschfield and joined by a group of Senators and Assemblymen. Confined to separate cars, the same trains carried more than eight hundred landlords, lawyers, real estate investors and developers.

Once the hearings convened, most tenant activists openly defied instructions to refrain from comment on New York City's housing shortage or soaring rents. For example, Alderman La Guardia drew an uproar from the assembly room audience when he declared, "I am here not to praise the landlord but to bury him." For a moment following his comments, it seemed as though the uproar might have degraded into an all out fistfight between La Guardia and a heckler in attendance as La Guardia was forced to vigorously and physically defended his comments. Joining La Guardia were a host of municipal Judges, clergymen, community organizers and a great many elected and appointed officials from both sides of the aisle, united in their efforts and advocacy on behalf of New York City's tenants.

As reported in the national press, this hearing "opened the eyes" of state legislators for the first time to the truly dire straits of tenants and the profiteering menace, that rent-hogging landlord. Recall, as well, how many people believed that the city's housing shortage, by virtue of its continued oppression of working-class tenants, fomented radicalism itself as it lay siege on the city in a *coup d'état* of the highest institutions of state government. Tenant advocates issued a stern warning during the open hearing in Albany—radicals waited in the wings, prepared to seize the state capital if New York's lawmakers took no action to ease the plight of city tenants. Alderman La Guardia, for his part, lent credence to this concern when he predicted that furious radical socialists would overtake the state legislature the following year if nothing was done. Judge Robitzek predicted that the Socialist vote in the Bronx would soar from 30,000 to 150,000! And after praising lawmakers for investigating those five Socialist Assemblymen ultimately ousted from the state legislature, Arthur J.W. Hilly urged legislators to "go one step further [and] eradicate the causes of Socialism by preventing rent profiteering."

With Moving Day 1920 approaching rapidly, state legislators had no time to lose, and lawmakers in Albany were time-pressed, at the eleventh hour, no less, to wade through some of the most tedious housing bills ever proposed in the state of New York.

Here's what I mean. The first bill of note would repeal the pesky Ottinger Law, effectively restoring the vitality of oral lease agreements and providing that, unless otherwise spelled out by agreement, no tenancy would expire until October 1, Moving Day.

A second proposed law would extend the notice requirement for any landlord seeking to end a lease agreement to 30 days, regardless of whether the tenancy was commercial or residential. Moreover, a landlord seeking to evict a tenant as "undesirable" would be required, if the law passed, to prove the tenant's undesirability.

Still, other proposed amendments proved to be more drastic measures. The first amendment would narrow the summary proceeding as a remedy for landlords, who could bring an action against a tenant for non-payment of rent only in cases where the rent had not been raised even a dollar over the previous month's or, alternatively, in excess of 20 percent over the preceding twelve months. Another proposed amendment provided that any landlord bringing a summary proceeding to evict a tenant for non-payment of a rent increase must prove, in each and every case, that the rent increase was reasonable and not some price-gouging measure. Finally, a proposed bill would empower New York's core of municipal Judges to grant a virtually unlimited stay of eviction where a tenant was willing to pay the old rent or, alternatively, agree to pay a new rent deemed reasonable by the court.

Unfortunately, New York City's tenantry was facing evictions by the thousands, a never-ending and ceaseless onslaught. The upshot was that a Joint Committee of the Senate and Assembly, for the first time in the state's history, voted to impose a form of rent control across the state in 1920 with focused measures directed to curbing rent profiteering in New York's dense urban enclaves.

The emergency rent laws, as enacted that April—referred to endearingly as the "April laws"—retained most proposals of the Lockwood Committee, proposals embodied in a lengthy report issued only a week earlier.

With respect to rent control, the marquee provision provided that a rent increase in excess of 25 percent over the previous month was presumptively unreasonable, requiring that a landlord imposing such an onerous rent increase prove, to the satisfaction of a municipal Judge, that the increase was justified. Furthermore, a landlord failing to furnish essential services such as heat or running water could, for the first time, be charged with a criminal misdemeanor, punishable by up to a $1,000 fine, a year in prison, or both. As well, state lawmakers repealed the pesky Ottinger Law, thereby restoring the integrity of the oral lease agreement on which so many tenants depended for recourse against landlords, overgrasping or otherwise. Finally, the new April laws empowered the state's core of municipal Judges to grant a tenant evicted for nonpayment of rent a judicial stay of eviction for up to nine months, provided that the tenant deposit the old rent with the court and show a diligent, though unfruitful, effort to secure alternative accommodations.

Most understood that a common conservative tactic in those days (as today) was to immediately build a test case to attack rent control on grounds that the nascent rent control measures violated both the New York Constitution and the *U.S. Constitution*.

To head off a constitutional challenge, New York's state legislature publicly justified the emergency rent laws as a short-term legislative remedy to address an ongoing emergency, one that continued to grip several major cities across the state. Rent control, in other words, was imposed to alleviate tenants from having to pay unjust and unreasonable rents, the harm coming not only in the form of rent so high as to require families to stint on food and other necessities, but also all but eliminating tenants' "freedom of contract," and creating a state of emergency that threatened public health, safety and welfare. Governor Smith signed these bills into law, to take effect shortly after midnight on April 1, 1920.

Landlords again went up in arms and, at least in part, may have had good reason to do so. Recall that rent hikes were symptomatic of a far deeper issue—the stubborn and unyielding drought in residential construction. As landlords were quick to point out, virtually everyone agreed that the only way to curb rent profiteering was to put up houses. Period, end of story. And yet, state lawmakers had voted during the regular legislative session to shelve the only two bills proposed to encourage builders to build and lenders to loosen credit. 'We would build,' you might overhear a real estate developer explain, 'but lenders won't lend and until they do there won't be any residential construction.'

On the other hand, supporters of the April laws stressed that it had never been their intention to solve the housing shortage, but only to provide temporary reprieve for tenants, and to do so in time to head off a growing crisis of public health. The pressing question, of course, was whether rent control would prove to be like pouring water on a grease fire or if the new measures indeed had any chance of smothering the city's housing crisis and stamping out rent profiteering once and for all.

Despite the outcry from landlords and those aligned with the real estate interest—and there was incredible outcry, bordering on uproar—the April laws were, in reality, not as imposing as they were portrayed in the court of public opinion. Consider that landlords could still raise rents, move for eviction, drag tenants through the mud of a summary proceeding, and all around still had far deeper pockets and closer political connections than the state's tenants.

On the other hand, tenants without a written lease were now less vulnerable that the Ottinger Law had been repealed. Landlords were still free to bring summary proceedings for non-payment of rent, though tenants were now empowered to offer a defense that the new rent was unreasonable.

Resolution of any dispute over a rent increase fell entirely to the state's core of municipal Judges who had to then navigate a burden-shifting scheme of proof whereby, if the rent increase is greater than 25 percent, the landlord carries the burden of proving that a rent increase is justified. Anything less than a 25 percent increase and the burden of proof fell to the tenant to show that a particular rent increase was, by contrast, unreasonable. Lastly, if a landlord brought a summary proceeding against a holdover tenant who continued living in a given apartment after the expiration of a particular lease agreement, municipal Judges were now empowered to grant tenants on the cusp of eviction a more generous stay of up to twelve months; provided the tenants could show they were unable to find another apartment and were willing to deposit the old rent with the court as collateral against legal fees.

Even with how fierce the debate proved to be, a question openly lingered—were the April laws ample enough a'measure to keep tenants in their apartments and deter rent profiteering? Would this monumental piece of New York legislation, imposing rent control for the first time, be the cure to the state's ills? No one could be sure, if only because this was the first time New York had, as a state, attempted to regulate rents by statute, an aspect of the tenant-landlord relationship traditionally reserved to definition by private contract.

Only time would tell.

## *HOLDING COURT*

Of all the criticism and uncertainty swirling around the nascent April laws, one thing was beyond a doubt—as enacted, the new laws contained no provision geared towards quelling litigation between New York City's landlords and tenants.

In the week or so after the April laws took effect, municipal courts across the state were inundated with a flood of landlord-tenant disputes. As reported in the national press, for example, "[m]ore than 1,000 litigants and their families jammed into the sidewalks, hallways and courtrooms" of Brooklyn's Seventh District. On April 6, 1920, more than a thousand people likewise tried to force their way into a Bronx courtroom with a maximum capacity of five hundred. And on April 8, 1920, the national press reported that "[m]ore than 450 litigants greeted Justice Harry Robitzek when he opened the Second Municipal Court" for business that day. Looking out over the hundreds of men, women and children jammed into his courtroom, Judge Robitzek recalled that he had "never witnessed such a scene."

And many viewed this overwhelming litigation between landlord and tenant over the metes and bounds of a "reasonable rent increase" as a futile exercise. Even the rare municipal Judge completely unswayed by political considerations struggled with resolving legal language left wholly undefined by lawmakers in Albany.

Why was it troublesome that state lawmakers had left "reasonable rent" undefined? Consider that the April laws, as one prominent municipal Judge pointed out, did not say whether a reasonable rent should be based on the market value of the property or the landlord's equity ownership of that property. Nor did the April laws specify what deductions should be made in calculating net income from a particular building, whether depreciation should be taken into account, how capital improvements and other "extraordinary expenditures" should be dealt with and "whether the landlord should be allowed to recoup the losses of previous years . . . [I]f so, over how long a period." To elicit this kind of information during court proceedings took a great deal of time, to be sure, an exercise that placed a tremendous burden on the city's core of municipal Judges, who generally lacked the manpower required to address such a crushing caseload.

It was simply a matter of numbers—municipal Judges just didn't have the hours each day they needed to work through each case on their dockets. Occasionally, when a municipal Judge took the time necessary for each party to enter all documents and testimony into evidence, even the most deliberate of Judges were often left with nothing more than contradictory statements of landlords and tenants that essentially broke down to a the familiar, but unresolvable case of, 'He said, she said.'

It was widely publicized at the time that landlords employed "many devious methods by which [they] tried to circumvent the recently enacted legislation and frighten tenants into paying inflated rents."

In an effort to oust holdover tenants, for example, some landlords claimed they wanted the apartment for themselves (a valid ground for eviction under the April laws), but in reality, had no intention of moving in. Landlords filed for permits to make alterations and renovations that they had no intention of completing or even starting! Some landlords converted large unfurnished apartments into two or more smaller furnished apartments, charging exorbitant rates for a few pieces of furniture and, in the process, replacing a tenant family with bachelors or even, in one outrageous case according to Arthur J.W. Hilly, replacing a married couple with a pet dog. Other landlords designated apartment buildings as office space, which had been carved out from coverage under the April laws as well.

Still other landlords listed their buildings on the market as cooperatives, which was done, at times, "to get tenants out quickly and to get others in at fabulous rentals [or], at other times, as a stock-jobbing scheme through which promoters hope to unload their property at highly inflated prices, at the same time perpetuating their management and control." Other, more brazen landlords simply attempted to justify rent increases in excess of 25 percent by inflating the old rentals and then submitting, during court proceedings, fraudulent receipts for non-existent expenses.

Aside from perjury and fraud, landlords still had the gall to complain publicly that the April laws left them at the mercy of municipal Judges who "have not the faintest idea of realty values" and whose sympathies "are entirely with the tenants." New York City's municipal courts were so busy, landlords charged, that even if they tried, Judges could not give each case the attention it deserved. Perhaps the city's municipal Judges, for their part, were helpless from the get-go. Perhaps they were set up to fail. Perhaps the April laws did not go far enough. Perhaps the state legislature underestimated the moral and ethical plasticity of landlords who were seemingly beholden only, as unhinged and predatory capitalists, to the almighty dollar.

In the background of this ongoing controversy over rent control, an entirely obvious aspect of the April laws again played out publicly—namely, that the April laws had done nothing to stimulate residential construction, which persisted in drought, not only in New York City, but also in Chicago and other cities across the country.

Turmoil persisted and many again called on New York's Governor to convene a special legislative session to address the deepening housing crisis. Despite calls for action, there was absolutely no consensus on how to address the crisis so obviously gripping New York City, bleeding working-class tenants dry. For example, some wanted to further broaden the discretion afforded to municipal Judges, while still others urged that state lawmakers set up an independent board that would administer rent control, much the same way that public utility commissions regulated rates in those days. Another pressing matter was that state legislators had left entirely undefined what constituted a "reasonable rent," other than to say that a rent increase in excess of 25 percent was presumptively "unreasonable." Still others called for a wholesale prohibition of any rent increase in excess of 12 percent. Some even went so far as to propose banning municipal Judges who were landlords themselves from presiding over a landlord-tenant dispute. Others proposed abolishing the summary proceeding altogether.

Likewise, there was no consensus on how to stimulate residential construction, particularly for low-income neighborhoods desperate for affordable housing.

## 'SPECIAL' SESSION REDUX

As New York City's housing shortage waged on, so too did immigrants continue to gush through America's borders at such a rapid clip as to leave many families with the bleak choice of cramming into over-crowded tenement buildings or else being forced to render make-shift living quarters among the city's many trash laden alleyways.

The influx alone of some 10,000 to 20,000 per week would be enough to pinch the housing supply of any city. Half-way through 1920, some estimated that New York City was short some 100,000 apartments, a shortage many predicted would dip to 125,000 by the same time the following year.

Even if we assume *arguendo* that the April laws had headed off an all-out calamity during that spring renting season, many still had doubts that the April laws alone were sufficient to head off another, more daunting crisis by the fall season. I don't mean to alarm you but landlords were still, in the face of this unprecedented legislation in New York, raising rents by leaps and bounds. What happened when tenants withheld their rent for the month? Lessees and landlords persisted in instituting summary proceedings in mind-numbing numbers.

The national press reported that, by mid-August 1920, the number of evictions was soaring, reaching one thousand per week in Brooklyn and between five and six hundred per week in Queens! Record-breaking evictions aside, something else started happening, too. Unprompted, landlords began serving tenants with notice that their leases would not be renewed come Moving Day, even for tenants who were fully willing and able to pay a substantial rent increase. Before long, landlords had served roughly 100,000 dispossess notices in New York City, again fueling fears of widespread evictions come the fall renting season.

Judge Robitzek commented publicly that, given the status quo, things would be even worse the following spring when as many as 40,000 families could be left homeless in the Bronx alone.

To the rescue? You guessed it, another special legislative session. Against the background of an election year, New York's Governor bowed to public pressure and called a special legislative session to convene on September 20, 1920, leaving legislators mere weeks to reach an agreement about what to do come Moving Day.

With so much disagreement swirling, it won't surprise you to learn that, once the special session convened, "both the Senate and Assembly were swamped with bills." The congestion came to a head in late September at a public hearing that was even more acerbic than the special session convened to debate the rash of bills passed as the "April laws."

Despite what many knew to be true, only one bill enacted out of the September special session was addressed to incentivizing private sector residential construction. Not once did the legislature so much as take up a proposed amendment to the New York Constitution, for example, required in order to allow for publicly subsidized residential construction. Under pressure from the state's conservative-leaning real estate interest, state lawmakers tabled bills to further tweak the Tenement House Act of 1901, which would have expedited conversion of single-family houses into multi-family tenement buildings.

That virtually nothing had been done to address the drought of residential construction gripping the city by no means detracted from the significance of September's special legislative session. The new laws that did pass a vote were implemented to protect tenants from greed-ridden landlords through November 1, 1922, a date when the laws were set to expire.

Here are the highlights. Chapter 942, which applied only to New York City's five boroughs and the surrounding counties, suspended a landlord's ability to bring a summary proceeding against a holdover tenant, meaning that, under ordinary circumstances, a landlord could no longer evict a tenant whose lease had expired for failure to pay a rent increase. According to Arthur J.W. Hilly, Chapter 942 abolished Moving Day for two years and "[t]he 100,000 dispossess notices sent out [that year] have been wiped out as if they never existed." As an aside, Hilly also pointed out, and rightfully so, that Chapter 942 deprived city marshals and schleppers of "their lucrative gold mine," *i.e.*, carrying out eviction warrants.

Chapter 944, which applied to New York City, Buffalo, Rochester and Westchester County, struck out from the April laws any reference to the 25 percent rule and, instead, provided that a landlord must, during any summary proceeding, prove to the court that any rent increase was justified, no matter the increase. To that end, this new provision required all landlords to submit a document known as a "bill of particulars" spelling out all revenues and expenses. The goal of this measure was to provide a new transparency to landlords' financials, a transparency unprecedented during the rough and tumble early years of immigrant banks and ethnic property ownership.

Chapter 945—to apply only to New York City, Buffalo, Rochester and Westchester County—stipulated that a landlord was prohibited from bringing any summary proceeding against a tenant for non-payment of rent unless the new rent was no higher than it had been in the preceding year. In other words, no tenant could be evicted for non-payment of rent unless the tenant failed completely to pay the old rent (a rare case) or completely refused to pay a rent determined as reasonable after full adjudication of a summary proceeding before a municipal Judge (also a rare case).

Finally, Chapter 947 provided that, in the event the savvy landlord brought an action for ejectment in state court, as opposed to a summary proceeding in municipal court, state court Judges would likewise be bound by the same rules as New York's core of municipal Judges.

On September 27, 1920, Governor Smith signed all ten bills that came out of September's special session into law, together taking effect as the "September laws."

The September laws, together with the April laws, came to be known collectively as the "emergency rent laws." There was no denying it by September 1920—the emergency rent laws constituted the most extensive revision of landlord-tenant law in New York since 1820, the year the summary proceeding was created!

How? Well, for one thing, a practical effect of the emergency rent laws was that most New Yorkers were now "statutory tenants," meaning that the State of New York regulated New York City's rents and delegated to the city's municipal Judges the task of mediating any dispute arising between landlord and tenant over rent. That this relationship was formerly governed by a private contractual agreement meant that any dispute under the former regime would've been confined to civil court. So when New York's state legislature made it a misdemeanor crime to fail in providing the basic guarantees of habitability (heat, running water, light, etc.), the emergency rent laws exposed landlords to an unheard of measure of criminal liability.

As statutory tenants, landlords had almost no ability to oust tenants from their apartments before November 1, 1922 unless the landlord could satisfy a municipal Judge that eviction was warranted under a series of narrow exceptions to the emergency rent laws. For example, a landlord could still oust an "undesirable" tenant, though the landlord must now prove the tenant's undesirability. A landlord also retained the right to seek an eviction where the landlord or an immediate family member sought to move into the particular apartment or, alternatively, that the building owner intended to demolish the building to replace it with newly constructed apartments. Finally, a landlord could seek to evict a tenant where he intended to convert the building into a cooperative ownership structure whose members intended to live as residents. Unless one of these narrow exceptions applied, a statutory tenant could only be evicted under the emergency rent laws for refusing to pay the old rent or a "reasonable rent" as determined by a municipal Judge.

"Our government is run by radicals!" many real estate investors proclaimed, apparently without realizing that New York's state legislature had not gone as far as France, Britain and other European countries that had imposed rent control and even gone so far as to build public housing.

That did not prevent sentiment towards the emergency rent laws from splintering along familiar lines. Those aligned with the real estate interest were in uproar that the emergency rent laws had gone too far. As reported in the national press, many attorneys regarded the emergency rent laws as "the most drastic measures ever enacted by the lawmaking body of this state." Many also found a troubling irony in the fact that the same legislature that began the year by ousting five Socialist Assemblymen would end it by enacting "the most socialistic legislation in the history of the commonwealth."

Others praised the emergency rent laws as "a great victory" for the city's tenants; many were more tempered, but nevertheless pleased. As observed by President of New York City's Board of Aldermen, Fiorello H. La Guardia, the emergency rent laws were "by no means perfect," but "as a first step, they were the most useful piece of legislation in the history of the State." There was no denying that the emergency rent laws were a landmark in the history of New York's landlord-tenant law.

But were these new provisions also a ticking time bomb? As Samuel Untermyer, Chief Counsel to the Lockwood Committee, pointed out, the emergency rent laws stretched the constitutional power of the legislature to "the utmost limit." Other New Yorkers foretold how the tenants' "great victory" would no doubt be short-lived. For, no sooner were the laws signed into law by Governor

Smith than did opponents of the emergency rent laws mount an expansive campaign of litigation, drumming up lawsuits that would dance across the desks of some of America's brightest legal minds.

**INTERLUDE**

---

EMPIRE STATE EXPRESS*

\*Fair warning, the following INTERLUDE should be read, despite its historical accuracy, as a piece of historical fiction for reasons of otherworldliness that should become immediately apparent.

## I.

*The scene is a disharmonious train car packed to the brim with boisterous passengers. Its destination? Albany, New York. This particular train car is operated by the Empire State Express and runs from Grand Central Station in Manhattan to Union Station in Albany, the state capital.*

*Chatter is loud, and the mood? Rambunctious with an acrimonious edge. There is a palpable anxiety circulating the railroad car, which is to be expected given the gravity of the public hearings being held upstate in Albany today, March 23, 1920. Two of the calmer (though no less embroiled in discussion) passengers are Fiorello H. La Guardia (President of New York City's Board of Aldermen) and Samuel Untermyer (Special Counsel to the state legislature's Joint Committee on Housing, also known as the Lockwood Committee.) While the passenger cars of the Empire State Express chug along, these, among the most prominent and outspoken of New York City's residents by 1920, are provoked to discourse by, at the same time, their respective sobriety (alcohol having been recently prohibited by constitutional amendment), and a housing shortage befalling New York City's five boroughs, engulfing the city in civil and political unrest. Fortunately (for there are serious matters to discuss), their efforts are sustained by dark and powerful coffee. Well, sustained for all in the car but one, Jacob Riis. One time muckraker and New York City's first photojournalist, Riis went to great lengths during his lifetime to document the plight of working-class tenants living in Manhattan's lower East Side tenement slums during the latter half of the nineteenth century.*

*Ol' Jacob suffers from an incurable disease, however. Don't worry though, he's not contagious—he's just deceased, freed of his mortal coil, his spirit adrift along the Empire State Express bound for Albany. Trapped in limbo arbitrarily aboard the Empire State Express Car No. 999, Jacob Riis drifts aimlessly as he eavesdrops on the lively chatter among some of New York's most prominent citizens.*

SAMUEL UNTERMYER: Fio, cut through the fog of speculation and your political ambitions and just tell me one thing. Will you give me your assurance—regardless of fact or circumstance—that you will limit your testimony in Albany to those matters affecting the debate at hand? You *absolutely cannot* provoke the audience with talk of New York City politics, be it housing shortages or the cost of living.

FIORELLO H. LA GUARDIA: Sam, my friend, rest assured. I may have been born in the West Village, but my parents are both Italian. I've lived in Trieste, and I've lived in Arizona. I will *absolutely* limit my comments in *no* such way. Would you ask Langston Hughes to stop writing poetry? Hughes is two cars up if you want to test your luck, but I'll warn you that it's likely to land you in fisticuffs.

UNTERMYER: Rest assured *yourself*, that those intentions of yours are sure to land *you* in fisticuffs. Be warned son, this is Albany we're bound for—the skirmishes of your boroughs are mere fodder for casual conversation in the state capital.

LA GUARDIA: Need I remind you that those skirmishes are not confined to the five boroughs of New York City? This conversation is a statewide issue, hence your destination, hence my destination. Hence Judge Robitzek's and Governor Smith's destination. Mayor Hylan would be there as well, if only his constituents were not on the verge of torching every tenement building in Manhattan's East Side neighborhoods and the Bronx. Did you even read *How the Other Half Lives*?!

UNTERMYER: I admire your commitment to principle, I'm just suspicious that your commitment to reform is misguided. The Lockwood Committee told us nothing we didn't already know, which means that nothing is changing. Rent control, to be sure, is not the answer—residential construction, the conservative solution, is what is needed. We need to keep everyone's attention on those legislative measures designed to address the redirection of capital investment back into residential mortgages. Into lending and residential construction, not rent control, as you so eloquently professed before the Mayor's Committee on Rent Profiteering. (*UNTERMYER's tone suggests sarcasm, but his facial expression hints otherwise.*)

LA GUARDIA: The state legislature's Lockwood Committee was a good start to the conversation, no two ways about it, but it left out one critical voice. The Committee failed to take stock of New York's most densely populated, most diseased, most impoverished demographic. These folks suffer at the behest of profiteering landlords the same as those in Buffalo, Albany, Seattle, Chicago, Paris and beyond. If I get the opportunity, you bet your grandfather's pocket watch I'm speaking up for my home state's most vulnerable population. Don't take for granted that the spring rental season is upon us. In mere months, tenants in all five of New York City's boroughs will face *WHOLESALE EVICTIONS DAMMIT!*

UNTERMYER: Slow your heart rate son, I can see the years peeling off you as we sit here. You'n I both know that, no matter how loud you yell, your precious city will not see rent control, if at all, until next year. None of the Lockwood Committee's Reports point to rent control as a feasible long-term option for permanently curbing rent profiteering and Mayor Hylan's administration certainly isn't up to the task of administering rent control. You think this conservative a'legislature is ready to give in to socialist pressures? Try telling Thaddeus Sweet that rent control is the answer and you're liable to end up on the street just like Charlie Solomon looks to be, on your ass. This legislative session, especially at this eleventh hour, has its eyes and ears shut to your city's plight.

LA GUARDIA: (*Overly facetious, almost in jest*) You raise a wise point old goose. But short of rent control what can ease the plight of "my city's" working class tenants, according to the Lockwood Committee's "Report"?

UNTERMYER: (*Paying La Guardia's facetiousness no notice*) Your City would do well to adopt every bill proposed by the Lockwood Committee's Report, I can tell you that much. But we both know that residential construction is the only answer, indeed anything short of that will drag this fiasco on for years and years to come. And, son, for the sake of your political career, I implore you one last time—*Don't provoke the crowd during your testimony!* This is the last time you'll hear that from me so heed it or not, but from here on in, you're on your own.

LA GUARDIA: Duly noted. As always Sam, I don't take your candor or loyalty for granted. You know how upstate conservatives rattle my cages.

UNTERMYER: Well, that's all I have for you on the business end. If I'm not mistaken, Stewart Browne stashed a liter of moonshine a few cars up, care to imbibe?

LA GUARDIA: Gladly.

*As* UNTERMYER *and* LA GUARDIA *shove off, Jacob Riis decides to hang back so that he can have a moment to take in his surroundings. 'How did I end up on this train?' he asks himself as he slumps in his chair and wanders off into reflection.*

*Not seconds later, Riis catches the shape of a woman passenger out of the corner of his eye. As the new passenger saunters in Riis' direction, he can't help but sense her imminent approach.*

*What happens next astonishes Riis. Without hesitation and no lack of grace, the newly boarded passenger stops directly in front of him, turns to sit, and descends weightlessly into and then through Riis' lap. Her hips settle into place. Riis can't feel any of this, mind you, but he surely can see it.*

*"MADAM!!" Riis calls out. Instinctually, Riis jolts to his feet—passing effortlessly through the woman's back—but losing his footing and stumbling backwards into the door separating a precarious walkway spanning between the railway cars.*

*'THUD!' The back of his head collides with the door.*

*The passengers look up quizzically from their newspapers, but seeing nothing, return to their reading.*

*'UNION STATION' rings out over the train's loudspeaker, 'OUR NEXT AND LAST STOP IS UNION STATION, ALBANY, NEW YORK. THANK YOU FOR RIDING WITH EMPIRE STATE EXPRESS.'*

THE SCENE *concludes as all aboard the train make for the railroad cars' exits, Riis included. Except that, Riis is unable to pass through the door! Trapped aboard the train, Riis has to cope with his surroundings—which become decidedly uneventful save for a band of children thieves on the loose.*

## II.

*As Riis acquaints himself with the Empire State Express, something else is happening at the assembly building in Albany on this, the morning of March 23, 1920. Hordes of landlords, tenants, real estate investors, municipal Judges, men of religion, men of money, women property owners (the list is truly endless) all file into the spectator's seating area surrounding the state Assembly's chambers, poised to hear, in a single day, debate on all nine housing bills introduced for a vote in the New York state legislature.*

SENATOR JOSHEPH MULLIN *presides as Chairman and calls, one by one, various witnesses to lend their two cents on the proposed housing bills; though not unexpectedly, many of the speakers take to their own agendas despite* CHARIMAN MULLINS' *best efforts. What ensues is truly a sight to behold as New York City's postwar housing crisis reaches what some might say is its climax, its crescendo, its signature moment when the tension truly boils over and city politics play out for all to see on the state's grandest political stage.*

SENATOR MULLIN (CHAIRMAN): Now, gentlemen, if you'll let me have your attention for a moment. This is a joint hearing of the Cities Committee of the Senate and of the Cities Committee of the Assembly in regard to our state's dire housing situation. We have a number of bills that have been introduced in both houses of the state legislature. It is the purpose of our committee assembled here today to consider all of the legislation presented, and, in addition, the bills presented by the Committee on Housing.

Before we go any further, I have this suggestion to make: that all speakers, whether for or against the bills, eliminate a description of the conditions as they exist either in New York City or any other city of the state from which you may come, because the committee is thoroughly familiar with those conditions. What we hope may result from a discussion today is some legislation which will relieve the situation. We invite your criticism of the bills as presented and we invite your suggestions as to any alternative method that might also bring about the desired result.

We realize that residents all over the state are facing a most unfortunate situation, and we realize that some relief must be accorded, so that if you will bear that in mind in talking to the committee it will save much valuable time.

(CHAIRMAN MULLIN *calls the first speaker,* JUSTICE FREDERICK SPIEGELBERG, *a municipal Judge sitting in Manhattan.*)

JUSTICE SPIEGELBERG: Mr. Chairman and gentlemen, my connection with this rent legislation is due to the fact that I was appointed chairman of a special committee on rent legislation for the municipal courts of New York City. Through that I came in contact with the Joint Legislative Committee on Housing, and it was my very good fortune to aid in the preparation of the bills.

As I understand the Chairman, nothing is to be said about the serious condition which confronts the people in the large cities of this state, and especially New York City. The situation has to be viewed from two standpoints. One is the ultimate solution of the housing shortage, and the other one is to give immediate relief to the tenants who are in need. Immediate relief has to be taken care of at once, and, as I understand, the bills which have been introduced are for the purpose of affording such relief. Now the programme, as I take it, which has been submitted by the Joint Legislative Housing Committee consists of a series of bills, one dovetailing into the other. I think there are nine in all. Some of the bills refer to the procedure only, and are of comparatively little importance.

Before explaining the main bills I want to refer to one of the bills that has been introduced providing for the repeal of what is commonly known as the Ottinger Law. Up to 1918, a contract could be made orally for the leasing of a residential apartment for not more than one year, no matter whether the lease agreement took effect immediately or at some future time. The Ottinger Law of 1918 repealed that statute, which had been on the books for a century or more, and it held that unless there was an agreement in writing, signed by both parties, that it shall be considered a month-to-month rental. I have no doubt that the purpose was a praiseworthy one, but it had rather disastrous results. Many tenants who were under the belief that they had a lease for a year, and were told that they could remain there until the end of the rental year, October 1st, were suddenly put out or were threatened with successive increases of rent.

The other bills, three of them, are of a radical and rather drastic nature. I think the committee is well aware of the fact that it is only the extraordinary conditions with which we are confronted that would and should call for emergency legislation of this kind. The committee as I understand, thought it necessary, and after due consideration, came to the conclusion that these bills now before the committee are the ones which will give the needed relief, and at the same time, do justice to the landlord. They attack the remedies which the legislature has given to landlords, the summary dispossess proceeding.

At issue first is the summary proceeding, the one remedy which the landlord avails himself in every case where he seeks to recover possession of their real estate from a tenant, either because the tenant held over or because the tenant failed to pay the stipulated rent. At the end of the day, it is important—critical even—to understand that the summary proceeding is a remedy which was given by the legislature and can be taken away by the legislature. It has been on the statute books, if I am not mistaken, since 1820. Before that time the landlord, when he sought to recover possession of real property, was relegated to the common law action of ejectment.

Now the legislature did not go and does not intend to go that far, as I understand, by taking away the right of summary proceedings, but it hedged it about with certain conditions.

So far as summary proceedings are concerned, effecting the holdover proceeding—in other words, where the landlord for one reason or another wishes to get the property back, the landlord's preferred remedy is not to ask for an increase of the rent but to give notice of twenty or thirty days, as the case may be, that the tenant should vacate the premises, with the result that the landlord and tenant come together and the landlord imposes conditions as to what rent should be charged if the tenant is to remain.

Now, under the proposed legislation, where there is a summary proceeding and the court holds that the landlord is entitled to a final order declaring that the tenant holdover, if the tenant applied for a stay and shows that he cannot get suitable premises in the neighborhood despite such a search, and that for other reasons it is fair that the warrant of execution be stayed, a municipal Judge has the right to stay the execution of the warrant, which is popularly called a dispossess, for such time as he may deem proper, upon condition that the tenant comply with the requirements that the court may lay down, and these requirements or conditions, as outlined in the bill, are that the tenant should pay a fair rent, which may be the rent which he has paid already plus such addition as may be reasonable, if any, and deposit that with the clerk of the court. That is one bill of very great importance.

Another bill refers also to that phase of the summary proceeding where a landlord seeks to recover the possession of property for nonpayment of rent. The proposed bill limits proceedings for nonpayment of rent to such cases where the landlord does not exact more than had been paid by the tenant the month prior or where the increase has not been more than 20 percent in the past year. In other words, the right of the landlord to bring proceedings of that kind is limited in that respect by the bill.

Now, it was necessary in order to prepare these bills to invoke great power which the state has to regulate private property where the public interest is involved, commonly called the police power. Under the police power of the state and the legislature, if this bill passes and an emergency arises it will be decreed that in an action for rent, where the landlord seeks to recover what he and the tenant had said should be paid as rent, that a defense may be set up by the tenant that the rent charged by the landlord is unreasonable, is unfair and is oppressive. In such case the landlord may prove the necessity or justification for the rent increase, if he so wishes, and may recover, a fair and reasonable rent.

Now these are the bills. There is nothing in the bills by which the Judge fixes the rent, though perhaps that may be the natural result of it. The committee realizes that no court has a right to make a new lease agreement for one which was already in existence. It has the right under certain circumstances under this bill to declare that the contract is oppressive and that therefore no contract was entered into in the first place, and then it is optional with the landlord to recover such rent as may be fair under the circumstances. Now this is, in short, the substance of the bills.

I am not here as an advocate either for landlords or tenants. I am not here for the purpose of picking flaws in the bills and showing how it might work hardship for one or the other; that these bills will bear harshly in some cases upon innocent parties. As to that there is very little doubt but the legislative committee was of the opinion that when it was confronted with such a menacing situation that emergency measures must be passed, and these are emergency measures pure and simple. They are not permanent. They are to remain in effect, under the present bills only until 1922.

These are the measures which the legislative committee thinks and hopes will relieve the present situation, and those who are concerned, and I think we are all vitally concerned as citizens in the increase of housing facilities—these are the measures—these measures which have been put in concrete and practical form and I have very little doubt, with every citizen, that the legislative committee will give those bills the same attention as they have given to the bills here.

Before closing I want to express my thanks to the legislative committee and to many of the Senators and Assemblymen for the aid that they have rendered, not alone to those who are interested in the matter, but the people of the state at large.

(*Exit* SPIEGELBERG, *enter* ASSEMBLYMAN MARTIN G. MCCUE, *a state Assemblyman hell bent, against all odds, to impress upon those present that residential construction is the only remedy for New York's housing crisis and that exempting real estate mortgages from taxation is the proper measure to that end.*)

ASSEMBLYMAN MCCUE: We can talk all we please about punishing over-grasping landlords; we can talk all we please about these dispossess notices and things of that kind, but when it is all said and done, in the final analysis, we have got to have more houses, plain and simple, and if these bills will induce builders to build, if this will induce the landlords or builders to build new houses we can very well excuse them from paying taxes for a term of seven years, and the taxes that we are depriving ourselves of for the next seven years will eventually be paid and eventually result in a benefit to the mass of the people. Mr. Chairman, as a result of conferences with men who are interested and men who know, I am of the opinion that this bill exempting mortgages from taxation for a period of seven years will go a long way to reducing the shortage of tenement houses in our cities. I hope you will give this bill your consideration. (*Applause.*)

(*Exit MCCUE, enter JUDGE JOSEPH M. CALLAHAN, a recently elected municipal Judge sitting in the Bronx.*)

JUDGE JOSEPH M. CALLAHAN: Mr. Chairman: May I ask your permission to take my odd place on the isle for about five minutes of your very valuable time.

Gentlemen, I wish to disagree, as I seldom have had the occasion to disagree with the last speaker. In this respect, I think my good friend, Mr. McCue, has made a mistake of confusing the two words "Cure" and "Relief." I agree with him that the only way to cure the present lack of housing facilities in this state is simply and unequivocally more houses. I believe there is, and their must be, and sovereign people of this state cannot and should not allow this session of the legislature to expire without saying that there shall be some relief from the present distressing situation facing tenants in the large cities of this state.

Now, I came up here last year on a committee from the Bronx endeavoring to get some legislation, but at that time sentiment was not nearly as crystalized as it is today. But it was my opinion then, and I am convinced now as well, that the only relief that we can give is by limiting the legal proceeding known as 'summary dispossess' proceedings, so that this remedy, this arm of the law shall not be taken up or used by a person who is attempting to take advantage of the large part of the population of the cities to inflict suffering on the vulnerable.

In other words, unless there is reform, municipal Judges across the state will be forced to use this arm of the law to make the vast majority of our state's residents suffer, not because the Judges want to do it, but because the Judges must do it, because the law affords absolutely no discretion, regardless of fact or circumstance.

Now, don't misunderstand me. I am just as much in favor of helping the real estate men, the builders, the property owners, as any man in this room. I realize just like all of you that the last few years have not been typical, that there has simply been a turn about in condition. But I say that there are some men who own real estate in New York City who are disgracing the vast majority of real estate owners to such an extent that the law must step in and prevent these men from gouging the general public.

I don't need to cite for you any number of examples of what is going on in this state. We haven't so much sympathy, perhaps, for the men whose wages have been so greatly increased in the last year. But it is the middle class of men upon whom the burden most gravely falls. Take, for instance, the municipal employee, a policeman of New York City. I know a policeman living two blocks from my house whose rent has more than doubled in the last two years. And I say, gentlemen, when that situation exists in New York City, we absolutely must find some relief for it.

As I say, I am convinced, I have been convinced right along, that the only relief will be to permit the courts, the municipal Judges to intervene and to say to the landlord, you are reasonable or you are unreasonable, and to refuse to give a summary dispossess warrant which will only serve to dump a man, his family, his worldly goods and everything that makes up his home out into the cold street on a few days notice. We must have a fair law that will permit him, the municipal Judge, to say that, "I will not do that if you, landlord, are gouging your neighbor and injuring your neighbor." I think this is what this program should do Mr. Chairman, and rightly so.

I don't care whether these bills are introduced by Republicans or Democrats. But it is, in my humble opinion, a most proper and basic idea that the summary dispossess proceeding shall not be used to oppress the great mass of citizens of these various working-class communities. And I say that the real estate owners, knowing as they do, the municipal Judges, can safely leave their cases in the hands of these judges, and the situation has got to be such that somebody must stand between the real estate owners and the Bolsheviki of this state, to see to it that justice is done on both sides and that property is not permitted in this state to oppress a citizen.

I am not going to spend any more time going through the bills—I sincerely trust that this program will receive approval of this committee and this legislature. (*Applause.*)

(*Exit* JUDGE CALLAHAN, *enter* JUDGE WILLIAM M. K. OLCOTT, *a former city Alderman and current municipal Judge who argues, rather controversially, that certain high-end apartment buildings should be exempt from any and all measures of rent control.)*

JUDGE OLCOTT: I will try to speak loud enough for all to hear. Gentlemen, I came up here, I might say in advance, representing an association of people who have been engaged in building and owning what are called "high class apartments" in New York City. Apartments such as you are familiar with—on Park Avenue, Riverside Drive and West End Avenue—I represent such an association. I make this statement in advance, sirs, because I must confess my attitude, my professional attitude in the matter, and yet I hope to demonstrate in the very few moments you are kind enough to allot me, that the feeling of my clients is broader and deeper than that of their own selfishness and that they are thinking of what is going to happen if they are subjected to legislative action which will interfere with the natural laws of supply and demand. (*Applause.*)

It is conceded by my very good friend, Judge Spiegelberg, whom I have known since we were school boys together in New York City, that this is a temporary suggestion that is embodied in these bills. It is an emergency measure, if you please, I take it that he means that, because it is to extend only for two years and a half, and that by that time the natural law of supply and demand can again become operative.

I think his reasoning is probably short-sighted, I dare say. He proposes to put this productive power of building at least certain classes of property on a basis without food for two and a half years and then expects them to function as if they had been fed during the entire period, and I assert here as an economical proposition and in all humility that there is about as little chance on November 1, 1922, after over two years of starvation, for the building industry to begin anew and in full vigor as would be the case if you starved a man for two and a half years. And yet, it is true, and here I want to get away from the selfish aspect in which my clients may stand because of the particular class of business that they do, it is true that there is a great and urgent requirement that something be done for the poor tenants who are at the mercy of irresponsible and over-grasping landlords.

Can it be done, sirs, by passing legislation, the constitutionality of which is so highly doubtful? I am too well aware, as is Judge Spiegelberg and all members of this committee, that what the legislature hath given the legislature is free to take away, and that you can amend your special proceedings and your summary proceedings, or hold them subject to conditions because you are the creative power of these very proceedings.

Again, I ask you gentlemen, whether it does not seem as if the conditions which the Judge said his bill sought to get away from, of making people repudiate the very contracts they themselves made, whether it does not seem that that condition is not met and that no such provision can be found in the bill?

Let me call your attention, just in passing, to a waiver section of the proposed laws. This section provides clearly that any provision of a lease whereby a lease or tenant waives any provision of this act shall be deemed against public policy as void.

Now, it seems to me that this is repudiating the traditional power to make contracts, and that if a man sane, and in possession of his senses, met another man in the same degree of mentality and says to him, "I will lease you this property, provided you will waive the provisions of this bill, provided that you will agree that you do not need police protection, provided that you will agree that your family can get along without that protection, then I will rent you the premises," and the legislature steps in and says, "No, if you make that agreement it is void as against public policy," it seems to me that that is an unconstitutional interference with the right of private parties to enter into private contracts of their own choosing.

But as I say, I do not propose to dwell upon the circumstances, because here is what I do say, and I am glad to find myself in agreement with the gentlemen of the committee who have been dealing with the thing. There is a police need for keeping people housed, no two ways about it. There is a police need for seeing that the poor man is not gouged by the rich landlord. Remember, however, that this is a narrow practice that should not be overgeneralized.

Further, it seems to me that certainly you would not need this police power, this power of protecting the poor, this police need of protecting the poor man, this police need of protecting the health of the family, and I would suggest, Senator Lockwood, the one who I think hand-crafted this bill.

(*To* SENATOR LOCKWOOD) I know your experience and your great ability and I hesitate to even ask for an amendment of anything that you have drafted, but I feel that so far as the police power is concerned, that it ought to stop with tenants in the more modern classes of apartments or in tenement houses. And I would like to ask whether or not it would be a fair amendment to your bill if otherwise you think it necessary to pass it, to say this bill shall not apply to tenancies and to premises bringing over $1,500 a year, if you please.

(SENATOR LOCKWOOD, *no longer able to contain his comments, jumps in.*)

SENATOR LOCKWOOD: Judge, then *you* might raise their rentals above fifteen hundred dollars! (*Applause and laughter.*) Wouldn't that make it unconstitutional too?!

JUDGE OLCOTT: As ever Senator, you are skilled in the repartee of discord. That can hardly be because supply and demand and reasonable values step in, and I can imagine no better fortune to fifty percent of the tenement house owners than to have the other fifty percent say that we won't rent you this twenty-five dollar apartment for less than one hundred and twenty-five. You see, it would not practically have that effect you speak of, and it would not be unconstitutional as making a difference between people of two different grades or financial position, because the very fundament of your bill is that the police authority and police power and health powers are for those who are not in a position to protect themselves; and certainly no man paying more than $1,500 in yearly rent needs police protection so far as his tenancy goes.

And I simply spoke of that figure because it seems to be an empiric one, and the man who pays $1,500 a year and who confesses that his family health is in danger and that he is in danger of being charged too high a rental can readily move to Jersey and get a cottage.

SENATOR LOCKWOOD: Judge Olcott, I only want to interrupt you for a moment. Last Friday, at the special hearing, a former fire commissioner came before the committee and complained that his rent had been raised from $2,000 to $5,000 a year, and that he had twenty-four tenants in the same apartment house with similar raises. He says he needs protection. (*Applause.*)

JUDGE OLCOTT: Now, it happens that the former fire commissioner's landlord is one of my clients (*Laughter and hisses*), and his statement to me was that the rent was raised from $2,100 to $2,800; $5,500 it was *absolutely* not.

Whether or not, Senator, and welcoming the discussion, I say that you know and the committee knows and the people within earshot of my voice know that any man who can afford to pay that amount of rent does not need police protection or protection of the Board of Health. (*Applause.*)

No, you cannot limit the power of a man to make a contract except on the ground that the tenant is in need of police protection. You have admitted it, and you know that any man who pays that amount of rent does not need it, and no court would sustain such a claim.

(*Another member of the committee,* SENATOR KAPLAN, *enters the fray.*)

SENATOR KAPLAN: Mr. Chairman, I would like to ask Judge Olcott a question. Your Honor, you say that the association you represent includes those who own apartment houses on Riverside Drive. Those sections of New York City are in my district. They held a meeting last evening at which were present some 2,000 people and a great many of them came from West End Avenue and Riverside Drive, and they are just as anxious for relief, and just as much in need of protection as the people in the poorer sections of the city. (*Applause.*)

JUDGE OLCOTT: I have no doubt, sir, that they are just as anxious for it, but it doesn't seem to me that you are in need of it.

I want to tell you that the idea of my clients, and certainly my idea, is to limit prohibition against production to a reasonable basis. That is what they want to do. They want to make it possible for people to again build something in New York City.

Now, let that thought, if you please, sink into you. Senator Lockwood and Senator Mullin, I do not want to corrupt you, but in my peroration here, I do want to ask you to believe that the urgency with which I speak is because I think you are confronted with a terrible possibility of cutting new residential construction in New York City, and I believe the biggest and the most constructive measure is that proposed by Senator McCue.

I think that New York, as a state, can afford to encourage the production of new buildings. They must do something to stimulate the checks and balances of supply and demand and it give us what we need even more than any modification of these proposed bills.

Now, I want to tell you something bearing on that, that throughout this country, there was in February 1919, sixty seven millions of buildings permitted, and February of 1920, one hundred and fourteen million, just short of double the permits. In the borough of Brooklyn, gentlemen, where Senator Lockwood hails from, there were permits in February of 1919 for seven million dollars worth of new buildings, and in February 1920, four million. In the borough of Manhattan, where I hail from, there were permits last year in February of $18,000,000 and this year, February, another $13,000,000 of new buildings.

Now, I want you to know, sirs, whether these figures, which were represented to me by an actuary, are not enough to make us pause?

Gentlemen, I ask of you whether my suggestion to limit the rental value of a premises as to which these new bills are to apply be the right remedy or not, to pause before you put the death hand even for two and a half years, upon production, because as the Mail and Express said in a short editorial and I like it for its terseness, "What we need in the world at large is production, production and still more production." What we need in the building world is building, building and still more building. Don't cripple the hands of the builders. Consider it carefully, gentlemen.

If I am wrong in the remedy that I suggest, do something about it, not with regard, of course, to my clients who are well able to take care of themselves, but with regard to all the buildings and trade industries which will be affected if limiting the possibility of money and capital going into the production of buildings.

*(Another member of the committee, SENATOR DUNNIGAN, interjects.)*

SENATOR DUNNIGAN: Judge Olcott, as an architect and builder I would like to ask you a question. As someone who has also spent eight or ten months upon this very investigation, I wish to say that your figures are absolutely correct as to the amount of money that is about to be spent or may someday be spent in Brooklyn, that there have been seventeen million and eight million and four million dollars of plans filed and permits issued for new construction. Indeed, I have filed some of those plans which call for the expenditure of some of that money myself, and I want to say that I do know about it, because I am in constant contact and have been every week with the Superintendent of Buildings in Brooklyn as well.

But I wish to clarify one important aspect of your statement—these figures represent *only* an amount for permits issued, but it does not mean that these buildings are under construction. In fact, I can inform you, of that seventeen million, there is possibly four or five million worth under construction today, the rest being unable to build until conditions change.

Now, in addition to that, I want to answer your criticism of the committee in so far as the possibility of the impression going abroad here that the committee thought that this crisis would be over by November 1, 1922. We know that it won't be over by November 1, 1922, but we are sure that if we leave these laws stand upon the books till then that we are, in effect, saying to builders, "Now, go on and build; we will let it stand until 1922, and if you don't build and these gouging landlords insist upon their tactics then we are going to say to you November 1, 1922, on the first of January next, 1923, we will enact these laws for two or three years more if necessary." In the meantime, we say to the builders, go ahead and build.

JUDGE OLCOTT: Don't misunderstand me Senator, that is exactly what they are afraid of, that you will re-enact it.

SENATOR DUNNIGAN:   No, no, no. We are making this law apply for two years, so they can build in the meantime if they so desire.

(*Exit* JUDGE OLCOTT, *enter* JUDGE JACOB STRAHL, *a municipal Judge sitting in the Bronx and outspoken advocate for tenants.*)

JUDGE JACOB STRAHL:   Mr. Chairman and gentlemen of the committee; If this meeting, or session was held in or near the borough of Brooklyn, the place would be overrun with tenants, but the trouble is, as far as their absence from the committee's eleventh hour proceedings is concerned, it is too expensive for them to come here and the roads are very bad for walking.

Now, I have just finished a few weeks in Brownsville Court of Brooklyn and I am not sitting in Williamsburg Court and my observation has been that the trouble lies with a certain class of men whom I will not honor the name of landlord but they are a class of men who are gambling in real estate. They are rent hogs. They refuse to give a lease for any period whatsoever because as soon as they give a lease to the tenants, the building is no longer vulnerable to speculation, deterring any future gambling on rent rolls. (*Applause.*)

Now, this rent hog or gambler in real estate, will hold the house for a month or two, then turn it over to a brother-in-law who then has the excuse to come in with the introduction, "I am the new landlord. I want more rent." Then the wife's brother-in-law (*Gesturing aimlessly with his hands*), and then comes in the son-in-law (*Shrugs his shoulders.*) In other words, it is a case of in-laws becoming outlaws at the expense of the community. (*Applause and laughter.*)

Now, as to the judges of the municipal courts. They want a stop-gap whereby they can stop these men from gambling in real estate. This gambler is a menace to society and it is on account of this class of men that most of our legislation will undoubtedly be passed.

So, my advice, to the extent this committee is looking for my input, is this:

Let the legitimate landlord join hands with the good citizens, the tenants, and the committee aiming for legislation that is going to drive this gambling landlord, this menacing rent hog, out of the gambling game in real estate, and let him gamble in something less essential to the American standard of life. (*Applause.*)

At the present time our hands are tied in municipal court. We can only grant a maximum stay of up to twenty days, and these gamblers know it and they come in there and say, "We demand the premises," and you can barely give over twenty days to these tenants.

I feel that this committee aught to permit the presiding justice of a municipal court to exercise his judgment and discretion in handling that kind of a menace to society. In other words let the judge decide how long that tenant can remain in possession during a hold-over proceeding, Municipal Judges can and should also have discretion to decide how long a stay he can grant, and perhaps you may limit the time of that stay in your Act to, say, nine months or, perhaps, six months, but remember it is not aimed nor will it be used by the Judges against these men and women who are legitimate landlords.

Then there is another provision. Let there be some legislation that will demand that there be a tenancy for a certain period, a year or nine months, for each and every party who occupies the place at a certain date. I mean by that there are some cases before your committee now, some bills, which imply a lease for a year. That will be sufficient to stop the gambling in real estate.

I say by way of anecdote that there is hardship being worked the city over and, as one example, consider that corruption is now rampant among residential building janitors, who accept premiums and bonuses to let out the apartment to the new tenants. I would favor legislation to the effect that anyone who offers, or any janitor who receives a premium or bonus for renting a new place should be punished as a criminal. (*Applause.*)

Now, my friends, cruel injustice is being done by the application of the law as it stands today. There is the gravest risk of wide spread disturbances in the lower district, in the poor districts. I have seen them. I have heard tenants stand up in city court and tell the Judge there, "I will not permit this landlord who refuses to give me a lease, and I want to pay an advanced rent, and I don't want to sleep out of doors at night; I wont' permit this landlord to throw my family and furniture out onto the street, except over my dead body."

Now, this is what confronts us today, and unless your committee will adopt legislation to guard against that condition it may be too late, and unless you do pass the right kinds of legislation I am satisfied that it will be necessary to call another session of the legislature, the same as last year.

So, I am going to ask the landlords here to come and join hands with the committee, give the justices some latitude; have confidence in them. The people have confidence in them when they elected them to this high position. You, too, have confidence in them. Pass legislation and if a judge does not do his duty then you have your remedy after that, and you can come here before the legislature and show just where a grave injustice has been worked.

I would also favor that there be a profit bill; in other words that the landlords receive or not be permitted to take more than a certain percentage profit. That law exists today in England. In 1915 Great Britain passed such a law to protect the people there and in April, 1919, they extended that law, and I feel it is the duty of the legislature to follow in their foot steps in that direction. (*'No, No, No,'* rings out from the audience, followed by roaring applause.)

(*Exit* JUDGE STRAHL, *enter* ARTHUR J. W. HILLY, *Assistant Corporation Counsel for the City of New York who, mere months prior to these proceedings in Albany, praised state legislators for investigating five elected Socialist Assemblymen with the goal of ousting them from their posts in the state legislature.*)

ASSISTANT CORPORATION COUNSEL ARTHUR J.W. HILLY: His Honor the Mayor, in a letter which he gave to me last evening, instructed me to come up here and favor legislation on, that is pending before this committee, that will have the effect, not to act as a deterrent or a dead hand, as it has been termed here, upon the future residential construction across New York's five boroughs. We all know and we all realize, and I feel that no one realizes it more than Mayor Hylan. You see we all realize that the real solution, the long-term route to a stable housing supply, at the present time is to address, by capital investment, a pervasive drought in residential construction. (*Low applause.*)

And, with that idea in mind, the Mayor had the foresight to call together all the interests that would readily be able to contribute to residential construction and is planning, as far as I know, to present a solution along those lines by way of written letter here today. And we have been open in our support of the Mayor's Committee on Rent Profiteering and its members' efforts to root out the cause of the war profiteer in New York City.

But—and I want to shift gears a little—there is another thing, above all else, that we favor as an association—and the thing which is most pressing at the moment—is to bring about relief from the speculating landlord and I feel that that measure of relief we're looking for is a measure that would provide this state's core of municipal Judges with the discretion to decide, during a summary dispossess proceeding, whether any given rent increase is reasonable or unreasonable. (*Light, well-rehearsed applause.*)

In closing, I would be remiss if I didn't again praise Mayor Hylan's efforts and remind everyone here today that these efforts have been in vain. Their strategy—examining the expenses for a given building along side the rent roll and endeavor, by persuasion, to convince city landlords to agree to charge only a reasonable rent—was foiled from the beginning.

Now, I feel that the time for persuasion has passed. (*Rising applause.*)

What we need at the present time is the firm and strong hand of the law. (*Roaring applause.*)

The laws of this state and the laws of our nation, including the robust history of common law down through the annals of history; there seems to be one motive in particular running down through it all, and that motive has been protection, at all costs, one of the oldest of America's rights—the right to ownership of private property. But I say in this twentieth century, under this government and beyond this government and in the name of all those who operated on the field of battle, that we ought to take one step forward and be guided by the other, and I feel that it is high time that this, the esteemed legislature of the state of New York, the foremost state in the Union, should be ready to take that step and put into the law the sacredness of humanity and the sacredness of the family. (*Cheers and hissing swirl the hall.*)

And that is the proposition I come to you in hand with today. This assembly of lawmakers has gone to extraordinary lengths to clear itself of the evil of socialism. I say you have done a good thing in that endeavor. But, and I can't emphasize this enough, this legislature must go further by eradicating, once and for all, the causes of socialism by preventing rent profiteering.

(*Those in attendance are pouring over the spectator railings, threatening to spill over onto the Assembly floor.* CHAIRMAN MULLIN *attempts to regain order in the assembly hall but his efforts, naturally, fall in vain.*)

There is one declaration that stands forth preeminent that has not been emphasized enough in our government and that declaration is in the *Declaration of Independence*, where it declares that men are entitled to life, liberty and the pursuit of happiness; and if men are entitled to life they are entitled to the means of life, and one of these means is a decent habitation. (*Applause and cheers.*)

Mr. Chairman and gentlemen of the committee: Rest assured, it is not my intention to incite violence, or even a demonstration; I intend only to express these sentiments here and now, and I believe that the proposed legislation being considered today will accomplish our stated purpose. You must act now.

If there are small injustices here and there let us wipe these injustices out, but the great big thing that we all desire is immediate relief from the oppressive conditions that confront us. (*Applause and cheers.*)

(*Exit* HILLY, *enter* ASSEMBLYMAN GEORGE N. JESSE, *sponsoring Assemblyman of the 'Jesse Bill' referenced to and argued over by various speakers as the proceedings march on.*)

ASSEMBLYMAN JESSE: Mr. Chairman and gentlemen of the committee: I won't talk to you very long, because I've got two good constituents here who can talk very much better than I can, but I want to say just a word and I want Judge Olcott to hear it.

(*To the audience*) Very early in the organization of this great commonwealth, as they have in all other commonwealths, we put upon the statute books of our state against burglary. That law did not concern nay man nor woman in this room, except as a measure of prevention and protection. (*Turning back to the rostrum.*) They do not care anything about it. That is the only interest they had in it. It only affected the man who committed a burglary and for that reason, landed the criminal, not the victim, in jail.

I want to say to you, landlords, that the laws which we propose to put on the statute books today, and as are outlined by this committee, have been drafted so as not to prevent the honest landlord from collecting a reasonable rent. For the rest of you over-grasping rent hogs, I hope that I'm not the first to tell you that when you come here and openly oppose these emergency measures, you confess to the public and this committee that you are afraid of just legislation in a time of great need. Unless you intend to violate the law yourself, you have nothing to fear. (*Hoot'n hollerin' from the rear rows, the outer rungs of the audience, growing more restless by the minute.*)

You, the dishonest landlord, who will be affected by this legislation, has something to fear, and that is the reason why you people now should go away from here and let us enact this legislation because, as my friend Mr. Hilly said, the cause of humanity is greater than the cause of property. It's high time the law reflect this social norm. (*Applause.*)

But, there is no reason why a single measure proposed in the nine bills should deter any legitimate landlord from investing his money in real property and building houses, and I defy any one of you to show me any reason why. There is no bill here that outlaws the legitimate landlord from collecting a reasonable rent. Any man who comes in here and opposes these bills comes prepared to confess that, "I want *more* than a reasonable rent." You should know that your opposition here today does not reflect well publicly.

Now, we have determined, so far as I am concerned at least, that all landlords may collect a reasonable rent, but in no case shall rent cost a dollar more, particularly when times are so dire in some corners of this state as to render a rent increase a matter of life and death. (*Cheers and hisses.*)

Now, Mr. Chairman, if you'll allow it, I want to give the balance of my limited time, first to Rev. Dr. Carsenden, Pastor of Holy Rood Church, City of New York, and then following him, the Reverend Lyman R. Hartley, of the Fort George Washington Presbyterian Church of New York City.

(*Exit* ASSEMBLYMAN JESSE, *enter* REVEREND CARSENDEN.)

REVEREND CARSENDEN: Mr. Chairman and gentlemen of the committee: I am mindful of the warning given by Chairman Mullin during his opening address—not to detail the living conditions, but instead to focus on the housing bills. Otherwise, I might reveal a situation which would make Rome howl, but I am here to contend on general principles against the affrontery of Mr. Stewart Brown as representing a number of his ilk, when he says, "Don't be content with receiving ten or twenty per cent, because if you aren't now, you will get more bye and bye." It reminds me of the boy who protested when his friend cut off a dog's tail all at once. He said, "Cut it off a little at a time and then it won't hurt so much."

I listened to what Judge Olcott said, too, about the natural laws of supply and demand. Now, supply and demand in this matter has been created as wash sales are created in the stock exchange. They corner the supply and they pretend that the demand is exceeding the supply.

I just want to give you an illustration of the nefarious proceedings of one agent who stands for the practices that we are contending against. To be clear, he is not an honest landlord. I hold a lease myself, which requires a notice of four months before expiration. I received notice ten days ago that I must report within ten days, otherwise my apartment will be leased over my head. Nothing was said about the raise of price. So, I went to this agent, this new agent, and the old agent, for his part, wouldn't consent to the dirty work that the new owner required of him. So I turned to him and said, "How much is the increase?" and he named a figure, 47 ½ percent.

I said, "Put that down in writing, please."

"No, I would rather not."

"Why not?"

"Because that has not been my custom."

"Well, it is my custom to demand black and white."

He said, "You won't get it."

"Well," I said, "You'll be sorry if you don't," and I used some very plain English with that man, and the next day I received a telephone message from him requiring an apology. I told him that what I had said—and I called him a thief and a liar—I told him that my characterization was well considered, well founded and reiteration would be the closest he would get to an apology, and if he wanted to hear an apology he could come to my church that morning and he would hear something more.

But, I did not see him in attendance. Later I received a telephone call from a man purporting to be a neighboring clergyman, but I have since found out it was not him at all; it was my friend the old agent. He tried to call me off and he begged me not to say anything about it, realizing that he was in the wrong, and that is the kind of cattle we have to deal with in the city of New York.

Now, Mr. Jesse has said, we are not here for any crusade against the honest landlord or against the honest agent, but we are here to stand against the affrontery, the thievery and the Bolshevism of the men who persist in victimizing tenants and their families.

Why, your legislature is here now engaged in bringing to task a mud slinging swashbuckler by the name of Anderson, but that man is innocent as an angel in heaven compared to some of these profiteering landlords.

I believe in law and order; I believe in doing all things honestly and in an orderly fashion but, you know, there will continue to be riots in the streets if you don't give us some relief. I am not a lawyer, I don't know the difference between the Constitution and the law of common sense; I suppose there is a difference. (*Laughter.*) But I do lay claim to a modicum of common sense and a conception of humanity, and I want to say this to you gentlemen, if you pass these bills you will bring comfort and peace to houses today which are dreading the back spectre of poverty and despair. If you pass these bills you will save the lives of millions of children, who cannot be ejected. If you don't give us some relief, of course you know what will happen.

Why, there are nursing-aged babies who go malnourished on account of rent-hogging landlords. Legions go so malnourished as to impose sudden and unexpected funeral expenses on the parents, which many families cannot, in turn, readily afford to pay because, for example, their landlord's agent extorted them, or they otherwise suffer at the hands of sneak thievery, pickpocketing and all around, the brutality of the highwayman.

That is the situation confronting us today. (*Applause.*)

(*Exit* REVEREND CARSENDEN, *enter* REVEREND LYMAN R. HARTLEY.)

REVEREND LYMAN R. HARTLEY: Brevity is the soul of wit and the core of attention. I will be brief. I have nothing against the landlords, and I am not a tenant smarting under the increase of my rent. I am the Pastor of a church, and I protest against the profiteering which today is going on. I protest loudly against it.

I am the pastor of Unity Church and my interest here today is in the people who are in need of relief. I am not interested in the middle class nor the rich who live in Riverside or on Madison Avenue, but in the poor of the slums, our state's most vulnerable population. I agree with Judge Olcott that the law of supply and demand is a fundamental law, but I believe there are emergencies when that law must be set aside and interfered with. We have had many such instances during the war and our Congress and our state legislature have responded in the past by setting aside those laws on account of such emergencies. Such an emergency exists in this present day and it exists in my community. The middle class of people are unable to pay any higher rent. Judge Olcott suggests they move to a beautiful little bungalow in the countryside of New Jersey. There is none such, and if there are, there will not be in one or two months. Something has got to be done now. Afterward, then take care of the law of supply and demand.

I do not see why there should not be power of discretion given to our judges, and I cannot see also why there should not be some limitation on the profits of the landlords.

There is a Senator of the United States who has houses over in Brooklyn and about three years ago he said he could make eleven per cent on his property if seventy-percent of his houses, his apartments were let. Since that time, about three months ago, which was my last information, he has only raised his rentals five dollars per tenant and they were then between thirty and forty dollars.

Now, why should the landlord get more than 20 percent when the ordinary interest on money is far less than that. Why shouldn't there be some limitation on the profit to the landlord. If he is reasonable and fair he will submit to legislation which will limit that amount. If he is not fair or honest, he will protest, and in the end, gentlemen of the committee, the citizens will have their way. There are twenty citizens at least, to every one landlord. Democracy requires representation of the majority. If some laws are not provided the citizens must, per force, for their very lives, take things into their own hands. This thing must not happen. We must, and at this very session of the legislature, have some definite action which will cure these evils from which we are suffering. (*Applause.*)

(*Exit* REVEREND LYMAN, *enter* DOCTOR H. W. BERG, *one of the most provocative speakers and outspoken critic of the housing bills.*)

DR. H. W. BERG: Mr. Chairman and gentlemen of the committee: There has been a great deal said on the part of the philanthropists and altruists and legislators that has to do with the making of this state and these cities, particularly the city of

New York, a proper place to live for the people. They blame the high rents and you have taken the trouble to outline a method of legislation by which you find it necessary to confiscate the rights of ownership and at the same time to absolutely retrieve anything it is possible to write in a contract in order to conserve—with the express purpose of conserving the welfare of the people, to meet an emergency.

I am afraid that you have forgotten that the emergency that is present is not only connected with the rent. The emergency that is present today, gentlemen, is that there are not enough apartments to go around amongst the people and the rent raises, don't forget, are a consequence—the raise in rent is a consequence of the fact that there are not enough apartments to go around. In other words, if you will take the trouble to pass such measures as will encourage the new production of additional rooms and additional housing, you will absolutely obviate and cure spontaneously the high rents.

Incidentally, I want to say that high rents are not limited to real estate, as far as the height is concerned, labor too, has charged infinitely higher in proportion as compared with the amount that it charged in 1914, than the most profiteering landlord has undertaken to charge as compared with the amount charged in 1914. I speak of labor in this instance not individually. I do not say that it is not possible that the price that they charge is the proper price. I simply say that the mere fact that labor enters into ninety per cent of all the commodities that are used in building, ninety per cent of that thing, labor, has charged two or three hundred percent than it was in 1914 and rents are, nobody has said that the maximum of rents, the average of rent has been much more than forty or fifty percent.

Now it is very important to understand that, if you have or if you were to have an increase in the amount of housing, you will have to have cheap labor. If real estate was really the good thing that some of my friends on my left think it is, wouldn't you think that the vast sums and fortunes and wealth lying downtown uninvested, would be invested in realty? If you can make twenty or twenty-five percent, why invest it at five and seven and eight per cent? The only reason that money refuses to go into real estate is because the twenty or twenty-five percent return is "purely fictitious and imaginary." It does not occur, and when you make these laws you are doing the very thing that is going to destroy and add the last clause to the prevention of capital going into real estate and curing the evil of which so much complaint is heard, that of high rents.

It is very important.

(*From the audience:* Will you permit a question?)

I will not submit to being interrogated until I am through. (*Hisses.*)

It is extremely important—

(DR. BERG *is abruptly interrupted by a forceful refrain:* "Will you permit a question?! CHAIRMAN MULLIN *quickly returns the proceedings to* DR. BERG*'s testimony.*)

CHAIRMAN MULLIN: Let they're be no interruption. Let the gentleman finish his statement. He has the right to be heard just as anybody else.

DR. BERG (*Pressing on, visibly shaken but otherwise undeterred*): It is extremely important that one should remember that if you are going to deprive real estate of capital investment that you are not going to add to the number of landlords and that you are going to diminish the opportunity for labor among the masses. Please remember that we are employing landlords; we hated landlords are employing vast masses of labor, labor that is being well-paid! If all these people who so hate a landlord—

(DR. BERG *is again interrupted by a voice from the crowd:* They love him! *'Who is this audience member referring to?' the inquisitive mind might ask. This question, however, does not occur to* DR. BERG, *whose determination is admirable but message not being well received.*)

DR. BERG: These people who think the landlord is such a disadvantage to the body social, I wonder why they didn't become landlords before 1914? That was the time when real estate was getting no profit, but getting a loss.

They don't even want to become landlords today. Today they feel that to become a landlord is an incubus from which they want to be absolutely deprived, and yet they are afraid that the landlord may get too much profit.

Now, there is a remedy and cure, and I am going to suggest it. There is a law, a United States law, which says that you must not permit the entrance in this country of an immigrant who cannot read or write and who cannot read a certain clause in his own language. The result has been that labor has been kept absolutely out of the country and today if you wish to lower rents you must give competition to the landlords, and if you legitimately wish to lower rents, not by the destruction of the constitutional rights of property, but if you wish to legitimately lower rents you must give competition to labor.

I can appreciate that the voting power of labor being so much greater than the voting power of the landlord, it takes a pretty brave legislator to oppose labor, but, I tell you that in the last analysis the day will come when such preposterous legislation as that proposed today will be absolutely inefficient, and you will have to do things that must be done to bring about the production of buildings, and you cannot introduce a building until you have competition to labor. Competition to labor will be brought about by repealing the literacy clause in the immigration law. That is the simple remedy. You will then get labor. They will work for reasonable figures. Real estate will become cheaper; real estate will rent for lower figures and as a by-product, everything that human beings use that requires labor will become reasonable in price.

Gentlemen, there have been no words said for the landlords here today, except that of derision, or of hatred, and you seem to think that certain restrictions are necessary. Have we, the landlords, got any power? Have we any unions? Is there any such combinations of unionism in landlords? Isn't it true that the wealth of New York today represented in real estate is more evenly distributed among the people of New York than any other commodity that you can think of? Isn't it true that there are individuals who own houses? And you legislators, I am sure you legislators when you legislate to tie to a given apartment a given tenant now existing there at a given rent, you forget that inasmuch as there is a dearth of apartments—an insufficiency I mean—you are tying eighty per cent of people to their apartments and you are leaving twenty per cent of the people *out in the cold*. This twenty per cent is entitled to the protection of the legislature as much as the others.

(Even SENATOR CHARLES C. LOCKWOOD, *Chairman of the Lockwood Committee, cannot hold back, jumping boldly into the fray.*)

SENATOR LOCKWOOD (*Referring to those tenants that* DR. BERG *says are being left 'out in the cold'*): Where would you leave them now?

DR. BERG (*Responding*): They still have the chance of competition but you are permitting their eviction for any reason whatsoever that is reasonable and the result is that you are leaving twenty per cent out in the cold and I predict, although I am no politician who has been connected with this kind of legislation, and I don't suppose it will affect any of you, but I predict that this twenty per cent and the thousands of owners of real estate in New York will be heard from the same extent as the people who are here in this room today. (*Hisses and applause from the audience.*)

(CHAIRMAN MULLIN *again tries to cut in and refocus the speaker, audience and panel.*)

CHAIRMAN MULLIN: I am afraid if you start this machinery going again, we won't get through! Please, Dr. Berg, your time is up. I will now call Stewart Browne.

(CHAIRMAN MULLIN's *efforts prove to be in vain as* DR. BERG *neglects his opportunity to stand down, and instead, lands himself in a cross-fire debate with* SENATOR DUNNIGAN.)

DR. BERG: I want to say as a citizen (*Hisses*), if this legislature cannot control this audience any better than it does I do not see how you can control the rent situation. This is a disgraceful proposition (*Hisses, groans.*)

SENATOR DUNNIGAN (*Chiming in quickly*): Disgraceful?! Disgraceful?! This is no more *disgraceful* than the meeting you real estate men held at the Hotel Astor last Sunday when your "Get All The Rent You Can Association" met there. When your "Association" met there and even your own President didn't agree with you!

DR. BERG (*Finally overtaken by his frustration*): I will hold you responsible for this! This is a disgraceful exhibition and only a proposition of votes!

SENATOR DUNNIGAN (*Speaking as though certain he will have the last word*): If you think these critical proceedings are just a matter of votes I want to say to you and those you represent that I would rather not come back here again than to be elected by your votes or anybody like you.

(*Frazzled, visibly shaken and heavily perspiring,* DR. BERG *exits; enter* STEWART BROWNE, *President of the United Real Estate Owners Association, a confederated association of local organizations representing tenement landlords, real estate owners and various others aligned with New York's real estate interest.*)

STEWART BROWNE: Mr. Chairman and gentlemen of the joint committee: I do not know what to say. I have read the newspapers and I have listened to a reverend gentleman refer to certain expressions to which I was supposed to give utterance which were better the reverse of what I did say than of what I felt or what I believe.

I have stated before the various committees of this legislature for the past month that I was aware that profiteering in rents was going on, that I was aware it was increasing and I felt that some check should be put on rent profiteering by the legislature. The bills that were introduced, I was opposed to.

They suggested that I should make some alterations, which, I'll be the first to admit, was perfectly right and proper. We had a meeting of the real estate owners in Astor the other night. I made the statement at that time that it was up to the real estate owners to see that justice was done between the tenants and landlords. That whatever legislation, if any, was passed, that the legislation should be fair to both side.

I then suggested, as bloon as it were, and because of the fact that there were certain bills in one of the committee that the net income of landlords should be limited to ten percent, I stated that ten percent was too low and that it ought to be made fifteen per cent and that I was of the opinion that anything between ten and fifteen per cent would be deemed as a reasonable return by the municipal courts. At the meeting at the Astor, simply to get an expression of opinion, I suggested that we make it twenty per cent. I wanted to get an endorsement of the maximum of twenty per cent and then come up here and suggest that, believing right well that the legislature would instead suggest fifteen per cent. Now, I am not in favor of twenty per cent, don't get me wrong. I never have been in favor of twenty per cent. Speaking personally I am not in favor of fifteen per cent but I am satisfied of this fact, that a liberal profit must be given to the landlord because of the other side of the question, there must be encouragement of new residential construction.

Now, Assemblyman McCue introduced a bill and another speaker has referred to the question of exemption from taxation and a statement was made as to what the New York Real Estate Board has done, and I want to say, for the United, when that bill was introduced they put themselves squarely on the record not only in favor of a tax exemption on new construction for five years but also for the exemption of taxation on the land on which the new building was built and that bill ought to be modified to that extent.

Now, we passed resolutions in opposition to those bills because there is a difference of opinion in the United on that subject and I am not going to do that, but I want to tell those people in this room that I am perfectly satisfied that the man must be put above the dollar. I say that the time has gone when property should have prior rights over that of mankind. (*Applause.*)

No, no. That day is gone and it has gone forever and it will never come back, and I agree with one of the senators who has said that we have got some drastic legislation because of the fact that the real estate owners of today have not made any suggestions to the legislative committee as to what ought to be done. I believe that. I said it at the meeting at the Astor. That unless they will agree on some sort of legislative program, instead of simply opposing all other recommendations, that they will get it in the neck and they will get laws passed that they will be sorry for and I repeat that here today. (*Calls of, 'Very good, very good' accompany a light applause from the audience.*)

Something must be done. But, the landlords, you must remember are entitled to a liberal rent because of the fact that, from 1909 to 1917, or possibly 1918 too, all real estate in New York City was rented at too low a'rate. No property owned during those years returned any more than possibly three percent, not on the value of the property but on the equity of the property.

Now, the landlord has got to get that back. They ought not to get it back in one year. They ought not to get it back in two years. It ought to be spread over a series of years. There is no question, though, the landlord should be allowed to get those losses back.

You want to remember this fact, that the cost of management and the cost of operation and the cost of maintenance and the rates of interest have gone up slightly, have probably doubled, or nearly doubled, since the war, and at the very lowest figure rentals ought to take care of that doubled cost at least, and something in addition to that. What that ought to be, I am not prepared to say.

I understand that the preferences of the United—with all due deference to the municipal courts—I don't know why, I have never had any personal experience in them, but the United would rather have the U.S. Supreme Court, if such a law is going to pass, they would rather have the Supreme Court Judges pass on the reasonableness of rents than the municipal Judges. Why, I don't know exactly, because I have never had any experience in dispossess proceedings in my life.

I want you people to know this above all else, though—that so far as the majority of the members of the United Real Estate Owners Association are concerned, I don't believe that out of ten thousand members there are over twelve or fifteen that are considered as profiteering landlords. I don't believe that outside of those fifteen that those landlords are getting even five percent on the value of their property. I don't believe that. I am satisfied as to it being so, but the whole trouble with it is that each and every one of them believes that property has certain sacred and inalienable rights that the legislature cannot and should not interfere with, and I don't agree with them at all. I believe it is not the business of the legislature to interfere with any of these rights. (*Calls of, 'That is right! Good for you!!' emanate from the audience along with a hearty applause.*)

(*Exit* BROWNE, *enter* SENATOR HENRY SHAKNO.)

SENATOR SHAKNO: Mr. Chairman: Now, in the limited time I have at my disposal I would like to answer Judge Olcott, if he is within earshot of my voice. I have a great deal of respect for Judge Olcott's knowledge of the law but it is an elementary principle of law and no one knows it better than Judge Olcott, that the legislature has a right to say whether or not a member of a community or inhabitant of the city of New York has a right to waive a statute which is created for his benefit.

I would call his attention, for example, to numerous pension laws and the exemption from taxation of the properties purchased with pension money received by soldiers and, as well, numerous other statutes exempting homesteads from execution under judgment.

Judge Olcott referred to the starving owners of building and said that two years or more from now when building is resumed they would be starved and could not function. The trouble with the owners of real property today and for the past year has been that they are overfed. (*Applause.*)

It is a pleasure for me to agree with Mr. Browne. He is the man who has been termed by the real estate owners association as the fanatic on the rent problem. I am glad to see that he at least agrees with me that there must be some point or another where the profit must cease, and if I am to believe the public press as to what happened at the meeting Saturday night, there is to be no limit so far as the owners of property are concerned and the members of this association, because when the question was raised they said, "We want all the money we can get."

To you, owners of real estate (*Addressing the audience*), let me say that the time has come and it is here right now, that you are not going to get all that you want. (*Applause.*)

Dr. Berg, in seeking to justify his argument, referred to the cost of buildings. I would like to know how many of these profiteering landlords own buildings that have been erected during the past three or four years. They are buildings that have been erected and have stood there for years and years. They have not paid a cent more for material, nor for wages and seek only to justify an exorbitant rental upon the plea that building construction has gone up, to my mind, which indicates clearly, not only the weakness of their position, but the robbery that they are committing on the people of the City of New York. (*Applause.*)

At the meeting on Saturday night of the United Real Estate Owners Association, and apparently they have been following their policy consistently during the past two or three years, one of the speakers suggested that, in the event of a rent increase, property owners and landlords must not jab it into the tenants too soon. No, you must not jab it in too soon. You have been jabbing it into them consistently and regularly during the past year and a half, every two or three months, and no one knows it better than you, but the time has come, if there is to be any jabbing, the members of the legislature of the State of New York are going to jab it into you first. (*Applause.*)

Dr. Berg referred to and asked whether there is a union of landlords. No, there is absolutely no union of landlords. We know the property owners association in the Bronx which I have the honor to represent in the Senate. We know what they have been doing. There is not such a thing as an honest landlord in the city of New York. (*Applause.*)

They are appearing here and pretending that there is a distinction between a good and a bad landlord.

(*Cheers and hisses rise above the audience to such an extent that CHAIRMAN MULLIN slams his gavel, demanding that "We must have order!" Still, cheers and hisses reverberate around the Assembly building, buzzing as a swarm of angry worker bees after an unwelcome disturbance of the hive. Eventually, a distinct voice rises above the crowd, "Who sent you here?! What are you a Socialist or a Bolshiviki?!" In his closing moments, Senator Shakno sneaks in a final word.*)

Well, if you had anything to do with it I would rather not come back again than come back with your assistance. What are *you*, one of these profiteering landlords?

(*Exit* SENATOR SHAKNO, *enter* FIORELLO H. LA GUARDIA, *President of New York City's Board of Alderman and outspoken tenant advocate.* CHAIRMAN MULLIN *admonishes* LA GUARDIA *that he limit his speaking to ten minutes, advice that, considering the nature of the proceedings, obviously goes unheeded.*)

FIORELLO H. LA GUARDIA: Ten minutes, okay got it Mr. Chairman. I want to make perfectly clear, Mr. Chairman and gentlemen of the committee, that I appear before you absolutely partisan in favor of the tenants. (*Cheers of "Good boy!" and hisses from the crowd.*)

I believe that the statement is necessary just as it was made by Judge Olcott when he appeared for the builders and the landlords. Now, to get right down to the matter at issue, I want to say at the very start that I come here not to praise the landlord but to bury him.

The bills before you, Mr. Chairman, are all right when the tenant gets into distress, but what we are trying to do is not to get the tenant into distress in the first place, but instead, to keep him out of court altogether.

It seems to me that the only remedy you have before you is when the tenant gets into court.

Permit me to point out bill No. 1286. Why, you legalize the existing exorbitant rents! Not only that, but you permit the landlord to add twenty-four percent more to the rent and also permit me to point out that the tenant can only avail himself of this bill when he is sued for the rent. So, if you pass Bill 1286 you legalize the existing exorbitant rents, permit the landlord to add twenty-four percent to that, even if it is unreasonable, and all that is left for you to do is to pass the McCue bill giving them an additional subsidy, exempt them from taxation, put a halo around their heads and wings on their shoulders and send them back to New York.

I was quite amused with the attitude of Dr. Berg, and he is typical of the new landlord. He says, "Give us more immigration so that we can go back to starvation wages, so that we can have more distress, more tenants in tenement houses and so they can make more money." (*Applause.*)

That was a fair statement from the landlords' view point, but I want to urge consideration by the committee of Senator Aberlee's proposed bills. (*Applause.*)

Mr. Chairman, that goes right to the heart of the situation and I am sure that the reputable, decent, law abiding landlord is willing to make ten percent clean on its investment.

(LA GUARDIA's *comment is met initially by silence and, after a moment, a voice chimes in:* Why don't the landlords applaud then?!)

No, they won't applaud to that. Ten per cent clean on the investment is sufficient and, Mr. Chairman, we are so generous that we are willing to take the landlord's own word as to the value of his property, when he goes down to the tax office, raises his hand to God Almighty and swears to the value of his property. (*Laughter and applause.*)

That is fair enough. Ten per cent on that, and then you say, Mr. Chairman, that decent and reputable capital will go into real estate.

The gentleman tells us why, it is congesting, it is the law of supply and demand that forces up the rent. (*Facetiously and in a mocking tone.*) Why, you naughty tenants, why do you force more rents on these landlords?

Mr. Chairman, the situation in New York is critical. We are trying to follow out in conjunction with this legislature a program of Americanism and we have embarked on a campaign of Americanization, and one of the first elements of Americanism is to permit the people to live up to the American standard of living. (*Applause.*) And you cannot live up to the American standard of living when so large a proportion of a man's earnings is taken for rent that he cannot give himself and his family sufficient and proper nourishment. (*Applause.*) And the people of New York have but two alternatives, either to deprive themselves of sufficient nourishment or to congest two or three families in one small apartment under unsanitary and unhygienic conditions. That is one of the principles of Americanism?!

I am much amused when I hear Judge Olcott invoke the *U.S. Constitution*. I have as much confidence in the invocation of the *Constitution* on the part of the tenant, and I have the idea that it is done for the same selfish reason and with the same mental reservation and ulterior purpose as led Emma Goldman and Alexander Berkmann when they invoked it to resist deportation. (*Applause.*)

Mr. Brown, whom I know intimately will admit, if he is not scared of his associates, that ten per cent net income is a fair return on the investment, and I do not doubt the constitutionality of that. Judge Boyle is here and will explain the law on that proposition.

Now, please give us that bill, which we require. We require immediate relief. It is not sufficient to extend the time when the unfortunate tenant comes into the municipal court. That is not enough. We must have relief. This situation in New York City is serious and even critical. No, Rev. Doctor, the babies in New York will not die. No sir, because if they don't get relief here, today, I will tell you Mr. Chairman that the tenants of New York will stop paying rents altogether! (*Applause and hisses.*)

Yes, hiss my friends. Hiss, my friends. You people who emigrated from the pales of Russia but a short time ago, you people who have come here—

(*A voice from the crowd butts in:* What about your own race?! LA GUARDIA *marches on, undeterred.*)

Yes! And I will tell you about them too. I am now referring to the gentleman there who hissed, and to him only, one of the newly made landlords. You are the type, sir, you can hiss, but I will tell you, that your day has come and is now passed. And I wonder if there is one in your family, a rent hog that is, and I would like to know what you did during the emergency and the crisis through which we have just passed. (*Calls of "Good boy!" emanate from the crowd, competing for attention with calls of "Cut out your personality!!"*)

I will not. You can indulge in all the personalities you wish and I will do the same. (*Hisses and applause.*)

It hurts, doesn't it? Oh, how it hurts! Why? Because I am striving to tell the truth. (*Hisses and applause are interrupted only by loud calls of, "Sit down! Sit down!"*)

I know it hurts. I didn't stay at home and become a rent profiteer during the war, you can be sure of that.

(*A desperate voice from the crowd:* No, you are a profiteer now! CHAIRMAN MULLIN, *sensing he is losing the room, implores* LA

GUARDIA: The speaker will confine himself to the question, which is the committee's program.
*Applause ensues, as do LaGuardia's efforts from rostrum.)*

The situation, Mr. Chairman, is such that there is not sufficient relief in the bills before you. I can only repeat what I said before that it only helps in the extreme case where the tenant finds himself in court.

We have in New York City a situation that you are well acquainted with, where these newly made landlords, not people that owned property for years and people who are satisfied with a reasonable return on their investment, but instead, people who are mulcting and who are exploiting their tenants, and that is why I ask you, Mr. Chairman, to please consider the Aberlee Bill or a bill of that kind, which will limit the return on a landlord or building owner's investment so that the tenant in New York may be able to live up to the American standard and find a decent place to live without working entirely for the benefit of the landlord. *(Applause.)*

*(For a moment, it seems as though the resulting uproar from the audience has degraded into fisticuffs between* LA GUARDIA *and a heckler from the audience.* LA GUARDIA *is forced to vigorously and physically defend his comments).*

LA GUARDIA *(Having descended into the crowd from the podium, tussling with the heckler)*: Buzz off you spineless shrew! *(Turning back to the podium.)* You upstate Conservatives don't understand that rent profiteering is only a symptom of a more chronic ailment. That radicals and Socialists haven't completely overtaken the capital of this state already is not surprising but a takeover is imminent and, when that happens, you'll see that we should be up here, in Albany, debating on behalf of the public instead of as a show of publicity.

(CHAIRMAN MULLIN *cuts off the furious* LA GUARDIA, *who returns to his seat, visibly perspiring, his face flush and glowing red. At long last,* CHAIRMAN MULLIN *regains order and calls* JUDGE AARON J. LEVY.)

JUDGE AARON J. LEVY: Mr. Chairman and gentlemen of this joint committee: This seems to be a dignified and deliberative assemblage. *(Laughter.)* I am entirely nonpartisan, interested in neither side and have not the wish to either freeze or bury the landlords and I feel that it is a sad misfortune that a gentlemen who rises to the importance of member of the Senate of this state saw fit to declare on this floor that there is not a single honest landlord in the great City of New York. *(Applause.)*

I beg you now to applaud. It is indeed a sad commentary on the New York situation and the hundreds, if not the thousands of perfectly conscionable, as conscientious men who not so long ago were far worse off than any tenant that I ever knew, and it is not that element that this legislation seeks to reach. It is this predominant number of honest men who for many years were unfortunate enough to own real estate in the city of New York that we are driving for. It is that rent hog whom I wish you could see as I see him, sitting as I do, upon the bench attempting to adjust these differences that arise by the hundred and thousand fold during the course of a year in our imperial city.

I had a notion when I came here that there was no great difference of opinion as to the needs of this emergency. I had the notion that a crisis existed and that everybody was agreeable to the fact that it did actually exist. I had the notion that there were diverse opinions as to the remedy that was essential to cure the conditions that sprung from that crisis. And so I came prepared to lend my view, of what little worth it might be, toward the solution of the problem that confronts this very hard worked committee, which has labored for eight or ten months on the subject and having inquired in a painstaking and careful and conscientious fashion into the actualities, that even-handed justice might be ultimately done to both sides but when I come here and see a bear garden it seems to me that this is not helpful toward that solution, and the least we can do is to be respectful of the relative difficulties that exist between the parties to this seemingly great conflict.

Now, at the outset, let me say that I have no patience with that rent hog, who gouges, as we have had it explained numerous times today, and who taxes the poor resident of the Bronx, Brownsville and Williamsburg and other sections, and who unjustly mulcts one month and then the next month and maybe the third and maybe eight times in ten months as I saw it recently before me in the court, all of which was done unjustly and wickedly and inequitably, of course.

I have no patience for that type of landlord and yet I refuse to subscribe to that other element, that element which for the purpose of political propaganda only seeks to disturb and create unrest among tenants as I have a hundred and thousand fold evidence. (*Applause.*)

So there are two conditions that we must face if we are to be practical, if we are to do constructive work. If we are to do this, let us look upon the situation impartially, not from the partisan point of view. We find the rent hog on the one hand and find the Bolshiviki Tenants League on the other and both must be wiped out.

(*A member of the Assembly,* ASSEMBLYMAN AMOS, *chimes in:* May I ask the gentleman just what he means by a 'Bolshiviki Tenant League?')

So you may intelligently hear what a Bolshiviki Tenants League, is I will gladly tell you sir. Anarchists and Bolshevists and socialists have combined in the city of New York in various congested parts for the purpose of disturbing the tenants in those parts and they organized what was known as a Tenants League, ostensibly in the interests of the tenants but actually to raise funds to help themselves in their political propaganda. (*Applause.*)

(*Another member of the audience joins the fray:* Isn't it a fact that Bolshiviki landlords have combined just as much and that the Bronxville Landlords Association has done as much if not more to disturb the tenants as the Tenants League?)

I have no desire, sir, to indulge in a controversy with you. I am explaining to the gentleman what I mean when I describe the Bolsheviki Tenant League, which is without exception an official socialist proposition and was organized in the headquarters of the socialists in a given community. The tenants in that community were organized within the houses of some member of the socialist or Bolsheviki organization in that community. They were led to the Socialist headquarters. Meetings were held and a fee of a dollar was levied for the purpose ostensibly of retaining counsel. Five dollars was collected from each tenant ostensibly as earnest money, as a bond that the tenants would stand together in this matter, to do whatever the majority willed, and the rents that were owing to the landlords were collected by these leagues in several instances, my friends, and I speak authoritatively and I repeat that I am speaking impartially, I hold briefs for neither side, my sympathies, I couldn't tell you where they are. I don't think I need tell you where they are. I don't own real estate.

(*A heckler from the audience persists:* You say you don't own real estate! You're an aristocrat!)

If you had any manners, you would not interrupt me. I cannot bark as you can. So, pardon me, if I do not engage with you in any undignified controversy. Whether I am an aristocrat or not I do not know, but you may have it if you so please. I am speaking from an observation and experience that is judicial, public and personal only.

I say, in many instances such fees were collected by these leaguers but were either never paid to the landlords or restored to the tenants from whom they were taken. This grand larceny under our civilized laws was committed by the authority of this brand of tenant league. So, when I came, for example, upon the bench on the East side in November last summer and I saw these conditions, I don't mind telling you that I stamped out the Bolsheviki Tenant League and dealt with the tenants as we did long before there was a tenant league of any kind and never was it protested in one single instance from any of the tenants on the hundreds and thousands of issues.

(*A voice from the crowd interjects.*)

SPECTATOR: Mr. Chairman, I wish to make a statement and a suggestion in the interest of the loyal Americans here assembled. I know Judge Levy well. In the interests of the people here assembled I am going to ask him to retract one thing. The people are real and true Americans and not one of them connected with the Tenants League. (*Applause.*) I want to apologize to Judge Levy for calling his attention to that.

JUDGE LEVY: I do not know why you should apologize to me because I never insulted you. I never said you were.

SPECTATOR: I thought you said so.

JUDGE LEVY: I beg your pardon. I did not. I don't know who you are. You may have the privilege and pleasure of knowing me. I haven't the same privilege. However it may be, I wish everyone here to understand that I made no reflection on any person here, because I don't know anyone here as far as this huge mass goes anyway, and you may all be good Americans, and if you are, I am very happy to know it.

SPECTATOR: All right, fair enough. Now, please talk about the rent profiteer.

JUDGE LEVY: Very well, I shall. I will now come to the point that is fundamental and vital and that is this, that I could not and would not subscribe to this legislation if I knew of something better. I could not and would not subscribe to this legislation if I knew a remedy that would be more effective. I think, in light of the existing conditions, in light of the evils of which we have heard so much, in view of the things that are going on—in view of all these things, I know of no remedy that is better than those proposed by this committee, and in the absence of that better remedy, I take personal delight in subscribing to this program of legislation except perhaps in one case, having examined four bills in particular, and I take slight exception to the proposed bill which prohibits in the maintaining of summary proceedings by a landlord unless the rent claimed in this petition is identical with the rent of the preceding month. That denies the honest landlord the honest privilege of making an honest defense where he is honestly deserving, and so it goes that I suggest to this committee that they reconsider that measure with a view to drafting an amendment which will be appropriate to provide this contingency of which I speak.

Now, President La Guardia has openly complained about the so-called "twenty-five percent" bill. He has not read the bill carefully enough, in my judgment, because the twenty-five per cent maximum fixes the shifting of the presumption or rather fixes the shifting of the evidence and creates a presumption. That is to say, under the measure, if enacted into law, the tenant would have the burden of establishing the rent as unreasonable and as to that feature of the bill, the landlord cannot complain. If the increase be in excess of twenty-five per cent that creates the presumption that it is unreasonable and relieves the tenant of the burden of proof, which is in favor of the tenant and not in favor of the landlord. So, the tenant, in my judgment, can have no objection to that feature of the measure.

That is all, thank you. (*Applause.*)

(*Exit* JUDGE LEVY, *enter* MRS. H. C. ARTHUR, *a property owner and landlord from the Bronx.*)

MRS. H. C. ARTHUR: Mr. Chairman and gentlemen of the committee: I want to endorse absolutely, completely and unqualifiedly the rent bills represented here by Peter Aberlee, Senator from the Bronx. (*Applause.*)

I also want to endorse unqualified the building bill put in by Assemblyman Martin McCue of Manhattan. (*Applause.*)

We have heard a lot lately about the price of housing being controlled by the natural laws of supply and demand. That does not apply today to the housing situation, particularly in New York State, because we do not have a natural condition, but you have, in fact, a decidedly abnormal condition following the war. (*Applause.*)

And we are trying to get on our feet and we are stumbling along and the result is that what might be extraordinary in normal times of peace *has* to be adopted today, because you cannot meet an extraordinary condition with ordinary methods.

I come from Bronx County where the housing condition is the worst in New York State. (*Applause.*) I am from the Third Assembly District. I come from the Twenty-First Senatorial District which Senator Aberlee represents where the housing condition is the worst, and Senator Aberlee knows, as nobody else can, the condition there and the kind of legislation needed to remedy things at the present time.

I understand all about the constitutional rights of property. I understand why we have got to be conservative, but that bill of Senator Aberlee limiting net profits to ten per cent is just such a'measure. (*Applause.*)

And I want to state that in that Twenty-First Senatorial District, where I am represented by Senator Aberlee, it was absolutely necessary that we have a fusion between both the Democrats and Republicans in order to prevent the Senate Chamber of the State of New York from being disgraced by a Socialist Senator. (*Applause.*)

Those people in the Twenty-First Senatorial District are just as good and just as clean and just as decent as the average American, but they work hard all day, and about all they know about representative government is that they elect an Assemblyman every year and a Senator every two years to represent them up here, in Albany, and when they are starving and houseless, all they can do is to register what they call a protest vote, and they don't realize what they are doing to American institutions. (*Applause.*)

I am not ashamed to tell you, gentlemen, I am a landlady. I am getting exactly the same from my property as I got fourteen years ago in rentals. (*Applause.*)

I sent a son overseas and he was shot in the head in breaking the Hindeberg line and upholding American institutions, and I am a woman who will go down into her pocket and who will wear clothes that are five years old to uphold American institutions and ideals down in the Bronx. (*Applause.*)

Now, I am through but have got just this to say. I am an American woman. The American form of government has never failed us since it was established and it will not fail us now, and you men will help us now that you realize and understand the situation down there. You are going to pass laws. You are going to protect the landlords. They have rights under the constitution just like anybody else. And you are going to help the rest of us, because I tell you, gentlemen, that between the Bolshevism of the poor, helpless, ignorant, illiterate alien, that came here believing that this was the golden land and finds out it is not, the landlord contributes plenty to the belief in Bolshevism among the people, that will squeeze every last dollar out of their fellow men and women and then in the name of patriotism, put it in liberty Bonds.

I am going to tell you that between the Bolshevism below and the Bolshevism up above, it is a case of God help the rest of us in the middle. (*Applause and laughter.*)

(*Exit* ARTHUR, *enter* JUDGE JOHN BOYLE, JR., *a municipal Judge sitting in the Bronx.*)

JUDGE JOHN BOYLE, JR: Mr. Chairman and gentlemen of the committee: I won't need more than five minutes of your time. I want to be clear that I wholeheartedly believe what Herbert Hoover says, that the way to get rid of the profiteer is to let him make the money and then tax it out of him.

Now, I am not one of those men who say there are no decent landlords; nor am I one that says that there are no decent tenants. That is the purpose of the bill. That is the purpose of the bill so far is it affects individuals under the Corporation Tax Law. Here, the income tax, not at all referring to corporations, it is a tax only on individuals, Section 210 of the Tax Law, don't know who put it in here, but corporations are exempt from this article.

Corporations which are engaged in the purchase, sale and building of real estate, if it is a holding corporation, whose principle income is derived from holding stocks and bonds of other corporations, all of these entities—including banks, savings banks, savings institutions, title, guaranty, insurance or surety companies, shall be exempt from the payment of the tax prescribed by this article.

Now, I suggest to amend that so as to include, as this bill does, the income from tenement houses.

To be sure, I am not here to make a spread eagle speech. But I am here to tell you that we need two things done. One is that we have got to stop the profiteer by limiting the amount of money that he can make and the second is that we have got to guaranty some permanence to the tenants. Now, will the bills of the committee do that? The four bills of the committee which I have seen I do not think will, because of what President La Guardia spoke about, so far as I see it, the present outrageous rents.

Now, when I say "outrageous rents," I mean it. I have here some cards that were handed up at the meeting that was held in the school house in the Bronx. I don't know who the people are. We asked them to put on here their names, their addresses, and the amount of money that their rent was raised, and what they paid to the landlord. I will read one of the cards: *July 1918, rent, $35.00. October, 1919, $70.00. Just doubled.*

(*A member of the audience speaks up:* Is that a matter of fact? Is the name on it?)

They were cards that were handed in. These are cards which the people handed in at the meeting to which I have referred.

Now, here is another one, I have in my pocket here, which was handed to me on the train this morning, a batch of dispossess notices for the first week of April. I want to tell you that it is wrong and I will leave it as to whether or not there are any of the landlords here. They went to the tenants with dispossess notices for the first week of April, unless they consented to an increase of ten dollars a month in the rent. Now, this one I have here is from a man who appeared before the Mayor's Committee, I can't, however, give you any idea as to what. I might say that I understand, from what I have here on the back of this envelope, that the rents from this house were $10,548, and there was not more than a four room flat in the entire fifty foot house. The rents were $10,548. His expenses included the interest on two mortgages, a first of $36,000 and a second of $14,000 and allowance for every repair, for coal, for everything he could think of, it brought his expenses for one year to $6,000.

He had a net on his investment of $4,548 in one year. He now demands an increased rental on the first of April to bring his return to $2,400 a year more, and his net return on an investment of $1,200 in one year will be $6,948, the $12,000 being the amount which he claims to have invested.

*(From the audience, coordinated chants of:* Yes! Yes!*)*

Now, another thing. Mr. Aberlee has drawn another bill which definitely covers this situation as to dispossess or summary proceedings, and hold over cases. I know that the judges of the municipal court—I have had the good fortune for a few months to serve as one myself—I think there are forty-seven now. Is that right?

No, I would a great deal rather stick to the old American principle that this is the country of law and not of men and I would like to see, Mr. Chairman, enacted a law that would guide the judges as to what they should do and not leave it to the individual discretion.

They told use in law school that the equity branch of the court was the King's Conscience, but it too frequently proved that the King's Conscience was affected by the breakfast of the Judge.

Let us have the law so that if we aggrieved, either tenant or landlord we can ask for something that will be definite as well as just and not depend upon what one Judge may do today and another of the forty-seven may do tomorrow. *(Applause.)*

Mind you, I am for the tenants, but I am first of all for fair play, but I believe that in telling you landlords, what these bills mean and what they stand for I am doing a service to the tenants as well as to you and to my own country. There is one bill, I do not say that I have read the bill but I have read an account of it in the papers, exempting a mortgage of $40,000 from taxation. Now I don't know whether that is so or not. I asked the Superintendent of Buildings, what it costs to build a building. You know, and we all know that if we are going to die we will go to heaven, but it is pretty tough living if you haven't got anything to live on until you get there.

Now, you talk about the ultimate relief being more building. Ninety per cent of the materials that go into any building come from outside the State of New York. Now, what can this legislature do with the control of the cost of materials outside of the state.

You see, we have a further situation too, that is the cost of building in the Bronx, and I am talking now about the Bronx because that is a county I know more about. We are not a place of homes. We have no apartments such as Judge Olcott talks about. We are five story walkups, usually four to six families on a floor. The cost of building one of these fifty, foot five story walkups to house twenty to thirty families in 1916, according to the Superintendent of Buildings of the Bronx was $700; $35,000.

(*A member of the audience interjects, engaging* JUDGE BOYLE *in discussion.*)

SPECTATOR:   $700 a front foot, you mean.

JUDGE BOYLE:   Yes, $700 a front foot. Today he says that the minimum cost of putting up on of these buildings is $2,700 a front foot.

SPECTATOR:   What is the size?

JUDGE BOYLE:   Fifty foot by a hundred. That is the statement of the Superintendent of the Buildings of the Bronx.

Now, what real estate man, what builder, what man associated with the building industry tries to kid anybody by telling him it is going to help building by having exempted from the State Income Tax a mortgage of $40,000? Do you know anybody who would loan on a building? Do you know any builder who would have the nerve to ask for a forty thousand dollar loan on a building that would cost $122,000?!

(SENATOR LOCKWOOD *interrupts:* The Committee never said that, Judge. *Even* CHAIRMAN MULLIN *appears confused, asking:* What is that?)

JUDGE BOYLE:   I am simply telling you what appeared in the newspapers. I have not seen your bill, I must admit. If that is not so, if I am not correct, and if there is any doubt in the Senator's mind, I drop the subject. I am simply recounting what was reported in the papers, that mortgages up to $40,000 were to be exempted from the State Income Tax for the purpose of encouraging building. Is that correct?

SENATOR LOCKWOOD: The interest on mortgage holding but the purpose is to get the Federal Income Tax also exempted in order to bring money into the market. All the money men say it will bring money into the market.

JUDGE BOYLE: No, I claim it will not.

(*Several members of the panel jump in.*)

SENATOR DUNNIGAN: It is so recognized by United States Senator Calder.

SENATOR LOCKWOOD: Yes, and also by the real estate board.

JUDGE BOYLE: I am frank to say whether U.S. Senator Calder said so or not, I am entitled to express my honest opinion that it will not, and I ask you to take it for what it's worth. It is an attempt on the part of mortgage companies to exempt their mortgages up to the point of $40,000 so that they may hold them out as a good investment because they are exempted from the income tax. It will not result in increased building or in the attraction of money to this field.

They tried to fix it and made the same plea in the briefs on which they went up to the courts and they had no right to tax these things, because they were holding this money out of the market.

Now, may I just say that I hope that the committee will look at these bills and strike out therefrom everything in the bill after the words, "On any income," making the bills read as follows: "On any income of more than ten percent there shall be levied a tax of one hundred per cent."

These two bills, in my opinion, gentlemen, will remedy the housing situation.

(*Exit* JUDGE BOYLE, *enter* SENATOR ABRAHAM KAPLAN *from Manhattan.*)

SENATOR KAPLAN: Mr. Chairman and gentlemen of the committee, brother and sister Americans: I have listened with a great deal of entertainment and interest to President La Guardia coming here and Judge Boyle and attempting to tear up the work of a committee that sat for one year down at the City Hall where

President La Guardia is. I should like to ask him why it was that during the sessions of that committee all summer that he did not have this kind of presence down there, to tell us something about this wonderful housing scheme that he can come here and speak about in four minutes and ask the committee to adopt it and at the same time attack the work of the committee that covered a period of nearly a year.

(LA GUARDIA, *never missing an opportunity to be heard:* I wish to inform the gentleman that I was not a member of the board sitting at City Hall.)

Don't you people from the Bronx understand that when he comes here and Judge Boyle comes here and they advocate a remedy by stating that they are here to bury the landlord, and that they intend to take from the landlord all of his income over ten per cent, that they are not burying the landlord for the benefit of the tenant, because that does not give the tenant or the tenant's family any more relief or any more food so essential as they contend, to meet the American standard of living.

They are here to bury the landlord for the benefit of the state. That is what they are trying to do with these bills.

When Judge Boyle comes here and says that you are going to determine the income of the landlord as ten percent, and then when he exceeds that you are going to take and tax that in a certain sum, and when he exceeds that you are going to take part of that and give the rest to the State of New York, when it is determined that the landlord has earned ten per cent or ninety per cent on his invested capital, you don't determine that until the end of the year. You don't determine that until the exacting rent profiteering landlord has in his pocket every last dollar that he means to exact from the tenant. You don't determine that until the tenant is suffering from a lack of ability to obtain a fair deal and a fair break from the landlord.

Those are not remedies. We stand here as members of this committee, I stand here as a member of the Housing Committee trying to find remedies that will do two things: Hit at the rent profiteering landlord, because he must be hit, and protect the tenant who desires to pay a reasonable rent and make it unnecessary for that tenant to pay any more.

Now on what theory can that be done: On what basis can that be done? It can be done, Mr. Chairman, on this theory, that the buildings of the city of New York are in the possession of people who control what might be regarded as a natural monopoly. You cannot tell me if a group of people were to take all the food in the City of New York and bring it down away from the city, and if the people of New York were without ability to take or get part of that food, that the legislature of the state of New York could not compel the people in control of that food to sell it at a reasonable price, because they were in control of a natural monopoly.

And so we say to the exacting and the rent profiteering landlord, you are in control of a natural monopoly. Justice Spiegelberg is perfectly right. The law has been written long before this, that when one is in control of a natural monopoly and is in a position to force down the throat of a bargaining party that kind of a bargain which is unfair, that sort of a bargaining is unjust, unfair and against public policy, that kind of a contract has been illegal at common law, and there is no doubt in my mind about the ability of the legislature to write into the law an act or provision that will so declare it, because it is no more or no less an unjust evasion of the common law.

I heard from Judge Olcott, who called attention to the fact that permits for building in amounts had decreased. Why is it that we have $19,000,000 available for building purposes a few years ago and only $13,000,000 available this year. Why is it that money interests do not invest their money in mortgages. That is a very important question. In the first place I will ask Judge Olcott why is it that the people complain when the rents are as high as they are today? If he wants to know, I will tell him. Why is it that these organizations, the life insurance companies and the banking associations do not invest in real estate when rents are so high? I will tell him why, because these concerns would rather invest their money in some other securities. They would rather buy a bond under par or stock under par. It is because the officers of the life insurance companies, the directors of the thirty odd subsidiaries in which the life insurance companies own bonds would rather invest the money at their disposal in that way, because in purchasing bonds under par they are in a position where they may obtain greater influence, they are in a position where they may obtain a greater value in direct return than they could possibly receive by investing the money under their control in real estate, even if rents are as high as they are.

That is one definite reason why builders cannot get money to erect their buildings with. The great important question here is not only the protection of the tenant, it is not only the creation of a situation which will make it impossible for this rent profiteering to continue, but the important thing to keep in mind, if you please, is to keep open the avenues for construction, because it is construction that is going to remedy this situation eventually, and you cannot open the avenues for construction unless you have some definite fund from which and out of which a building may be constructed.

I will also say in answer to Mr. Judge Olcott, that we ought to go one step further and that step to take is to say that the life insurance company and the savings banks who are in possession of the money and who have got the money because they receive their premiums in advance, to be kept until you die and I die, we ought to say to those companies that they are in possession of the reserves of the people of the State of New York; that we are in a crisis, which we are at this time and we ought to turn to them and say you are in possession of our money, to the extent of hundreds of thousands of millions of dollars and all that treasury belongs to the people and realizing that the people are going through a crisis and must be compelled to take that money and put it into new construction. And if you did that in addition to these plans adopted by the committee, if you went back one step further, if you said to these financial institutions that you have got to give this money belonging to the people of the state of New York, you have got to use the money for the purpose of building houses, because they must have houses, which, I say we have the right to say to them, the time would come very shortly when the situation would be permanently relieved.

I feel that the legislature has the right to adopt such a law and that it has the right to do that in view of the fact that we have this situation and, if we did it we would have a situation where we would get new buildings in the Bronx, we would get new buildings in Manhattan and we would get new buildings in Brooklyn, and this committee could feel that its work was well done because the people could move into these new apartments and the construction of new apartments would force rent down naturally to a proper and fair basis. (*Applause.*)

(*Exit* SENATOR KAPLAN, *enter* ALEXANDER S. GRESHLER, *spokesman for the Brooklyn Board of Real Estate Brokers.*)

ALEXANDER S. GRESHLER: Mr. Chairman, members of the committee: There is no doubting the nature of this crisis, the only question seems to be a matter of degree.

Well, I'm here to tell you that I watched my district in Brownsville grow from a population of twenty thousand to a population of three hundred thousand during 1910 and 1911 by virtue of the fact that there were buildings erected from time to time as a result of the right encouragement. We want to get the investor, we want to get the man who is willing to put his money into homes and we cannot induce him to do it as long as present conditions exist and there is a lack of encouragement, so without taking up your time Mr. Chairman and gentlemen I am going to file a brief with this committee.

But from the sentimental standpoint, from the humanitarian standpoint, from the standpoint of expediency, every one sees we must remedy the conditions. We cannot remedy them unless we have places to put people, places to house them. Let us take them away from the situation that exists in Manhattan, let us spread them out.

In the Brownsville district alone, in Brooklyn, when I was alderman there, in 1910 and 1911, we had three school houses. Now we have 15 school houses, a teeming population and we must not arrest development, gentlemen. We must be fair about this thing. I agree with Judge Levy in what he says. A certain class are taking advantage of the situation, and a certain element today are stirring up the people, rousing them I might say to the border line of revolution, and I think there are some in this chamber today who are endeavoring to stir up this strife. I have reference to those demagogues who stand on soapboxes and who do nothing else but excite the populace. I have faith in this committee. I have faith in Senator Lockwood, of Brooklyn, whom we all love, and I do say this is a constructive piece of legislation.

The moment you encourage these mortgage investors to go to Brooklyn and the Bronx and to build small homes, you are creating a condition so that the state can see that it is getting an income out of this and will be getting more into the treasury than it will lose, because as a matter of finance, as a financial proposition, it is a matter of dollars and cents and I hope Mr. Chairman and gentlemen that when the smoke sweeps away and you go into solemn conclave, you do not forget you must encourage the honest and respectable investor—I do not mean the Bolsheviki profiteer, because if you will examine and inquire you will find a good many of these shoestring landlords down deep in their hearts do not believe in our institutions. I know from personal knowledge if you walk into the municipal courts and see them take the stand as landlords, you look with amazement at them.

That said, I will conclude. I want to say Mr. Chairman that the people who are making a big hulloa about this thing are not good loyal Americans.

(*Exit* GRESHLER, *enter* ISIDORE M. LEVY, *a resident professional lessee in New York City.*)

ISIDORE M. LEVY: Mr. Chairman, ladies and gentlemen: I shall take the liberty of believing that the tenants and the landlords have come here for the purpose of seeing legislation passed to drive the indecent landlord into perdition, to encourage the decent landlord to eliminate the indecent tenant and to give the decent tenant fair play.

Ladies and gentlemen it is the type of landlord that has resorted to oppressive methods that has created a situation such as exists this afternoon, and the decent landlords are compelled to suffer, because perchance, there are rotten indecent men who for some reason or other own property and abuse their fellow human beings. I say that these indecent landlords are more than 12 or 15 and I disagree with Judge Olcott who said that on the west side the tenants do not need protection. The worst landlords in New York are to be found on the West side and in Washington Heights operating among the better class tenants. The landlords have gotten to a point where they say they won't bother with cold water tenants—we won't bother with the poor tenant, we don't want to have anything to do with him, we are only going to tackle the fellow that we can jack up one hundred percent and he is going to pay because he won't suffer the humiliation or the indignity of protesting against it too much.

Now my friends at the Greater New York Taxpayers Association asked me to speak for them. They consist principally of the landlords of the poorer tenements, and I said gentlemen I am a tenant as well as a landlord, I am a tenant in a high class house, and I stated, gentlemen, I am perfectly willing to speak before this honorable committee, provided you let me speak as a citizen, to see that justice is done throughout the community fairly and squarely to the landlord and the tenant, and you won't ask me to speak to protect the selfish or corrupt interest, and I want to say ladies and gentlemen that when Dr. Berg spoke I was very much interested in what he said, but I felt ashamed to think that an intelligent man like Dr. Berg would reflect upon this committee by threatening them and insinuating to them that they should beware of their actions unless it lies along certain lines or they will meet with chastisement by a certain class of voters in New York.

I want to say to you gentlemen on behalf of the tenants I represent and on behalf of the class of tenement house owners that I represent that we feel you have a tremendous problem before you, that you have spent eight or ten months in studying it, and, God be with you, it is a problem that requires the ablest minds in order to solve it, not only for the purpose of keeping rents reasonable, because that is one thing we want to do, but also for the purpose of furnishing a future remedy, to see that new buildings are erected, to furnish accommodations for the new tenants, so that if a young man and a young woman choose to marry each other they may feel that they can marry and have a decent place to live and raise their family.

May it please you gentlemen of the committee let us do what they have done in Washington with the farmers of this country in order to encourage agricultural pursuits. They created a Farm Loan Board. Let the state of New York follow suit and likewise create a loan board or let them urge the national government to create a loan board so that a tenant with two or three thousand dollars will be able, by reason of financial assistance that he will get from his government to build a little house for himself and the larger operator will also be enabled to put up proper buildings.

The second suggestion that I have to make, may it please your honorable body, is that the bill proposed by your honorable body which vests in the board of justices discretion to grant an unlimited stay is sufficient to meet the entire situation. I think if you gentlemen confined yourself to that bill you would find that if a tenant was unjustly attached, as undoubtedly he will continue to be unless some relief legislation is passed, he can go into municipal court and ask the judge to listen to both sides of the story and to give him a stay not of ten days, twenty days, thirty days, sixty days, but a year if necessary.

I say to you Mr. Chairman and gentlemen that from my knowledge of realty that if you vest this state's core of municipal Judges with the power to grant a stay of a year, you will drive every speculator out of business because no speculator can operate with profit if he cannot dispose of his property within a year and so I say to you Mr. Chairman and gentlemen, on behalf of the tenants and on behalf of the property owners, the way to preserve the respect of our fellow citizens, is to pass this legislative enactment vesting discretion in the board of Justices to limit that stay to one year, and also to modify that bill so that if a completely new set of conditions occurs it shall be possible to submit the case to the Judge for further justice if the situation warrants.

That is my amendment, Mr. Chairman.

(*Exit* LEVY, *enter* JUDGE HARRY ROBITZEK, *a municipal Judge sitting in the Bronx.*)

JUDGE ROBITZEK: Mr. Chairman the time is late. I appreciate it. I presume that I have had as many landlord and tenant summary proceedings before me as any other judge in the City of New York by reason of the acute situation in the City of New York and particularly in the borough of the Bronx. I say that advisedly. I was not looking for those summary proceedings, I try to avoid them where I can. I try to make adjustment where possible and I want to say in due fairness to the landlords and tenants that the majority of the landlords that come before me are fair and reasonable, but it is the minority of landlords that you members of the committee are, in duty, bound to the people of the state to get rid of, and if these laws are not stringent enough then other laws must be and shall be enacted to bring about justice as between landlord and tenant.

I will recite but a few incidents that have come before me, personal experiences, and I think you will agree with me that it must be stopped. We municipal Judges haven't the power. We have tried everything by way of persuasion. We have done it by duress. We have threatened some landlords with every possible means, but of course we haven't the power to do in those things. What in God's name are we to do when we see men and women and children, thousands and thousands of them where we require the police department of the City of New York to keep law and order coming not only in the court rooms but in the streets leading to the court rooms—what are we to do unless we appeal to the legislature of the state of New York to give us the power to relieve the situation?

I had one case, and I think it is striking, where a landlord could not even speak the language, as many of them cannot, and this landlord came before me and the tenants, 22 in number, said this landlord is a new man now but he owned the property 8 months ago, and I said to him, come up here I want to speak to you. I said Mr. Smith or Lefkowitz, or whatever his name might be, they tell me you owned this property before, 8 months ago, and at that time your rents in this apartment were $20 on an average for a four or five room apartment. This rent probably was reasonable at the time. Who did you sell this property to 8 months ago? He said he sold it to some man, he had forgotten at the moment. I asked this landlord if he and the new owner were related? He said not exactly. I said what do you mean not exactly?

To make a long story short, there had been 8 specific transfers in 8 months and every landlord was a relative of his, either directly or indirectly, and everyone gave the tenants a boost so that today in that house he was trying to raise the tenants, the last time from $55 to $65 and apartment.

What power did I have to relieve the situation? Then he had the audacity to tell me he was losing money on his house. Now I have been following this matter for a year and a half. I was up here last year. I am sorry to say that a great many of those that are appearing here today did not come with me today. They did not see the necessity for this legislation. I was up here then urging these very measures, that is, that the court have the power to ascertain whether the rent demanded was fair and reasonable, and I say there is not a judge in the municipal court of New York who cannot be relied upon to give a square deal to the landlord and to the tenant. I will say that every Judge will see to it that those who preach Bolshevism under the auspices of tenant's leagues or any other league will be ousted from the control of property, and I have done as much as any man in the City of New York to rid the city of these tenant's leagues and to drive Bolshevism from the county of the Bronx.

But if you don't give us this legislation, and I am as much a believer in this constitutional form of government as any member in the assembly, I say if you do not give us this legislation I have no hesitancy in telling you that you cannot prevent the socialist voting population in the Bronx from increasing from 30,000 in the last election to *ONE HUNDRED AND FIFTY THOUSAND AND WHAT IN GOD'S NAME IS TO PREVENT IT?!*

I have gone over these bills, the committee bills. I have urged these bills for the past year and a half. Let's pass them. Don't wait until tomorrow to enact these laws. On April 1st, I am going to have no less than three thousand tenants before me personally, and I am only one Judge in the City of New York. I am asking now—I am not speaking on behalf of the tenants alone—I am asking you on behalf of these landlords that are reasonable—and I state at the outset the majority are—and if they don't see the light today then the alternate, and there is an alternate, is to obliterate the summary proceeding and let landlords go to ejectment, a state court remedy, which will take two years.

I will stake my reputation as a lawyer and a judge, and I have been at the bar sixteen years, before I became a judge, I will stake my reputation on this, that you have the power to enact every one of these measures, and for God's sake, *go to it!*

(*Exit* JUDGE ROBITZEK, *enter* H. M. PHILLIPS.)

H. M. PHILLIPS:   Mr. Chairman, ladies and gentlemen, when judges get excited in discussing a political and economic question it is about time to ask ourselves what hope is there for any reasonable solution?  Judges, temperate men, men who are expected to hold even the balance between one faction and a question in the general interest of the public. Now, don't let anyone misunderstand me. I agree there is an acute situation, but I also hope everybody will agree that you are not going to cure injustice by perpetrating still greater and more lasting injustice. Let us see if a way cannot be found to do a fair thing in a fair way and not be carried away and swayed by the excitement of the moment.

One man said (*Referring to Arthur J. W. Hilly*), and he complimented the Assembly and Senate, upon ousting the Socialists, and then he goes ahead and says you have to oust them, but do the very things they recommend. He says the easiest way to fight temptation is by yielding to it. Those men say, take from those that have and give to those that have not, and the question is to what extent that is a proper principle.

I agree to a certain extent it is a proper principle, but it is not a proper principle to take it in the way that these bills propose, and let me take each one of these bills and I will show you.

Now, don't get excited. I am trying hard not to be myself and I do not think I will be and I do not think the audience is going to be. I will take each one of these bills and I will show you that from the moment you enact each one of these measures you have absolutely taken away every element of the ownership of property from the men that own it.

Take the bill which says that municipal Judges shall have the power to stay execution as long as they please. I ask you, haven't you by that act taken away the element of ownership and placed it in the discretion of the Judges. There is a proviso in that bill. I am coming to that. There is a proviso in that bill that the discretion of the Judge is limited only to an order requiring the payment of rent—again in the discretion of the Judges—according to what was reasonable or what was the past rent. Haven't you, by that act, I repeat, taken away nearly every element of ownership and placed it in the discretion of Judges? I do not say those Judges are not men whose discretion I will trust at this time, but who knows, who knows who can be trusted? Is there any human being that can be trusted with such wide discretion when the clamor of the public is at him and insists upon his exercising it in a certain way? I would not want to be trusted with that kind of discretion and I think I would try hard to do my duty, but I fear that the power of the newspapers and the general power of the clamor of the people who are heard who sway me, as near as I would try to do my duty as I see it—

(*A voice from the audience interrupts:* Aren't Judges to be more trusted than landlords?)

Perhaps, but at what cost? Consider a bill permitting a tenant a stay and requiring the tenant to pay into court the rent at the old rate, and such additional sum as the Judge may deem fair. Any clause in the lease waving these provisions is to be void too, etcetera, etcetera. Now one man asks me—Aren't the judges more to be trusted than the owners? Well, if we have reached that stage in our political development that we are going to enact legislation which expresses in itself the choice between one class of citizens and another, as to which is to be trusted most, I think we have reached the parting of the ways in our constitution's form of government.

Another of these bills provides for the amending of the code of civil procedure. We have some other bills of like character. One which says no summary proceeding to dispossess a tenant for non-payment of rent at an increased rent shall be maintainable unless the petitioner alleges in the petition and process that the rent of the premises described in the petition is no greater than the amount paid by the tenant for the month preceding the default for which the proceeding is brought, or has not been increased more than twenty per centum over the rent as it existed one year prior to the time of the petition.

I agree with you now that certain rentals in certain houses have been so increased that it may be that twenty per cent additional increase would be about as far as the landlord ought to go. But what will you do for that owner who has not yet increased, and who has not been able to, and probably did not want to increase his rent to such a point.

(*Cries from the audience interrupt again:* Where is he?! Where is this honest owner?? Here is one, have his picture taken!)

I can point to you in our association, three thousand of such owners. But aside from that question what standard have you, and what standard is there in these bills as to what is a fair rental? At one time, when I went to school, I recall the teacher said about twenty to twenty-five per cent of one's income may be spent in rent. Has any one of the committee examined the present standard of living and the earnings of the various tenants and determined whether it exceeds that amount? I say if an examination were made it would be found that the standard of earnings have so increased in the past two years that, though the rising rents have also been steady, it has not yet reached that twenty or twenty-five per cent that has heretofore been taken up in rents.

I know this to be true in our association from the number of houses we examined. We found although the increase in rentals has been going on, at the same time the tenants have been so improved because of increased earnings that their income is more than four times as much as their expense for rent. I recall that in parceling out a man's income some years ago, he used to figure so much for clothing, so much for food, so much for rent, and I tell you that the increase in the family's expenditure for clothing is far in excess of the increase in rents.

(*A voice from the crowd:* We will fight them next!)

Ah, there is the solution! Is this Legislature prepared to encourage a fight against one class of ownership this year and another next year, and is it prepared to encourage that kind of legislation?

I ask that the Legislature consider an amendment to all these bills allowing a certain maximum of profit over and above expenses based upon cost or upon valuation to be determined by a commission in each case.

(CHAIRMAN MULLIN *jumps in, informing* PHILLIPS *that his time at the rostrum is up, but his efforts prove to be in vain as both* SENATOR ABELEE *and a* MR. WILBUR EASTLAKE *interject abruptly.*)

SENATOR ABELEE: What's the matter with the assessed valuation of the property?

PHILLIPS: That might do, but it again leaves someone in power to assess as he pleases. I am not prepared to say now who shall be the arbiter of values, but some bill along that line ought to be suggested and a committee should be appointed. I believe a committee is far, *far* better than taking the assessed valuation because I know how the assessed valuation is sometimes made.

MR. WILBUR EASTLAKE: Do you mean to tell me, carefully and earnestly, that the Landlord's Association of the City of New York has appointed a committee to investigate into the wages earned of the income of their tenants?

PHILLIPS: I mean that the greater New York Tax Payers Association have had for the past several months from various of their owners reports as to increases in rents and we find the increase far less in proportion to the increase in wages.

EASTLAKE: Will you kindly tell me the membership of the Greater New York Tax Payers Association?

PHILLIPS: It has a membership of 2,600 south of 42$^{nd}$ Street and east of Third Avenue, mostly tenement house property.

EASTLAKE: I think your association has rather a misnomer for your name.

(*Exit* PHILLIPS, *enter* JAMES B. HOLLAND, *the final speaker of the proceedings.*)

JAMES B. HOLLAND: Mr. Chairman, I am my own landlord and I don't increase rents either. I have a tenant, or tenants in my house now. You can telephone over there and ask if the rent has been increased in the last year.

(*A voice from the crowd speaks up:* Was it increased before that? If you had five hundred tenants then you would raise the rent!)

No I would not. It is you grafters in the real estate business that raise the rents. You let me alone or I will go after you in good shape. Mr. Chairman, nobody knows about profiteering better than the Assemblyman and Senators in the different neighborhoods from which they come. I live in Rockaway Beach, 234 and 236 Washington Avenue. I own that property. I have got tenants on that property. They have been there for three years at the same rent they went in for three years ago. A telephone is there. I will give you their names and addresses. Ask them. Nobody knows it better than the working people the way the rents have been increased. My own brother doesn't own his home, but unfortunately, he has been like a good many more—he is the father of a big family and he cannot get into a house in Manhattan in view of the number of children he has. The landlords won't let him in. And the landlord he has jumped his rent from twenty-one dollars a month to forty-five.

(*A voice again butts in from the crowd:* How about his wages? And what did you pay three years ago for a ton of coal and what do you pay today?!)

Never mind what his wages are. You are going to take it away from them anyhow, aren't you? You are going to take the wages away from them? I know a fireman in the Fire Department of the City of New York who received an increase last year of $425.00. The landlord gets $325.00 of it! What are the wages, you ask?! That's where the wages are going.

In reference to the ton of coal, some landlords have taken out the boilers and put in electric stoves and gas stoves at the expense of the tenant, and you cannot deny it. There are some Jewish boys up there who come from the east side. They will tell this man who asks, "What are the wages?" They will tell him. They are members of our organization. They will tell you what the wages are and they will tell you how much of that wage you have taken for your rent.

Mr. Chairman, this Assembly and this Senate have *got* to do something for the people who pay rent in the City of New York and in the State of New York. There would not be this turmoil here today in this city and this State if the rents were not jacked up and jacked up and jacked up, every dollar a man earns taken away from him. Some of these landlords have talked about clothing. Those that own the tenement houses are even taking the clothing.

One gentleman said if you own five hundred, you're more likely to raise the rents! *THERE IS THE TROUBLE!!* If the real estate shark was taken out and the individual owner were to rent his own home in place of the real estate shark there would not be any jacking up of rents. That is where the wages go.

(HOLLAND'S *comments provoke a debate with a member of the audience.*)

SPECTATOR: Allow me to jump in. On July 19th, 1919, I employed a contractor to work for me. He employed Union men. I employ Union men only on my jobs.

HOLLAND: You couldn't get anything else in the City of New York.

SPECTATOR: I gave the contractor a payment of a thousand dollars on Saturday. He took the money to pay the men. The men saw me pay him. The men stayed there until six o'clock that night. They demanded their money from me. I went to the Union and they laughed at me and said you must pay the men the money and pay them for waiting time, and pay them for Sunday, Monday and Tuesday. I paid them. If they would work decently and lay eighteen hundred brick a day instead of eight hundred—

HOLLAND (*Interrupting, but meaning only to appease the spectator*): You had a right to pay the laborers for the work and not the contractor.

SPECTATOR: I asked you to keep that contractor out of the Union and you said nothing to it, they are employing our men.

(*As the spectator drifts further and further off topic,* CHAIRMAN MULLIN *jumps in:* This hasn't anything to do with the bill.)

HOLLAND: Mr. Chairman, Stewart Browne sits here and he let the cat out of the bag when he appeared before the committee of the Assembly on the Jesse Bill, and when one of the Assembly men asked him, "You are getting the rents?" he said we are getting because the getting is good!

(*Naturally,* HOLLAND'S *comment provokes* STEWART BROWNE *to enter the fray*).

STEWART BROWN: That's not it.

HOLLAND: That is absolutely true Stewart, and you cannot get away from it. If what you said in the public press is true, Mr. Stewart Browne, it has again quoted you even behind closed doors—

BROWNE (*Jumping to his own defense*): Not closed doors!

HOLLAND: Closed to nobody but the rent payer. Mr. Real Estate Shark is here, the rent-hogging landlord is here—that's the man you want to watch, Mr. Landlord, the runner that is going from place to place finding out what a man is paying, what one man is paying and the other man is paying, and the landlord leases the house next day and up goes the rent again. That's where some of the wages are going.

Years ago, in the last five or seven years, a working man working at his trade even as a laborer gave one week's wages to the landlord for one month's rent. There isn't a rent payer within the sound of my voice that does not know this is true. Today he has to put aside two weeks' salary for his monthly rent. He has got to do it. If I was a Judge, and if this matter was put up to me I would handle it whether it was constitutional or not. Let the higher courts state whether it is. You can take fifty lawyers and perhaps you will get fifty different opinions. You have *got* to do something for the rent payers of the City of New York, and *you've got to do it today!* It has to be now.

That is not alone in New York but it is true in Buffalo, Albany, Syracuse and Rochester. In considering the Jesse Bill we have had them from Rochester. They said the rents were not jacked up there.

(CHAIRMAN MULLIN *interrupts so as to clarify:* Yes, the rents have been jacked up in Rochester.)

HOLLAND: The Assemblymen from Syracuse know that rents have been jacked up in Syracuse as far as working people are concerned. The fellow that can pay thirteen and fourteen and fifteen dollars a month, he isn't crying, but the poor fellow who has to work from Monday morning to Saturday night to get a week's wages, whether it is forty or sixty dollars a week, the landlord takes it away from him. Now let the working man who has been trying to get away from that sort of thing, and saving a few dollars to build his home, give him a chance.

*With that, the proceedings conclude and all gathered in Albany that day make for home, visibly exhausted.*

## III.

*JACOB RIIS rolls along on the Empire State Express Car No. 999, his second round trip of this, his first full day in limbo. The hours have begun to stretch out as if time, itself, were beginning to mock Riis, testing his temper. And the worst part is that he's tormented incessantly by a restless energy burning inside his belly that will neither allow him to catch any shut-eye nor even to take a load off. By now, Riis has realized that this restless energy serves a purpose—to afford him the gumption to seek out and handle whatever unfinished business lay before him, blocking his path to the afterlife.*

*Riis is meandering down a crowded aisle, passing blithely through the passengers without fear of the narrow confines experienced by those living passengers crammed into the stifling walkways. "There he is again! Wait, where'd he get off to this time?!" Riis calls aloud as he catches another tantalizing glimpse of a child pickpocket he'd been attempting to follow for the last few hours. Of course, no one could hear Riis' voice. Riis had caught an early glimpse of the young boy, perhaps seven or eight years of age, shifting among the passengers, making people move, blowing in an ear, and when they shift, he adeptly exploits their momentum, distracting them just long enough to filch coins, sneak a loose ring, remove a pocket watch.*

*It's in haphazard pursuit of the juvenile thief that Jacob Riis discovers that he has the ability to move between train cars, despite not being able to exit the train in Albany. Riis struggles to kill time on his return trip to Grand Central Station and reminisces about his time exploring and documenting the 'Bend.' At the forefront of his thoughts are a rum-running, growler-schlepping, pick-pocketing band of children that quietly supplemented their families' income through an organized crime ring.*

*Riis' reminiscions are interrupted abruptly by the sound of train doors opening as the train pulls into Grand Central and a crowd of loud, lewd and boisterous passengers all swarm to get off the train. To his utter astonishment, Riis is gathered in the herd and hoisted from the train car onto the platform. Before he can gather himself, the child Riis had been chasing appears suddenly before him and taps his wrist as if asking for Riis to check the time. When Riis looks down, he realizes that his pocket watch is no longer chained to his vest. He's been robbed!*

*Riis, surprised that the child can actually see him given his being devoid of life in the earthly sense, Riis pursues the thief, who runs*

## ROARING TWENTIES

off swiftly through the crowd. Riis passes easily through the crowd but somehow loses sight of the boy.

THUD!

Riis is clocked in the back of the head by a dense, metallic object. Reaching down he realizes the bludgeon was, in fact, his pocket watch! Checking the time, panic sets in as Riis realizes that, if he wants to be up in Albany when the Joint Committee hearings adjourn, he has to get a move on. The young thief is nowhere to be found.

"But wait," Riis blurts out aloud, "why is it that I can get off the train at Grand Central and not in Albany? And how did that boy see me, for one thing, and manage to grab my watch for another!?"

'ALL ABOARD!'

The conductor rings out over the loud speaker, the final boarding call for the next train back upstate. Were Riis to miss this one, he may never have a chance to hear how the hearings pan out. He has no time to lose and makes a break for it. By the nick of time, Riis steps off the platform as the train doors close, the door catching his leg and sending a shot of pain from his calf, up through his back. The other passengers freeze, unable to see what, exactly, is keeping the door from fully closing. As the door snaps open, Riis falls free, collapsing onto the train car floor.

"Fiouf!" Riis exclaims aloud as the train begins its journey upstate to Albany.

By the time DR. BERG and STEWART BROWNE board the Empire State Express train car for their return trip to Grand Central Station in Manhattan, it is well past 9 o'clock. All aboard are discouraged and confrontational. These, New York City's landlords, real estate moguls and others, persist in trying to speak over one another, resulting in uproarious remorse for the case made out by their hired advocates. This collective remorse is the only point of consensus amongst the group; otherwise they bicker among one another as hyenas do when food is running low.

The crowd calms when BROWNE's voice rises above the rest, turning to scold DR. BERG.

STEWART BROWNE: You cannot be serious when you say, 'Bring competition to labor by writing out literacy as a requirement of citizenship.'

I mean honestly, could'ya have made yourself look more like'a cook cackling from a tree up there?

Is it your intention to drag us all down with you?! Because, if so, I'll just as soon have you escorted off this train, never mind that you're a doctor, if you catch my drift.

*(The train door blows open, knocking Riis aside. BROWNE and BERG are broken in on by a newcomer, an unwelcome visitor—imposingly tall, a pale woman with a flash of steel in her hair. It is H. C. ARTHUR, and she is agitated.)*

H. C. ARTHUR: But you're always speaking out of both sides of your mouth, Stew.

STEWART BROWNE: Have a seat and take a moment to gather yourself, that grey streak is growing by the day.

ARTHUR: I'll sit but only for my own sake.

*(With grace, ARTHUR is sauntering in Riis' direction when he recognizes, for the first time, that this woman is the same passenger from his maiden voyage to Albany along the Empire State Express that morning. "Had she really been clever enough to stash herself, undetected by even by those no longer of this Earth, in the train car full of tenant advocates, some of New York City's most prominent politicians and their security details among them?" Riis wonders aloud.*

*As before, ARTHUR again sits directly onto Riis' lap, startling him and bringing him to his feet. Just before settling, she peels a glare in Riis' direction, pausing to smirk, and quickly returns her gaze and attention to BROWNE.)*

ARTHUR: It's too bad that neither of you have a clue what you're doing. I don't mean to be crass, but both of you would do well to realize exactly what happened today. Thanks to your bamboozling, gentlemen, we'll most assuredly have rent control this coming season. Do not take my warning lightly—go easy on your tenants this renting season, for the sake of us all.

BROWNE: With this, good Doctor, I must absolutely agree.

*THE SCENE concludes as all aboard the train make for the railroad cars' exits, the Empire State Express having reached it's final destination at Grand Central Station in Manhattan. Riis looks on longingly at the exiting passengers, fully aware that this northbound Empire Express will be altogether uneventful. With that, H.C. ARTHUR walks directly into Riis and abruptly knocks him off the Empire*

*State Express out onto the platform at Grand Central Station. The doors creak shut and Riis finds himself out among the hustle and bustle of Grand Central.*

—FIN—

# BOOK THREE

## RISE OF THE TENANT ARMY

*As the moon rose higher the inessential houses began to melt away until gradually I became aware of the old island here that flowered once for Dutch sailors' eyes—a fresh, green breast of the new world. Its vanished trees, the trees that had made way for Gatsby's house, had once pandered in the whispers to the last and greatest of all human dreams; for a transitory enchanted moment man must have held his breath in the presence of this continent, compelled into an aesthetic contemplation he neither understood nor desired, face to face for the last time in history with something commensurate to his capacity for wonder.*

-F. Scott Fitzgerald

## **CONSTRUCTIVE EVICTION**

You may have guessed by now, but I should tell you that I'm an attorney. Maybe I should've let you in on that sooner but the reality is that, at least in my experience, American people, by and large, hold a strong partiality against attorneys, and though it may sound vain, I remained silent for fear that just such a predisposition might cause you to abruptly stop reading, putting this story down forever and missing its conclusion. I've been around attorneys my entire life and I've known them to come in all shapes and sizes, and of all varieties of disposition and intention. Rest assured, I have no intention of picking your pockets or committing any number other of conniving or Machiavellian tactics often associated with the bottom rungs of the profession. No, no. My intention is only to share a story that, despite its transformative effect on history, is truly incapable of telling itself.

You're on the last leg of this story, the final Act, so to speak. I'm compelled to share with you a quote by Harrison Tweed, an attorney who had a career as well known for it's legal prowess—Tweed having served as counsel to both the Chase Manhattan Bank and the Rockefeller family—as it was for its strong orientation towards civil service. Tweed's bias is apparent immediately (having been an attorney, after all), but his words ring true—

> I have a high opinion of lawyers. With all of their faults, they stack up well against those in every other occupation or profession. They are better to work with or play with or fight with or drink with than most other varieties of mankind.

With that, let's jump back in.


I may have mentioned this earlier, but the owner of my first Manhattan apartment building lives in Florida and, on more than one occasion, allowed our fourth-floor flat (my two roommates' and mine) to degrade into such disrepair that I had to evict myself! 'How is that possible? Why would you evict yourself?' you might naturally be wondering.

Well, one of the oldest remedies available to a tenant, today as in the 1920's, whose landlord so neglects an apartment that the living space, in effect, becomes unsuitable for human life, is to simply move out, jump ship, whatever you want to call it—but know this, a neglectful landlord always remains subject to an age-old tenant remedy known as, "constructive eviction." Here's what I mean. No matter how bad living conditions get for a given apartment, courts without fail require a tenant insisting on remaining in the apartment to pay some measure of rent, whether adjusted by a court or not. Only when a tenant flees and, importantly, seeks out other accommodations, can that tenant lay claim to the remedy of constructive eviction, which essentially allows the tenant to treat any lease agreement with the landlord as null and void. Even as far back as 1920, if not earlier, New York City's municipal courts allowed a tenant deprived of peaceful possession to stop paying rent to a neglectful landlord so long as the tenant gave up the apartment, effectively forced to abandon the uninhabitable space in favor of other accommodations.

And that's exactly what I did when, one day while in the midst of my morning shower, our bathroom ceiling caved in, releasing an avalanche of gravel and dirt onto my head before coating me in a layer of rock, dust and grime. I'd had enough! No longer possessed of the belief that my apartment could sustain life, I fled with a full six months left on my lease and never looked back. Believe me when I tell you that I don't intend to pay another cent towards rent at 153 Suffolk Street, and not out of recklessness or overreaction, but because I can comfortably rely on a claim of constructive eviction should my landlord ever try to collect back rent for the remaining months on our lease agreement.

And who knows? Had it not been for those courageous efforts of New York City's tenantry during the 1920's, having overcome seemingly insurmountable odds to bring, in hindsight, some minor semblance of relief during an all out housing crisis plaguing the state, I may never have been able, almost a century later, to absolve myself of those unlivable housing conditions in the way I did. For that, I owe a debt of gratitude to that long-lost generation of New York City tenants. *Adieu*. That said, I don't need to remind you that the battle for rent control and other tenant-oriented measures was a fierce one to say the least, and a hard-fought victory for New York's tenantry. Nevertheless, with a barrage of legal challenges, the battle waged on long after the emergency rent laws first took effect in 1920.

## *AMERICAN FEDERALISM*

There's something absolutely fundamental about our national form of government and how it works that you hopefully know by now but that bares repeating. To say that the *U.S. Constitution* established a "Union" during the 1780's would be technically correct, though, as you know, not in the same sense that "union" was meant by America's citizenry during the 1920's. You would also be correct if you said that the *U.S. Constitution*, through the *Tenth Amendment*, ensured America as we know it today would be founded on a federalist form of national government. So that we can be on the same page, the *Tenth Amendment* reads:

> The powers not delegated to the United States by the Constitution, nor prohibited by it to the states, are reserved to the states respectively, or to the people.

Over two centuries since its enactment, the *Tenth Amendment* has matured, guiding the U.S. into a form of government based on principles of federalism. Depending on the geographic region, federalism (the political kind), is carried out by and between a national government, said to be at the "federal" level, and overlapping provincial or state governments, each sharing authority to govern different aspects of citizens' lives. This authority at the federal level is said to amount to "national sovereignty," which confers the basic power to govern national citizens. You already know that there might also be additional, lower levels of government like municipalities and even a Board of Aldermen (yikes!), so we won't belabor the point.

To be sure, the U.S. relies on a written constitution as the operative document implementing her secular trinity of American federalism—the United States (federal government); the states; the People. In this way, the New York State Constitution, by contrast, covers different aspects of each citizen's national sovereignty than the *U.S. Constitution*, though you should know that state constitutions are ultimately subordinate to the *U.S. Constitution* at the direction of a separate provision called the Supremacy Clause.

In the interest of full disclosure, I'll mention by way of anecdote that "federalism" didn't always mean what it's come to be known by since ratification of the *Tenth Amendment*. During the French Revolution in the 1790s, for example, "federalism" referred, instead, to a grass-roots movement to weaken the nation's central government sitting in Paris by divesting national sovereignty to the provincial governments.

In effect, the *Tenth Amendment* presumes that the power to govern, or national sovereignty, can and should be carved up in some orderly way among national and state governments and, in effect, provides a framework for doing so. Here's what I mean. The authors of the *U.S. Constitution* envisioned a world where, as opposed to their British counterparts, the national government of the U.S. would be one of comparatively limited authority, a measure to combat the ills of boundless authority reminiscent of the British monarchy.

To that end, the *U.S. Constitution* was drafted so as to vest the federal government with only that limited authority granted expressly to it by the *U.S. Constitution*, reserving all other aspects of sovereignty to the state governments or to the People themselves. In this way, the *Tenth Amendment* birthed a regime that blossomed into a national government with limited authority relative to the breadth of authority reserved to each individual state.

A decidedly traditional power reserved to the state level is what has, through the years, come to be known as the "police power," a grant of authority so wide in its application as to justify the state government acting in almost any way for the betterment of the citizenry's health, safety, morals and general welfare.

In 1920, proponents of the emergency rent laws in New York, for example, maintained against adamant opposition that New York's state government stepping in to regulate the housing market by, among other measures, imposing rent control was a valid exercise of the state's police power. As everyone knew by this time, tenant families all over the state were sleeping on the sidewalk or, worse, in the streets, rendered homeless by unapologetic landlords seeking eviction. Surely, such measures could be justified on the grounds of the state's police power, necessary in those years to maintain some semblance of "general welfare," right?

I should mention that, for as broad as a state's police power can be, it's also absolutely not, by any stretch, to be thought of as boundless. No, no. There are restrictions and for good reason.

Let's say, for example, that you owned an apartment building in the Bronx in 1914. Things would be undoubtedly going great for you in the sense that you never had to worry about filling your apartment units with paying tenants because there was a relative scarcity of livable apartments in the Bronx during those years as compared to the relative abundance of tenant families. In fact, not only would you have tenant families lined up out the door and around the corner to rent your apartments, but those tenants that did risk occupying your building were so leery about absolute homelessness that they would pay almost any increase in rent that you imposed on them. In the rare event that a tenant refused to pay rent in full, well, hell, you'd just get an eviction warrant from the courthouse up the street and remove those pesky tenants yourself! And for anyone that looked at you sideways, implored you to consider the fate of those tenant families living in your building, you simply could turn the other cheek, albeit not before uttering, 'It's a free country! I own the joint, this building is mine. Buzz off!' Maybe you'd be more coy about it, maybe not; but hopefully you see the truth—that you, as a building owner, valued, above all else in many ways, the primacy of private ownership and neither the federal government nor any state or municipal government had the authority to interfere with private real estate ownership in particular, one of the most sacred of property rights in the U.S., even today.

'How dare those upstate lawmakers from Albany tell me how to run my tenement building?! Where do they get off?' you might shout from your bedroom window as a building owner only a few years later, by 1922, when the scope of rent control had most certainly reached your corner of the city. As a building owner in 1922, you wouldn't be alone in your consternation and frustration with New York's state lawmakers who, despite your best lobbying efforts, continued to impose regulation over a greater and greater share of real estate ownership during the early years of the 1920's. You might challenge the emergency rent laws as an improper use of the state's police power, for example. After all, rents were rising all over the country, not just in New York, and the real threat to the "general welfare" was the high cost of building materials and stingy lenders, and you, for your part, were forced to respond to those natural market forces of supply and demand just like anyone else. However, you would soon realize that, indeed, there was no denying that, with so many homeless tenants packed into every corner of the state, to say that the "general welfare" of New York's tenantry wasn't suffering at the hands of a housing crisis would be a losing argument to say the least.

That said, you might resort to another traditional limitation on New York State's police power as a challenge to the emergency rent laws—the Contracts Clause of the *U.S. Constitution*. True, that this obscure language, housed in Article I, section 10, is rarely invoked, but given that state lawmakers' upstate efforts so thoroughly prevented you from enforcing the lease agreement of *your* choosing with *your* tenants, no one would look at you sideways if you determined that the situation seemed ripe for such a challenge. Here's what I mean. The Contracts Clause of the *U.S. Constitution* effectively prevents a state from passing any law that retroactively impairs an existing contract between private citizens. In this way, you might say that lawmakers upstate in Albany, by passing a set of laws essentially prohibiting you from charging market rates in rent or managing your building according to your usual lease agreements, have so interfered with your right of private contract as to violate the *U.S. Constitution*!

Even so, you might also argue that the emergency rent laws deprived you, the building owner, of the full value of ownership to such an extent that this deprivation was tantamount to the state government seizing your property altogether and leaving you without two nickels to rub together. Surely, if state lawmakers were as well-intentioned as they claimed, passing the emergency rent laws to temporarily lower the cost of living in the face of a housing crisis, they should've found a way to also compensate you, the building owner, in some way, right? I mean, why should tenants all over the state be given a break in these trying times and not landlords too?! You might say that such an unwarranted seizure of your private property without any compensation violates the Takings Clause of the *Fifth Amendment*, which (through the *Fourteenth Amendment*) prohibits a state government from appropriating private property without fair compensation. A proper exercise of eminent domain would, by contrast, require compensation in some way, and you wouldn't be alone if you took issue with New York's emergency rent laws on this ground.

Given your frustration, you might even go so far as to want to dispute the constitutionality of New York's emergency rent laws on these grounds in a court of law. If so, you wouldn't be alone, either. In fact, as soon as the emergency rent laws took full effect in 1920, the state's conservative leaning real estate interest mounted a campaign of lawsuits geared towards cutting the rent laws out at the knees, or at least blunting their impact. The all out blitz on the new laws occurred in both state and federal courts, extending well beyond New York's judicial system. In point of fact, the coordinated campaign against rent control was by no means confined to New York's state courts and the conflict over whether and to what extent a housing crisis justified government intervention soon squarely reached the U.S. Supreme Court, eventually having to be settled by then Chief Justice, Oliver Wendell Holmes.

## *OLIVER WENDELL HOLMES & THE DC RENT COMMISSION*

Do you remember Chief Justice Oliver Wendell Holmes? Perhaps not, but all's well and good. Do you recall the Espionage Act or the Sedition Act? Remember the case of Charles Schenck and the unanimous decision penned by Chief Justice Holmes in that case? In the event you're in need of a gentle reminder, there was a similar case to Schenck's that made it to Chief Justice Holmes' storied desk, the case of Eugene Debs, also brought by federal U.S. prosecutors in 1918 for federal crimes related to sedition.

If you recall those pesky Wobblies at all, you remember that Eugene Victor Debs was a founding member of the Industrial Workers of the World (IWW) union. You won't be surprised to learn that Debs was also a five-time candidate of the Socialist party for President of the United States. At the time of his arrest in 1918, Debs was one of the most prominent Socialists serving in the U.S. Government.

Police officers arrested Debs for nearly inciting a riot outside of a prison in Ohio where, for more than two hours, he enthralled a gathering crowd with a speech that the U.S. Government charged as an obstruction of the federal Conscription Act, punishable as a federal offense. As so many others before him, Debs too was convicted of obstructing U.S. draft efforts and enlistment service for the American military, punishable by imprisonment. In the end, Debs' undoing was ultimately that there were draft-age young men amongst the audience gathered to hear his speech the day he was arrested.

You might see it as ironic that Debs was arrested for his speech on that particular day, especially if you have even a passing familiarity with others among his body of public speeches. Take, for example, the following excerpt from a speech Debs gave to a boisterous audience of Socialist party members along one of his many stops on the campaign trail—

> Yes, in good time we [Socialists] are going to sweep into power in this nation and throughout the world. We are going to destroy all enslaving and degrading capitalist institutions and re-create them as free and humanizing institutions. The world is daily changing before our eyes. The sun of capitalism is setting; the Sun of socialism is rising ... In due time the hour will strike and this great cause triumphant ... will proclaim the emancipation of the working class and the brotherhood of all mankind.

Debs' speeches were, regardless of audience, usually received by thunderous and prolonged applause. Leading up to his day in court, Debs denied nothing about his message outside of the Ohio prison. At trial, Debs refused to take the stand in his own defense, or even to call a single witness! Instead, Debs addressed the trial Judge before sentencing—

> Your honor, years ago I recognized my kinship with all living things, and I made up my mind that I was not one bit better than the meanest on earth. I said then, and I say now, that while there is a lower class, I am in it; while there is a criminal element, I am of it; while there is a soul in prison, I am not free.

Not surprisingly, a jury of his peers found Debs guilty of obstructing the Conscription Act and the trial Judge, before sentencing Debs to ten years in federal prison, denounced from the bench anyone in the courtroom "who would strike the sword from the hand of this nation while she is engaged in defending herself against a foreign and brutal power."

By the time Chief Justice Holmes heard Debs' appeal in 1919, the U.S. had withdrawn from war hostilities overseas. That, by no means, prevented Holmes and the rest of a unanimous U.S. Supreme Court from affirming Debs' conviction and prison sentence on appeal. For a unanimous majority, Chief Justice Holmes wrote that Debs had "expressed opposition to Prussian militarism in a way that naturally might have been thought to be intended to include the mode of proceeding in the United States." The unanimous *Debs* Court went on to rule that Debs espoused "the usual contrasts between capitalists and laboring men . . . with the implication running through it all that the working men are not concerned in the war."

Upholding his conviction, the *Debs* majority found that the "natural and intended effect of Debs' speech was to obstruct recruiting for the war effort," a federal crime punishable under the Sedition Act. Debs spent thirty-two months in prison until 1921 when, at the age of sixty-six, he was pardoned by President Warren G. Harding and released from prison.

By March 3, 1921, when the U.S. Supreme Court heard oral argument on a case of first impression, *Block v. Hirsch*, those lawmakers, advocates and New York residents gathered in New York's state capital (as well as the rest of the country) looked on intently as Chief

Justice Holmes again delivered the opinion of a unanimous court a mere month after oral arguments, an opinion that cut to the heart of the nationwide housing crisis.

At issue in *Block v. Hirsh* was the Ball Rent Act, a law passed by Congress for Washington, D.C. that granted to D.C. tenants during those trying times the right to remain living in a rented apartment after the end of a given lease so long as the tenant continued to pay rent and otherwise perform all obligations under the original lease or, alternatively, agree to a rent fixed by the D.C. Rent Commission, as it came to be called. The D.C. Rent Commission was an independent rent commission tasked with the authority to fix a "fair and reasonable rent" in the event of a dispute over a residential lease agreement. Notably, a landlord or building owner only had a rather limited right under the Ball Rent Act, to dispossess a tenant "for actual and *bona fide* occupancy by himself or his wife, children or dependents." This right to *bona fide* occupancy was qualified only to the extent that a landlord was required to give each tenant 30 days' notice in writing prior to ending the lease agreement.

So on December 15, 1919, when Hirsh, the owner of a building on F Street in D.C., notified his tenant, Block, of his intent to retake possession of the unit for his own *bona fide* use after expiration of their lease agreement only 15 days later—December 31, 1919— Block naturally refused, maintaining that he should be allowed to remain past the expiration date of his lease agreement under the Ball Rent Act because Hirsh hadn't afforded him the proper 30 days' notice. There were so few livable apartments in D.C. at the time that Block faced a daunting prospect of homelessness in the event his challenge proved unsuccessful.

The dispute came before the D.C. Rent Commission, which sided with Block and ruled that he could remain in his apartment, not for any special circumstance, but the outcome dictated simply by a black-letter application of the Ball Rent Act. Hirsch then brought an action to recover possession in trial court, arguing that, in fact, he was entitled to dispossess Block on such short notice because the Ball Rent Act itself violated several key provisions of the *U.S. Constitution*. If successful, Hirsh's argument threatened the continuing vitality of rent control across the country.

The dispute eventually landed before the D.C. Court of Appeals where a majority of the appellate Justices ruled that the Ball Rent Act did violate the *U.S. Constitution*, entitling Hirsh to give Block the boot, effective immediately. Block appealed and, after consolidation with a companion case that raised many of the same issues, Chief Justice

Oliver Wendell Holmes and his contemporaries on the bench of the U.S. Supreme Court voted to hear the appeal.

In a decision that sharply split the Court 5-4, a majority of the Justices voted to uphold the Ball Rent Act as "made necessary by emergencies growing out of [World War I], resulting in rental conditions in [D.C.] dangerous to the public health and burdensome to public officers." In this way, Chief Justice Holmes wrote, "circumstances have clothed the letting of buildings in [D.C.] with a public interest so great as to justify regulation by law" that which would otherwise "be a matter of purely private concern." That Congress passed the Ball Rent Act as an "emergency measure" to address, albeit temporarily, an ongoing threat to the public health alleviated any concerns the *Hirsh* Court may have had that rent control, as administered by the D.C. Rent Commission, deprived building owners of the value of their property without fair compensation, due process of law, or otherwise interfered with existing lease agreements between the city's landlords and tenants. In the end, Chief Justice Holmes and the slim *Hirsch* majority held that the Ball Rent Act was "justified only as a temporary measure."

With that, a nationwide precedent had been set—the government could step in and regulate rents in the name of the public interest when the circumstances called for it. And a gripping nationwide housing shortage certainly qualified.

Chief Justice Holmes' *Hirsh* opinion, as it turned out, would go on to shape the plight of working-class tenants all over the country. Thus approved by the U.S. Supreme Court, rent control was here to stay, at least for now.

## *MUNICIPAL JUDGES AT THE HELM*

No two ways about it, the question everyone was asking in those early days of the 1920's—especially in New York City in the wake of *Block v. Hirsh*—was how to effectively administer rent control among landlords and tenants, two groups of urban residents who couldn't be more disagreeable towards on another.

New York's state lawmakers, for their part, had labored—working overtime hours down through 1919 and 1920, and were fatigued, no two ways about it. That state legislators didn't entirely fold to riotous, persistent real estate lobby groups should not go understated. Achieving any measure of rent control for New York City in those years was nothing short of remarkable when you consider the virulent opposition from the state's conservative leaning real estate interest, well-funded and on a mission in both Albany and New York City.

Following a lopsided tenant victory during the Lockwood Committee Hearings in 1920, it also seemed like a real possibility that New York might adopt a statewide rent commission to administratively resolve rent control. New York's state Senators and Assemblymen, however, declined the opportunity and, instead, voted down a measure that would have delegated authority over administration and enforcement to a specialized independent rent commission.

Instead, New York's state legislature voted to have rent control administered, not by an independent rent commission, but by the city's core of municipal Judges. In fact, had it not been for New York's real estate interest, who knows? Maybe New York residents would have seen a state-wide rent commission to administratively resolve rent control, *à la* Congress when it voted to administer rent control in the nation's capital district through an independent rent commission.

In so doing, New York's conservative (supposedly) state legislature voted against what would have been a well-established delegation of authority over enforcement of law to a legislative or executive agency and, instead, opted in favor of a state-wide rent control regime administered, not by any specialized body to be sure, but rather, state lawmakers left rent control in the hands of New York City's core of municipal Judges.

In the first few days of rent control in New York, few municipal Judges knew the gravity of their assigned task. It soon became clear that, given the opposition, New York's core of state and municipal

Judges would not only have to administer rent control in an even-handed way, but also would have to entertain the many constitutional challenges being leveled against New York's emergency rent laws, which continued even after the U.S. Supreme Court decided *Block v. Hirsch*. In point of fact, attorneys for landlords and the state's real estate interest challenged the validity and definition of nearly every word making up the emergency rent laws.

Even the most basic of questions was up for grabs. For example, one of the thorniest issues proved to be figuring out which apartment buildings, exactly, were covered by the state's new laws. Say that a particular apartment building was built before the laws were enacted—this older building would no doubt be subject to the emergency rent laws, including the nascent rent control provisions. By contrast, consider a building that went up after the rent laws were enacted—this newer building would be exempt from rent control. Fine, easy enough, right? The problem, to be sure, was that many building owners would renovate or otherwise undertake various construction projects that the owners argued should not only justify a rent increase but also that these "new" buildings should be exempt from the emergency rent laws. Municipal Judges also had to decide whether a building owner's justifications for raising rent were legitimate or, more often, whether the landlord was saying one thing as a pretext for skirting rent control and raising the rent higher than the new laws allowed.

As you might imagine, these questions were of great moment, for unless a tenant's apartment building fell under the emergency rent laws, a tenant could not compel a landlord who sought to raise the rent by more than 25 percent to prove that the rent increase was reasonable (or else be forced to drop the summary proceeding).

Piece by piece, the emergency rent laws were upheld and, thanks in no small part to the remarkable even-handedness of most of New York City's municipal Judges, rent control was administered in as balanced a way as was possible given the circumstances. That, by no means, meant the job was easy.

Given the thorny and often unworkable world of legal precepts, dispossess notices and summary proceedings, some critics charged that New York's emergency rent laws farcically relegated enforcement to the state's core of municipal Judges. Moreover, many more were outspoken about the fact that Judges didn't rule objectively, but based on personal sensibility or preference for landlords or tenants. There was some merit to this charge. In the court of public opinion, the city's municipal Judges broke down, broadly, into two camps. The first camp consisted of those Judges that ruled decidedly in favor of tenants on the one hand and, on the other, Judges that ruled consistently in favor of landlords.

'But enough already, let's meet some of these revered New York City municipal Judges!' you might have gasped just now. Maybe not.

Maybe we'll begin with a Judge from the Bronx whose name you'll likely recognize—Judge Jacob Strahl. Indeed, the national press once openly described Judge Strahl as "the tenants' friend." Widely outspoken, Judge Strahl was known to be hard on what he perceived as rapacious, greedy landlords. Indeed, one of Judge Strahl's contemporaries on the bench once accused Strahl of coming down in favor of tenants "merely for the purpose of gaining public applause."

This accusation aside, Judge Strahl did issue several distinctly significant rulings that came out favorably for the Bronx's urban tenantry.

Recall that New York's emergency rent laws implemented a statutory presumption that any rent increase in excess of 25 percent over the previous month's rent was "unreasonable" unless proven otherwise by the landlord. If that doesn't ring a bell, consider the case of one landlord who refused to settle a summary proceeding for a rent hike of 25 percent on the nose. With little hesitation, Judge Strahl declared that the rent increase would be cut to 10 percent and, just as blithely, Strahl went on to enjoin this particular landlord from raising the rent any higher within the next 12 months.

Consider also, the case of another landlord who refused to settle with a group of sixteen tenants for a $2 increase in monthly rent per tenant. Judge Strahl strong-armed this recalcitrant landlord, ultimately convincing him to permit all sixteen tenants to remain in their apartment units at the old rent by threating to charge the landlord court costs of $10 per tenant. Shortly after the emergency rent laws took effect, Judge Strahl also publicly announced that exactly zero eviction warrants would be issued from his bench on Moving Day, later clarifying that he wouldn't rule to dispossess any tenants for failing to pay a rent increase in full each month.

In fairness to his critics, Judge Strahl rarely left any doubt as to the basis for his rulings, often commenting openly from the bench about why he came out one way or another. For example, when Artilio Callaro, a mother of six, entered Judge Strahl's courtroom at the behest of her landlord, Angelina Buogioni, Judge Strahl asked Ms.

Buogioni directly why she brought a summary proceeding to oust Ms. Callaro and her six children. In open court, Ms. Buogioni declared, "I want the rooms for my niece," who was also a mother of four children. Judge Strahl didn't hesitate to deny the landlord's request for an eviction warrant, espousing openly the reason for his stance: "Let [Ms. Buongioni] stay in New York. Brooklyn has plenty of rent problems of its own without importing more."

Another so-called, "tenant judge" sat on the Bronx bench. Judge William Morris (no, not the British author and activist) garnered admiration from many a'tenant corralled like sheep in his courtroom. By some accounts, tenants found Judge Morris to always be deeply compassionate and even, at the opportune time, wildly entertaining while he carried out his duties from the bench.

Just as tenants admired Judge Morris, so too did landlords despise him and his tenant-friendly tactics, which left Judge Morris a frequent target for criticism. Particularly vocal critics took to writing "poison-pen letters" that leveled so many ridiculous epithets and *ad hominem* attacks as to be dismissed by Judge Morris' chambers as farce. Taking issue with Judge Morris' courtroom rulings, a disgruntled attorney once charged that Judge Morris had, by ruling against him, acted in active furtherance of damning prejudice against his landlord client, in not so many words. With a tap of his gavel, Judge Morris dismissed the disgruntled attorney's case, though not before responding that he had nothing against landlords on the whole, just certain profiteering landlords in particular.

Another attorney became so roused by Judge Morris' decision to adjourn proceedings—just for the day—on account of oppressive heat that caused all present in the courtroom that day to perspire furiously. Cursing the Judge's brief adjournment, this particular attorney threatened to apply for a *writ of mandamus*, which would have compelled Judge Morris to hear the attorney's case despite sauna-like conditions in the courtroom and chambers, to which Judge Morris retorted, "I'll mandamus you in the nose!" Naturally, Judge Morris' retort was received with thunderous applause and laughter from tenants in his audience that day.

There is even one documented instance of Judge Morris telling a recalcitrant attorney to "Go to hell," before adding, "I think more of one little finger of one of the children of those tenants than of all the bleeding, grasping landlords combined." It's easy to see why Judge Morris might be confused for a tenant-friendly jurist.

At the other end of the spectrum from Judge Morris and Judge Strahl were other of the city's municipal Judges who, generally speaking, disfavored tenants during summary proceedings, ruling in favor of tenants only rarely during long judicial careers punctuated by landlord-friendly practices and rulings.

For instance, Judge Michael J. Scanlan was sitting as a Bronx municipal Judge in the fall of 1919 when Private Beril Bogomolia entered his courtroom at the behest of his landlord, David Goodman, who owned the building where Private Bogomolia lived with his wife and three young children. Private Bogomolia had enlisted in the U.S. military shortly after the draft. During his tour of duty, Private Bogomolia's family had to make due with nothing but a military stipend of $55 per month.

During his tour of military duty, as well, Private Bogomolia suffered chronic injuries, having been caught as a sitting duck amidst the gunfire of a German machine gun nest. Following an honorable discharge accompanied by a Purple Heart Award, the soldier returned to his family in pieces and, upon arrival back to the U.S., military personnel rushed Bogomolia immediately to a hospital for medical treatment.

With Private Bogomolia confined to a hospital bed, David Goodman, Bogomolia's landlord, notified his tenants that he was raising the monthly rent from $25 to $35. Mrs. Bogomolia, for her part, pleaded with the landlord to postpone the increase, her efforts ultimately in vain. Fearing eviction, she conceited and paid the rent increase. Private Bogomolia, barely out of a hospital bed, was not so generous and, instead, overruled his wife. Shortly thereafter, he informed his landlord that the new, higher rent was unreasonable and that his family would be withholding rent until further notice.

Despite his unstable health, Private Bogomolia was summoned before Judge Scanlan. To get to the witness stand, the pale and emaciated soldier, now crippled, had to enlist the help of two women just so that he could hobble through the spectator's gallery. Once sworn in as a witness, Private Bogomolia pleaded with Judge Scanlan while on the verge of collapsing from the witness stand's stool. To the vocal dismay of spectators, Judge Scanlan ruled in favor of the landlord and, although vested with authority to grant the soldier and his family a stay of up to twelve months, Judge Scanlan ordered that the family pay rent in full within five days' time or else face eviction.

If you're fearful for Private Bogomolia's family, you should know that Judge Scanlan's decision generated such a fervor that the Mayor's Committee on Rent Profiteering stepped in to intervene, managing to secure a stay of ten days for the Bogomolias and an injunction preventing city marshals from carrying out an eviction warrant during that time.


Besides the openly landlord-biased Judge Scanlan, to say definitively whether a particular municipal Judge was landlord-friendly would, in all reality, require you to be an interpreter of winks, smiles and backdoor deals. The chances of that are slim so I guess I'll save you the trouble. Few Judges, if any, ruled as consistently in favor of landlords as Judges Strahl and Morris ruled in favor of tenants.

In point of fact, to say that Judge Harry Robitzek, also sitting in the Bronx, was a landlord-friendly Judge would be to get caught up in a case of misidentification. A former New York City Alderman, Judge Robitzek won election to the municipal bench in 1917.

It's true that Judge Robitzek, a native New Yorker, was regarded by some as a landlord-friendly Judge. Occasionally, Judge Robitzek would issue a well-deserved eviction warrant against tenants who, in the name of reprisal, refused to pay rent to their landlord altogether. It's also true that Judge Robitzek had, on documented occasions, issued an eviction warrant for certain recalcitrant tenants that his court found to be "undesirable." It's even true that Judge Robitzek liberally allowed landlords to raise rents, even as high as 20 to 25 percent.

But those critics overlook the efficiency and even-handedness with which Judge Robitzek administered rent control from the Bronx municipal bench once the emergency rent laws went into effect. Judge Robitzek's rulings made a unique but altogether logical adjustment by looking, not for an "unreasonable" rent increase, but instead a rent that represents an "unjustified rent increase" after being adjusted for inflation. Judge Robitzek's formula for determining an "unjustified rent increase" proved more efficient than its predecessors and allowed municipal Judges in the Bronx to rule on summary proceedings at a notable pace. Quick resolution of the summary proceeding favored tenants and, acting to further expedite summary proceedings in the Bronx, Judge Robitzek also held the parties to a strict schedule of mandatory settlement conferences.

In favor of tenants, Judge Robitzek freely granted stays of eviction, sometimes for as long as 12 months. His court also refused to enforce a landlord's request for eviction if the facts exposed the landlord's request as a measure to circumvent New York's emergency rent laws. Judge Robitzek's innovative approach to administering rent control tilted the balance of summary proceedings further in favor of New York City's tenants, including such measures as requiring landlords seeking eviction for purposes of remodeling to submit architectural drawings, building and environmental permits, or any other method of proof.

Perhaps New York City's municipal Judges were stacked against insurmountable odds; perhaps they were set up to fail. Perhaps not. Perhaps it was unrealistic for state lawmakers to delegate such a broad range of responsibility for administering rent control to New York's judicial branch of state government. Perhaps not.

Any way you cut it, even the sharpest, most experienced of municipal Judges were ill-equipped to administer every aspect of rent control—particularly in New York City where pressure exerted by conservative leaning real estate lobbyists in Albany continued to reverberate downstate to New York City's municipal court houses.

## *EXTENDED EMERGENCY?*

At last, some reprieve. By 1923, residential construction in New York City had roared back and was so well underway, in fact, that some foresaw a housing surplus for that year, which meant a promising increase in New York City of "the range of choice and the bargaining power of tenants."

That these rosy predictions were circulating around New York City just as the emergency rent laws were set to expire raised the natural question—was New York City still in the midst of an emergency that would justify extending rent control? To decide the question required, of course, another public hearing held at the state legislature in Albany. Though called by a new name, the Stein Commission came to many of the same conclusions as had the Lockwood Commission a few years earlier.

As prior investigations revealed, some of which dated back as far as the mid-nineteenth century, "to speak of housing for the unskilled workers as an 'emergency' was to obscure the real situation" because "[t]here have never been enough decent houses at a price that the poorest paid can afford." The Stein Commission confirmed that the poorest among New York City's working class have always had to inhabit tenement buildings that were overcrowded, filthy, dilapidated, dark and lacking in basic necessities like plumbing, heat and even breathable air! The rent laws "cannot avail much against a situation which has been lacking with us for decades and has grown more difficult in recent years." In this way, the Stein Commission confirmed what most knew to be true—it was not that rents were too high but that wages were too low. In other words, the chronic problem underlying the housing crisis was systemic and pervasive poverty, not rent profiteering or an epidemic of over-grasping landlords.

Much of the debate that dominated the 1923 Stein Commission hearings focused on whether rent control should be extended or, alternatively, if it was time to address this underlying issue of New York City's chronic housing shortage by some more directed measure. Despite the Stein Commission's findings with respect to the real driver of New York City's plight, the Commission did make more targeted findings on whether the current state of affairs warranted an extension of the emergency rent laws and, ultimately, rent control.

To that end, the Stein Commission addressed three pointed questions:

(1) Are unjust, unreasonable and oppressive agreements now exacted by landlords from tenants under stress of prevailing conditions?

(2) Is freedom of contract between landlord and tenant now restored?

(3) Has the housing congestion prevalent in 1920 been relieved sufficiently so that it no longer menaces public health, welfare and morals?

If these questions seem subjective and difficult to measure to you, then you're not alone in your observation. If it seems to you now that the Stein Commission should've focused on more objective and measurable criteria—like whether rents were out of reach for most New Yorkers taking account of family income or, alternatively, whether and how many New Yorkers were forced to live on the streets as a result of eviction proceedings—you share much in common with those who followed the Stein Commission closely once it was called to session in 1923.

As subjective as the Stein Commission's points of inquiry sound on first blush, however, the Commission did collect data on these pointed questions and ultimately reached a clear conclusion, which was articulated in an extensive report. For example, one indication that freedom of contract had not been restored between landlords and tenants was the city's overall vacancy rate. New York City's vacancy rate hovered at 0.33 percent at a time when many believed that the vacancy rate required to maintain the bargaining power of the city's tenants was 5 percent!

The Stein Commission also had no trouble measuring the city's over-congestion, which it found was still worsening by the day, particularly in low-income neighborhoods. Here's what I mean. It was still common during 1922 and 1923 for two or three families to share one three-room apartment or, alternatively, for nine or more people to live in as few as three or four rooms. Many of these rooms, for as crowded as they were, were also so dark that gas lamps had to be burned during all hours of the day. The air in these apartments became so stifling, particularly during the summer months, that families were left no choice but to sleep on the roof. And sanitary conditions had not improved since 1920 either, growing worse and, according to the Stein Commission's report, exhibiting a "progressive deterioration, readily attributable to the housing emergency."

Given that the housing shortage was having such a woeful impact on the city's health, welfare and morals, those presiding over the Stein Commission were not at all surprised that speaker after speaker called for an extension of the emergency rent laws.

Following the Stein Commission hearings, Congressman La Guardia, a leading advocate of rent control in both New York City and the District of Columbia by this time, declared, "The tenants have made out a perfect case" for the extension of rent control while landlords, by contrast, had made a "sad spectacle" of themselves during these first Stein Commission hearings. And any chance that landlords may have had was quickly dashed given that there was so much discord among the various factions of landlords, building owners and real estate investors. Those advocates spearheading the conservative-leaning real estate interest simply could not get on the same page and, as a result, seemed resigned to their shortcomings before the Stein Commission. That by no means prevented them from complaining, as many landlords did, that "the greatest outdoor sport in the metropolis has been the hurling of bricks at New York landlords."

The Stein Commission concluded that, "if the emergency rent laws were needed in 1920 they were even more necessary at the present time," in 1923. The Commission recommended that the emergency rent laws be extended immediately for two years and, to ensure that no time was lost in allaying tenants' anxiety, that the laws be re-enacted without amendment.

After the Stein Commission published its report, the fate of New York City's tenants again fell to the hands of New York's state lawmakers who, according to Congressman La Guardia, had more than enough information to propose legislation and come to a vote on whether to extend the emergency rent laws.

To that end, the state legislature subsequently passed the Dunnigan Act, which extended New York's emergency rent laws without amendment through February 15, 1926. Like the emergency rent laws that had been passed in 1920, the Dunnigan Act similarly faced a barrage of legal challenges based on alleged violations of the New York State Constitution and the *U.S. Constitution*. Given the Stein Commission's report and that the state legislature extended the prior laws without amendment, it should come as no surprise that the Dunnigan Act survived all legal challenges.

## *RISE OF THE TENANT ARMY*

What happened next put on full display just how much influence the state of affairs in New York City had on the politics of the rest of the state. Equally, it was a testament to just how formidable a force New York City's tenantry and their spokesmen had become.

To begin with, it's important to know that a residential construction surge was underway in New York City as of 1925 and early 1926, the likes of which hadn't been seen since 1906 and 1907 when construction boomed in the frothy wake of the Tenement House Act of 1901. With institutional investors (banks and insurance companies) flush, building materials plentiful and labor relations relatively peaceful, builders rushed to capitalize on the pent-up demand for space in new apartment houses, which, notably, were not all covered in the same way by the emergency rent laws.

In 1924, a year in which all records were broken, some 3,900 apartment buildings sprouted up through the city's five boroughs, adding nearly 55,000 apartment units to the city's housing stock. The very next year saw construction of an additional 2,800 apartment buildings, adding some 42,000 additional apartment units. Significantly, the vacancy rate climbed from a dire 0.37 percent in March 1923 to as high as 3.46 percent by January 1926. By all accounts, the surge in residential construction faced no immediate barriers to progress.

This too, in a year that the emergency rent laws, already extended once, were set to expire again. Many had reason to believe that the emergency rent laws wouldn't be extended again, in large part because it seemed a stretch for the state legislature to find that an emergency still existed as late as 1925 and 1926.

Moreover, there was reason to believe that, in 1926, New York City's municipal Judges might well find another extension of the emergency rent laws to be in violation of both the state and federal constitutions. On April 24, 1924, some three years after issuing *Block v. Hirsch*, the U.S. Supreme Court handed down its decision in *Charleston v. Sinclair*. The dispute involved the Charleston Corporation, which owned an upscale apartment building in the nation's capital, Washington, D.C. Just as in *Block v. Hirsh*, so too did the Charleston Corporation challenge a decision by the D.C. Rent Commission to allow a tenant to remain in a rented apartment past the end of his lease on the grounds that Congress, by that point, had exceeded its authority by extending the Ball Rent Act a second time. Both the D.C. Supreme Court and D.C. Court of Appeals sided with the

D.C. Rent Commission and upheld the Ball Rent Act, finding that the District of Columbia still faced an ongoing public health emergency that justified an extension of rent control.

The U.S. Supreme Court, by contrast, disagreed. Writing for the majority, Chief Justice Oliver Wendell Holmes, who had authored the majority opinion in *Block v. Hirsch*, held that, based on the facts presented to the Court, there was no longer evidence sufficient to demonstrate that an emergency still existed in the nation's capital. After the *Charleston* case was sent back to the lower courts, the D.C. Court of Appeals was unequivocal—the nation's capital had no option but to hold that the wartime emergency was over, that the Ball Rent Act was no longer valid and that the D.C. Rent Commission no longer had any authority to administer rent control.

Initially, it was entirely unclear what impact the *Charleston* decision might have in New York City.

Despite a revitalization of residential construction and the *Charleston* decision, rent control proved so deeply entrenched in New York City's social fabric by this time that it was going to be difficult to shake. Edith Elmer Wood wrote that, for tenants, rent control had become like other "habit-forming drugs." Notably, city tenants also numbered in the millions and at least one author likened the bunch to a veritable "Tenant Army" whose neighborhood, borough and city-wide tenant leagues covered much of Manhattan, Brooklyn and the Bronx, actively insulating the city from succumbing to pressure and arguments against the continuing vitality of rent control.

Tenants also had friends in high places by this time, not the least of whom was Congressman La Guardia. Tenants' efforts even secured the sympathies of long-time political rivals, garnering almost universal support in New York's state legislature.

In fact, in the eyes of nearly all New York politicians—state, municipal, Democrat and Republican alike—the city's tenantry was a force to be reckoned with and would come to shape the elections in 1924. Indeed, in the days leading up to the November election of 1924, in which all seats in the State Assembly were up for grabs, one candidate after another running for the state legislature pledged his or her vote to extend the emergency rent laws in New York, regardless of their stance on whether and to what extent an emergency persisted at the city or state level.

Notwithstanding the political sway that city tenants may have garnered going into the November election, there was still no doubt about the strength of their case for the continued existence of an emergency in New York City. It was true that residential construction as booming. Of the apartments that went up, however, there were essentially none that rented for less than $15 per room in monthly rent, which was significantly more than most New Yorkers could afford, particularly those poor working-class tenants who had, through the entirety of the 1920's and beyond, been forced to live in the same dilapidated and almost entirely unlivable slums.

Rents were still undoubtedly on the rise in many buildings too, though not rising as rapidly as in the years immediately following World War I. The vacancy rate, a familiar metric, still hovered well below 5.6 percent, which was widely viewed as less than "necessary to allow freedom of movement with normal turnover." As before, most of the city's vacant apartments were either in well-to-do apartment buildings, few of which were within the reach of working-class tenant families, or in old-law tenement houses that remained uninhabitable and had fallen into disrepair beyond reproach.

The debate over whether to extend the emergency rent laws came to a head in October 1925 when the Stein Commission announced that it would hold another round of hearings. Despite the outspoken political support garnered by tenants the city over, the 1925 hearings, this time held at New York City's City Hall, drew an even larger and more acrimonious crowd than did the first Stein Commission hearings only two years before. An estimated 1,500 people, most of whom were tenants, stormed City Hall. As reported by the national press, women—mothers and housewives—were still on the front lines of the rent laws debate, attending the Stein Commission hearings in droves "with children in their arms." The crowd was so large that it overflowed down the steps of City Hall and onto the street, bringing pedestrian traffic to a complete halt.

This round of Stein Commission hearings were, at times, moving, particularly when some witnesses broke down, "mingling tears and threats as they pleaded for an extension." Drawing on personal experiences and neighborhood surveys, one witness after another told the Stein Commission that there was still a severe shortage in apartments, especially those that rented for $10 a room or less per month. Capitalizing on the shortage, landlords were still unapologetically raising rents, sometimes by as much as 100 percent, causing serious concern, particularly at a time when wages continued to fall with no end in sight. Especially offensive were the many landlords who took advantage of those exceptions under Chapter 942 of the September laws to oust old tenants and replace them with new ones, most of whom had no choice but to pay a higher rent. Tenants were forced to continue to cut back on food and clothing, in addition to taking in borders and lodgers to make ends meet. Said many social workers who testified before the Stein Commission, the city's tenement houses were more congested than ever.

Landlords still had no incentive to make even necessary repairs and, given that the Tenement House Department was unable or unwilling to enforce the Tenement House Act, sanitary conditions were worse than ever as well.

Perhaps more ominous were the observations that some landlords were biding their time, awaiting the ideal opportunity for reprisal against the city's tenants who had so tactfully evaded rent increases and evictions over the last few years. Some predicted that, should the emergency rent laws expire, tenants would be left at the mercy of vicious landlords who had no reservations about continuing to aggressively raise rents. The risk, as in years past, was "wholesale evictions," and some went further, predicting that there would be riots and bloodshed in the streets. As reported by the national press, some witnesses warned that if the rent laws were allowed to lapse, landlords "would be found dead in the streets" and property owners "would be met by tenants with shotguns."

The city's landlords, through various spokesmen and witnesses told a different, but by then, familiar story. The crux of the problem, one prominent witness explained, was that at no time in the history of New York City, especially not since the passage of the Tenement House Act of 1901, had apartment buildings been built for the city's poorest, working-class tenants. This was a chronic problem, not an emergency.

The star of the show, so to speak, was Samuel Untermyer, who had served as counsel to the Lockwood Committee in the early 1920's and perhaps knew more about the emergency rent laws than any witness that stepped before the Stein Commission in 1925. Untermyer was one of the nation's most prominent attorneys by this time and when he took the stand on November 12, 1925, the fourth day of hearings, his testimony drew the keen attention of all in the room.

The takeaway from Untermyer's testimony was that he saw no reason to extend New York's emergency rent laws beyond February

1926 for apartments that rented for $15 a room or more in monthly rent. To his mind, there was a serious shortage of housing for low-income tenants and "there always will be," barring an overhaul of the city's poverty-stricken neighborhoods. Although Untermyer favored extending the emergency rent laws for apartments that rented monthly for $12 a room or less, he warned the Stein Commission that if the laws were renewed until vacant apartments became available at $4 or $8 a room, they would need to be extended indefinitely.

Untermyer was not the first New Yorker to argue that high-rent apartments should be exempt from rent control. In October 1923, during the first round of Stein Commission hearings, for example, the Commission acknowledged that there was no longer an emergency in the case of apartments that rented for $20 a room or more; however, it found no dividing line above which rent control could be allowed to expire and still maintain the safety of vulnerable tenants. Suffice to say, that when the Stein Commission held its second round of hearings in New York City two years later, it came under a good deal of pressure to find such a dividing line.

By the time the Stein Commission closed its second round of hearings in 1925, its members had heard more than two hundred witnesses, received several hundred exhibits and taken over nine hundred pages of testimony in New York City alone.

The Stein Commission submitted its report to New York's state legislature in late December, a report that ran more than one hundred pages. The report found that conditions in New York City had improved since March 1925, no two ways about it. The recent surge in residential construction was "without precedent" and left the city with roughly a 20 percent increase in the residential apartment stock since 1920. The Stein Commission also reported that the city's vacancy rate was "approaching the pre-war normal" of roughly 5 percent.

Despite the recent surge in residential construction, however, the Stein Commission estimated that only 2.4 percent of those apartments completed in 1924 rented for less than $12.50 a room per month, and likewise, that only 19.7 percent rented for less than $15.50 in monthly rent. Accordingly, the Commission concluded that nearly all new apartments were still well out of reach for most New Yorkers, especially those poverty-stricken tenants for whom the emergency rent laws were initially passed to address.

As for the vacancy rate, the Stein Commission acknowledged that it was approaching normal, but that, as before, the percentage was skewed to the extent that many of New York City's vacant apartments were so obviously in disrepair as to be almost entirely unsuitable for human occupancy. As an indication of the wretched condition of these apartments, the Commission pointed to a rundown, ill-lighted and poorly ventilated tenement house in Manhattan's lower East Side neighborhood that was fully occupied even though its halls were wet and slimy, its courtyard covered with refuse and its fire escape so old and begrimed that it was scarcely recognizable against other scrap metal jutting out from the sides, front and rear of the building. And the laws notwithstanding, average rent increases were some 68 percent higher here than in Manhattan's more well-to-do neighborhoods!

On the basis of these findings, the Stein Commission recommended for the first time that New York gradually "de-control" rents, a measure that would facilitate "the return to a free market" by allowing the emergency rent laws to expire first for apartments that rented for $20 a room per month and then gradually for all apartments. Governor Alfred Smith sent the Stein Commission's report to state lawmakers in early January and publicly announced that, unlike in years past, he would completely defer to state lawmakers regarding any extension of the emergency rent laws and sign, without opposition, any bills that made it through a vote.

Accordingly, whether the emergency rent laws were extended beyond February 15, 1926 depended almost exclusively on the vote of Republican legislators, notorious for their opposition to the rent laws dating as far back is 1920.

What eventually passed came to be known as "Chapter 6," which was widely viewed as another victory for New York City's tenantry who, for their part, had managed to exert so much influence over state-level politics by this time as to corral a surprising number of Republican adversaries (all of them) to vote in favor of extending rent control again, albeit in a more limited form. The new statute exempted from rent control all of the city's apartments that rented for $20 a room per month or more. Practically speaking, by exempting these apartments from the emergency rent laws, Chapter 6 significantly reduced the number of New Yorkers who had a stake in the continuing vitality of rent control.

"Regulation is commendable in an emergency . . . but we are getting beyond the emergency and coming face to face with the chronic housing problem that New York has never solved," declared

Governor Smith. Given that rent control seemed to be on its way out, Governor Smith admonished New York's state lawmakers that the time for "temporizing" the housing shortage was over and it was finally time for lawmakers to address the city's "dark, ill-ventilated, overcrowded, unsafe tenement houses," apartment buildings that continued to pose an ominous "menace to the health and morals of the community."

It was now up to public authority to do that which private enterprise had proved inept—provide much needed housing for low-income families and overhaul the state's congested and unsanitary neighborhoods, especially pervasive on Manhattan's lower East Side.

The Nicoll-Hofstadter bill, as it came to be called after its two sponsoring lawmakers, was drafted to stimulate construction of affordable housing "within congested areas for wage earners by private capital at reasonable rents." Easier said than done, no doubt, especially considering that the shortage of decent housing for low-income families had plagued the city for the better part of 200 years.

Nevertheless, state lawmakers persisted. To carry out this ambitious plan, the bill called for the creation of a State Housing Board, a State Housing Bank and a number of low-dividend housing companies to spurn on publicly-subsidized housing.

The new scheme would go something like this. The Housing Board would be empowered to designate neighborhoods in which private enterprise was unable to provide livable accommodations for working class families at a reasonable rent. The Board would then enter into an agreement with a limited-dividend company which, in return for the opportunity to erect and manage a new building, would be required to raise one-third of the capital needed for construction, fix rents according to the new law and, to blunt the incentive for profiteering, make distributions of no more than 6 percent per year to stakeholders.

Any construction projects would also have to be approved by New York's Housing Bank, which was authorized to issue bonds and apply the proceeds to the remaining two-thirds of the capital required for construction. New York's Housing Bank would also retain the right to reclaim the property by eminent domain in the event that the private owners were unwilling to sell. If a city or town was so inclined, the Housing Board could also exempt any newly-constructed apartment building from state property taxes.

Over vocal objections from New York City's real estate interest, New York's state legislators passed the Nicoll-Hofstadter Bill in April 1926 and Governor Smith signed it into law in May, less than a month later. Governor Smith conceded that the bill was "not perfect" but praised it as "the beginning of a lasting movement to wipe out of our State those blots upon civilization," the old law tenements that had, for so long, been "unfit for human habitation."

## *REIGN OF THE TENANT ARMY*

Shortly after Governor Smith signed the Nicoll-Hofstadter bill into law, the Stein Commission was replaced by the State Board of Housing, whose mandate was to promote low-income housing and slum clearance. As successor to the Stein Commission, the State Board of Housing had the unenviable task of advising Governor Smith and state lawmakers about whether the emergency rent laws should again be extended, this time beyond May 1927.

To that end, the State Board of Housing held two days of hearings in mid-February, again hosted at New York's City Hall. Not surprisingly, the hearings revealed that the emergency justifying statewide rent control had subsided and, accordingly, there was little need for further extension of the emergency rent laws. In fact, the hearings revealed that many recognized New York's emergency rent laws had actually done little to improve living conditions for the poor in the past, rent control being merely a bandage on an otherwise more chronic and gaping injury. Nor was there reason to believe that, if the emergency rent laws were extended, that they would do much in the future to that end. Now that the city's vacancy rate was approaching 5.2 percent, up from just 3.5 percent a year earlier, the Board of Housing seemingly had no choice but to allow the rent laws to expire on June 1, 1927.

The Housing Board issued its report in mid-March, finding that vacancy rates had almost reached pre-war levels, market rents were no longer rising and the "bargaining power" of city tenants had climbed back to normal. The Board reasoned, "[i]f the present forces continue to operate as they have in the past year, no further rent control will be needed."

This didn't prevent the Board from acknowledging that there was still a pervasive shortage of low-priced apartments and that the expiration of the emergency rent laws risked doing "irreparable damage to the health and welfare of a great many tenants." Hence, the Board recommended that in the meantime, New York's state legislators adhere to the same policy of gradual decontrol that had been devised by the Stein Commission and extend the emergency rent laws for one more year, though only in the case of apartments that rented for $15 a room or less per month, and only for the five boroughs of New York City. Governor Smith, having been reelected in 1926, endorsed the Board of Housing's report and urged state legislators to enact the recommendations.

In the end, the Board's recommendations were incorporated into a bill that passed New York's Senate on March 2, 1927 and, incredibly, passed without a single dissenting vote. The State Assembly followed suit two days later. Governor Smith signed the bill into law a month on, thereby providing protection for a good many New Yorkers while no doubt troubling a good many others. Wrote the *New York Times*, if an emergency still persists after several years of "exceptional prosperity" and bountiful residential construction, it was here to stay. "In fact, then, if not in name, we have Government control of rents not as a temporary arrangement but as a permanent policy."

As the Board of Housing predicted, residential construction continued to surge back all over New York, but particularly in New York City, which experienced residential construction at a record pace in 1927. As before, driving the surge were speculative builders from the private sector who had little trouble raising capital and found it easy to sell their buildings quickly at a profit, if not before construction was completed, then immediately thereafter.

Surprisingly, however, it remained unclear in 1927 whether the legislature was ready to completely repeal rent control. For all the rhetoric and opposition through the years, Republicans again voted to extend the emergency rent laws, but this time with seemingly one goal in mind—garnering support in an election year from the hundreds of thousands of foot soldiers forming the formidable "Tenant Army." As reported by the national press, rent control in New York City had become a "habit" that would be hard to break and would drive state politics again during an election year.

The issue came to a head in February 1928 when the Board of Housing submitted a second report to New York's state legislators for consideration. The Board found that New York City had seen "further improvement in the general housing situation in New York City." Residential construction was, to be sure, robust and continued at a torrid pace. Between October 1, 1926 and October 1, 1927, there was a net addition of more than 94,000 apartments to the city's housing stock with more than 74,000 new-law apartments, all of which were exempt from rent control, with the remainder being one and two-family houses.

As a result of the city's booming residential construction, coupled with the attendant slow down of European immigration, the number of vacant apartments in New York City had surged from as low as 8,000 in 1924 to more than 83,000 vacant apartments by January

1928. And the vacancy rate, which lingered under 1.0 percent in January 1924, climbed to more than 6.6 percent in January 1928.

By early March 1928, it seemed that the emergency rent laws might finally be set for repeal. Recall, however, that rent control had been so fiercely politicized and fought for so courageously by tenants from all corners of the city that Republicans not only succumbed to a renewal of the emergency rent laws again, but drove the renewal themselves! In a surprising turn of events, Republican leaders decided it was too risky to allow the emergency rent laws to expire during a year in which, not only the state legislature, but also the U.S Presidency and other political offices were up for grabs. There were several Republican candidates "who now aspire to State offices and who, if they thought voting in favor of the emergency rent law extension would improve their prospect of election, would not hesitate to do so."

On the final day of the regular legislative session that year, two bills reached the floor of New York's Senate and Assembly. One of the bills proposed to extend the emergency rent laws for New York City apartments that rented for $15 a room per month or less. The other bill would, if enacted, extend the discretion of municipal Judges to grant a stay of up to six months in cases where a landlord attempted to oust a tenant for non-payment of rent. Incredibly, the two bills were passed "by unanimous vote and without debate." Some commented that it would have been logical for the legislature to let the emergency rent laws "die a natural death," but "the temptation to play politics proved too great."

Governor Smith signed the bills into law within two weeks of passing a vote in the Assembly and Senate, explaining "that there must be a gradual decontrol and that we cannot terminate protection of these laws without creating a most serious condition" for hundreds of thousands of tenants. Governor Smith went on, "when we set up a new and drastic form of protection of tenants on account of an emergency due to lack of housing we cannot consistently throw these tenants out on the street or force them to move overnight without allowing reasonable time for them to find vacant places into which they can move." The legislature had acted wisely, added Governor Smith.

With the 1928 election in the books, Republican leaders had no reason, political or otherwise, to accommodate New York City's low-income tenants any longer. Franklin D. Roosevelt, former Duchess County State Senator, Assistant Secretary of the Navy and eventual candidate for U.S. President, was elected Governor of New York in 1928. He had more on his mind than rent control.

In early March, moreover, the State Board of Housing released yet another report in which it found that housing conditions were improving for New York, residential construction was booming and vacancy rates were still on the rise. Any continuation of the emergency rent laws would do nothing to provide decent housing for the more than 1.7 million New Yorkers who still lived in dilapidated old-law tenements. As the State Board of Housing put it, to say that there is still an emergency "deprives the word of any special force," and to enact laws to that end was "to endorse price fixing as a normal policy of legislation."

On June 1, 1929, the national press reported that New York's emergency rent laws had expired at midnight the day before, May 31, some nine years after they had been first enacted. Though, strictly speaking, this was not the full story. Many of the emergency rent laws passed by New York's state lawmakers were permanent and persist in existence today, almost a century later. For example, unless otherwise specified, a tenancy does not expire until October 1st, whether the lease agreement is oral or written. Landlords must still prove that a tenant against whom he brought a summary proceeding on the ground that he is "undesirable" is, in point of fact, so recalcitrant as to warrant eviction. And, perhaps most importantly, Chapter 951 remained on the books, which made it a criminal misdemeanor for a landlord to deprive a tenant of heat and other essential services. Any continued deprivation of essential services provides suitable grounds for constructive eviction still to this day, no two ways about it.

Enacted in the aftermath of World War I, it shouldn't be lost on you that the emergency rent laws were allowed to expire on the eve of the Great Depression, a time when New York City's housing market would be tested as never before in American history.

First imposed by the state legislature as "a war baby," wrote Edith Elmer Wood, rent control would later be re-imposed by the U.S. Office of Price Administration as part of the federal government's effort to curb inflation during World War II.

But that's a story for another day.

—FIN—

Made in the USA
Lexington, KY
17 June 2016